G000242244

MY DARLING DIARY

My Darling Diary

A wartime journal -
Vienna 1937-39, Falmouth 1939-44

Ingrid Jacoby

UNITED WRITERS
Cornwall

UNITED WRITERS PUBLICATIONS LTD
Ailsa, Castle Gate, Penzance, Cornwall.

*All Rights Reserved. No part of this publication
may be reproduced, stored in a retrieval system,
or transmitted, in any form or by any means, elec-
tronic, mechanical, photocopying, recording or
otherwise, without the prior permission of the
Copyright owner.*

British Library Cataloguing in Publication Data:
A catalogue record for this book is
available from the British Library.

ISBN 1 85200 080 5

All the characters and incidents in this
book are entirely authentic, and any
resemblances to fictitious persons or
events are purely coincidental.

Copyright © 1998 Ingrid Jacoby

Printed in Great Britain by
United Writers Publications Ltd
Cornwall.

In memory of my mother.

Introduction

For ten months before the Second World War there was an organised movement, formed in Great Britain, which brought 10,000 mainly Jewish children between the ages of three months and 17 years out of Nazi-occupied Austria, Germany and Czechoslovakia to the safety of this country. It was called 'Kindertransport' (children's transport) and it saved the lives of children who would otherwise have perished in concentration camps. Only a few of the children spoke English, and even fewer ever saw their families again. They went to hostels, and private houses across Britain. My sister and I were among the 'lucky' ones who went to a private home in one of the loveliest parts of England.

Human beings, and especially children, have an infinite capacity to adapt to their surroundings. And so my misery and homesickness were gradually overlaid by an enjoyment of new friends and, ultimately, even by a superficial feeling of belonging. After more than half a century I look back on those five years in Falmouth as being among the happiest of my life. For this reason I wanted to show my gratitude to the town which gave me refuge, and I do so now with this record of my time spent there.

Vienna 1937-1939

30th December 1937

One day I caught lice from a girl at school. Ulli, our governess, washed them away with paraffin. It wasn't very pleasant. This year I had flu during the summer holidays. Olli, our cook, has a sore throat.

I've only been skating twice because I was ill. I didn't fall down on either occasion.

Last Friday I went to the theatre with Mummy and Lieselotte to see *Prinzessin Prinz*. Lieselotte and I were to go alone but Mummy accompanied us to the theatre. When we arrived we asked her to stay and see the play with us. Luckily there was still a ticket available. When we were in our seats a gentleman came to collect our tickets. He said: "These tickets are for tomorrow. Your seats are taken for today." We went quickly to change our tickets and returned just in time to see the curtain go up. When the play was over we saw that a dreadful snow-storm was raging outside. My hat nearly blew away. We took a taxi and were soon home.

Most of the following entries are undated:

I have written a poem about a boy called Peter who was always naughty, and very lazy at school. He reformed only when his mother threatened to die. It all ends well. I also wrote a poem

9

about Shirley Temple, my favourite film star.

1938:

Today, Thursday the 9th of March, my birthday, Helli, whose sick mother died a few months ago, slept at our house. I wanted a new red diary for my birthday, but forgot to ask for it. I have a red handbag and everything in it is red, too - mirror, purse, pocket diary, lucky alligator, comb and propelling pencil. My handbag has my initials *I.P.* on it. I wish my initials were M.S. They look and sound nicer.

Ruth, my best friend, and I were walking in the Kärtner Strasse when we met Gerti Gutfreund and her boyfriend. Suddenly on the opposite side of the street, a horse fell down. The boyfriend wrenched himself away from Gerti and ran across the road, leaving Gerti standing alone. We thought this very rude and ill-mannered, and I said to Ruth:

"He should have said to Gerti: 'Come beloved, a horse has collapsed on the other side of the road', instead of leaving her so abruptly."

We laughed about it for the rest of the afternoon.

I love drawing children - best of all girls in short dresses or pleated skirts. I love the colour red and spring and visitors. My favourite months are May and January. My favourite names are Annemarie and Peter. My favourite authors are Else Uri and Erich Kästner. My favourite games are Spekulation, Ludo and Diablotin. And I love music best of all. It makes me think of all that is good and beautiful in the world, and of nature. If only people were different.

My father is in a terrible state because Hitler has marched into Austria. I shall never forget the day of the Anschluss. Austria belongs to Germany now. It happened two days after my birthday and I couldn't have my party. I cried.

Still no period. I've looked three times today. When, when,when will my period start? I pray for it, but Gromi said it's wicked to think of God in the lavatory.

After Daddy went to Italy because of Hitler, Mummy had to let a room in our flat because she needs the money. Our first lodger was Otto Seifert. He was forty years old. The times we spent together were the most wonderful I ever had. He often kissed me and called me "my sweet, golden one" and in the evenings I sat on his lap. He sometimes referred to me as his young bride and often brought me presents home - chocolates, crayons, books and such things. We loved each other very much. Then, one day he was arrested and sent to Dachau. I cried for him every day. How to get him out? We tried everything. I was in despair - and then, one evening the door opened and he walked in! They had released him! He looked thinner and paler but he was still my lovely Otto Seifert. But as usual in life - I've learnt that much since the Anschluss - happiness was not to last. He had to leave Austria and has gone to China! All the things he left here he left to me, as well as a box of chocolates. I gave him my favourite propelling pencil, and a drawing I'd done, which he stuck in his passport so as not to lose it.

"You see, Ingerle, whenever I have to show my passport at the frontier, I'll think of you," he said. There was such a sadness in his face when he spoke that I thought my heart would break. I thought we would never be able to part from each other. But when he went up to everyone in turn and kissed them goodbye - even my sister - and finally me, I knew it had to be. I miss him most dreadfully. The first days without him were unbearable. Now I'm longing for Christmas because he promised to write then. I kiss his photograph every evening and I have written a book about him called: *With Him to China*. It is five weeks now since he left. I know he loves me, even though he is in China. After all, I'm his bride. We had a long letter from him, but we didn't get the previous one he mentions, only a post card. The letter of course was written to Mummy - but guess what he says in it, diary: 'I miss my little bride so much. How is she? Please give her a big kiss for me!'

Lieselotte is not a bit interested in boys. Incidentally, she has changed considerably, to her disadvantage. We are always quarrelling these days. I don't know what's the matter with her. She's so virtuous. It must be her age.

I'd like to have six children when I marry. I'd like to live in North America, preferably in a villa near New York. I want my husband and my children to have blond hair and blue eyes, and to be tall and slim. Perhaps it will come true one day - fingers crossed!

2nd July 1938

Up to my tenth birthday I had very few worries. Apart from the fact that my parents often quarrel, and little troubles with school friends, everything was fine. Then Hitler came, and Otto Seifert went to China - and now I've found out that my best friend Ruth can be horrible! When we were in the third year she was always very nice, but when in the fourth year a loathsome girl called Louise Herzberg-Frankel joined the class, Ruth began to ignore me and I noticed that she was insincere. The first time this happened - when Ruth ignored me and wouldn't speak to me for a week - I was broken hearted, especially as I had given her no reason. I sat on the lavatory and cried a lot of the time. My parents comforted me but in vain. When she spoke to me again I was unspeakably happy. She promised me never to be horrible to me again and said that Louise was to blame and had put her up to it. But it happened at least ten more times and now I know that I can't trust her.

Last summer Ruth came on holiday to Waldegg with us. She was very moody there and not always nice to me. My mother agreed that was not the way to behave. Ruth is never nasty to Louise, or Susi Roth (another school friend). She is the most popular girl in our gang and always gets her way. We all do what she says and don't question it. It must have gone to her head. I see now that we used to get on well together but no longer do. But I have a new friend, Eva Urbach, who is a sweet and kind girl. After my experiences with Ruth, I saw from the start that, compared to her, Eva was childish, harmless and sincere. Our mothers are also good friends (but Ruth's and my mother had a stupid quarrel and are not on speaking terms!). When Ruth realised I had a new best friend she became jealous and tried to come between us. I told Eva everything about Ruth and we decided to avoid her. That was before Hitler invaded Austria. After the Anschluss we made it up with her, and so it has gone on ever since - friends, not friends, friends, not friends.

I'm a very jealous girl and I don't want Ruth and Eva to become friends. Eva and I are together every Sunday. Last Sunday she didn't ring and I was very sad. The Urbachs live in the second 'Bezirk' where Jews are badly persecuted and sometimes they have to hide. When I went to the Urbachs' house a few days ago, how changed I found Eva's parents! Instead of the happy, cheerful couple, they were in a grave mood and looked grey, old and unkempt. Eva was sulky. By the way, she has blonde pig-tails! Lucky Eva.

We have a new lodger, Herr Feldmann. At first I liked him a lot. Imagine it, diary - almost as much as Otto - but now I hate him. Comparing them is like comparing an elephant and a flea. Lieselotte never liked him.

9th January 1939

I now go to the Sechskrügelgasse, the school, to which all Jewish children from this district must go, and I have a new friend, whom I knew from my previous school. I always admired her, and now we are friends! Her name is Lotte Lustig. She is very nice and so far I have not yet detected one bad characteristic in her. She knows a lot about boys and has explained the facts of life to me. I didn't believe her at first but Ruth confirmed them on Monday, 2nd January 1939. Now I think I know everything. Eva is the exact opposite of Lotte and has no interest in such things. Lotte is beautiful and very popular. She has been able to skate and ski expertly since she was five years old and has often performed and had her photograph in the newspaper. Until last year she attended a drama school and she knows Traudl Stark well! Traudl Stark is my next favourite film star after Shirley Temple. I am very proud to be Lotte's friend.

Girlfriends are a lot of trouble - how will it be with boys?

Liesolotte's best friend is called Muschi. Sometimes I wish I had a friend like that. They are inseparable.

Today, after school, Lotte and I went home together as usual. Unfortunately we met three boys of whom Lotte knows two well, as she goes to English lessons with them. They teased and annoyed us, as boys always do. One of them brushed against me and opened my satchel. Two of them were very nice-looking and the one Lotte didn't know was ugly. What a strange coincidence! They walked behind us and made us laugh with their silly talk of marriage etc. Then two boys departed and one of the nice looking ones continued to follow us. When Lotte and I said goodbye the fellow pretended to look at a shop window and waited till we went our separate ways. I shall never know which one of us he followed.

31st January 1939

Today Mrs Bielitz telephoned and said she had almost certainly found a solicitor's family in England for me who were willing to take me and another girl who's sixteen years old. Wonderful! Eva is in Sweden with a family and doesn't like it there. She writes me very nice letters. Her parents told me that she likes me very much, but is not a person who can show her love.

Lotte has gone to Shanghai with her parents! On the boat she met an Indian who gave her twenty pounds and his address. I always knew that something special would happen to Lotte.

Ruth and I are best friends again. We even write our diaries together. Fingers crossed that it stays like that!

4th March 1939

Today the Urbachs came to say goodbye. They are going to England. It was terrible. Lieselotte wept bitterly, but I bravely controlled my tears. Bravely? I don't know about that. I don't think that I can cry any more. I've shed so many tears for Otto Seifert that I've none left. There are no bottomless barrels. When Mr Urbach kissed me goodbye I was reminded of Otto's departure and his kisses, and I couldn't bear it.

I think a lot about Eva now that she has gone. She was very

14

wild. We often romped and fought. When there were other children with us she never took my part in an argument. That's not how a friend should be.

Ruth often shows me parts of her diary, and I show her mine. Hers is mostly about boys. Lotte never showed me her diary but she once told me that it contained something about a wicked mother-in-law.

I don't think I've loved a person as I love my dear, dear Otto, and I'm sure I never shall again. I long for him, I love talking about him. Only those who have experienced love and longing can understand how it feels. It is terrible, simply terrible. But I know he loves me too, I know it, oh I know it!

Another letter has come from him. He wrote to each one of us - Mummy, Lieselotte, Gromi (my grandmother) and me. What he wrote to me was so lovely that I can't bear it. I have copied the letter and it is in my secret drawer number two. (The keys for this are at the bottom of my dolls' clothes cupboard, under a pile of paper). Oh Otto, will I never, never see you again? Why can't I marry you? In this letter you have shown me your love, and I know where I stand.

9th March 1939

Today, Thursday, is my twelfth birthday. Feldmann didn't even wish me many happy returns. I don't care. I hate him. A few days ago, as I wasn't with any of my friends, I stupidly went out with him and Lieselotte. First we went to the British consulate and then to the Bondyheim, where his daughter lives. On the way there things were all right, but since one can't get on with Feldmann for long, we argued all the way back. This is how it was: he bought a little piece of roast goose for himself (my favourite dish) and promised to give me a bit. I said thank you. Lieselotte said jokingly to him: "Take care that *'I'* doesn't eat it *all* up." He replied: "Oh, I'm not a mean person. She might do well to copy my example." Whereupon I, not lost for words, said, "What example?" That's how the argument started. I was very cheeky to him and when he accused me of always being cheeky to Gromi, I seethed with rage and said some very rude things.

Of course, I had to accept the bit of goose but from now on I shall ignore Feldmann. I shall greet him and no more.

Mein lieben kleines Ingelein,

Heuer ist es das erste Mal, dass ich an Deinem Geburtstag nicht mit Euch sein kann und so muss ich Dir leider nur auf die Entfernung meine Geburtstagswünsche übermitteln. Sie sind deshalb nicht weniger herzlich, im Gegenteil, noch nie habe ich Dir so sehr alles Gute gewünscht, wie gerade dieses Jahr, von dem ich hoffe und was mein allererster Wunsch für Dich und uns alle ist, dass es uns wieder vereinen und vor Allem Dich bald nach Paris oder England bringen wird.

Du bist jetzt schon 12 Jahre alt, also schon ein grosses Kind, beinahe schon ein kleines Mäulein und verstehst sicher Vieles von dem Schweren, was wir alle durchzumachen haben und besuchst Dich, möglichst viel zu lernen, besonders Praktisches, und Dich nicht zu freuen, wenn Du keinen Unterricht hast, denn das was Du jetzt leicht lernst, würdest Du, je älter Du wirst, desto schwerer lernen und alles, was Du kannst, ist für Dein Leben ein grosses Glück, denn leider bleibt uns heute nichts mehr, um unser Leben zu fristen, als unser Können, unsere Bildung und vor Allem unser Verstand. Bemühe Dich daher, viel allein zu denken und nicht gedankenlos zu fragen, sondern Deinen Verstand zu üben, damit Du später in schwierigen Lagen, in denen Du auf Dich allein angewiesen sein wirst, Dir auch durch Deinen eigenen Verstand helfen kannst.

A birthday letter from my father.
Below is a translation of the full letter.

My dear little '*I*',

This is the first time that I can't be with you on your birthday and so unfortunately I have to convey my good wishes from afar. They are no less sincere, however, on the contrary, never before have good wishes been so important as this year which, I hope - and this is my dearest wish for you and all of us - will reunite us and bring you to Paris or England.

You are now 12 years old, a big child, almost a young girl, and you certainly understand some of the suffering we have to endure. I hope you are trying hard to learn all you can, especially practical things. Don't be pleased at having to miss lessons because what you learn easily now is much harder later. Every skill and all knowledge will be an advantage to you in life. Sadly there is nothing else left for us which cannot be taken away. Try hard, therefore, to think things out for yourself instead of asking thoughtless questions. Use your intelligence so that later, in difficult situations in which you have to rely on yourself, you will be able to help yourself.

This advice, and my best wishes, are unfortunately almost the only things I can give you for your birthday, except for the small item which Mummy will give you for me. I hope you will use it wisely and that it will come in useful for your journey.

Continue to be a good girl. I am sure you enjoyed your birthday cake if you were able to have one. I'd like to have been there to see you stuff it, (but only this once, next time I'd scold you again, you are probably thinking). I would also have allowed you two silly questions. That's a good birthday present, isn't it? But the best one would of course be a visa for France or England, where you will be able to have a proper education again.

So once again, all the best, greetings to Lieselotte, Mummy and Gromi, and write me a full account of how you spent your birthday.

Many kisses from
Your loving Daddy.

Fingers crossed that I can keep to my resolution.

31st March 1939

Ruth was at my house today, and, guess what, diary - she told me a boy has kissed her! There, I've told you now, but it's a dead secret to which I am sworn, so no snitching. The boy was Walter Stern, and she loves him! Of course it's all in fun, but I would like that fun, too. A pity, a pity, it can't be.

What is it all about, actually, this boy and girl business? Oh, I know exactly what it is about, and yet I don't, I don't. It's that world famous love, I suppose, but what is that?

Britta, another girl in my class, also knows the facts of life. I wonder who told her? When Ruth and I go for walks we always laugh a lot. Everything makes us laugh, and when there isn't anything one of us says: "Come, beloved, a horse has collapsed on the other side of the road," and that sets us off.

4th April 1939

Today I wore my spring coat for the first time.

I've kept my resolution and barely speak to Feldmann. He said to me: "You don't like me, do you, *'I'*, and think all sorts of bad things about me just because I often tell you the truth?" I made no reply, even after he repeated it all three times. I'm glad he has noticed. The mean fellow always has me fetch a glass of water for him, and once Ruth and I wanted to put salt in it. We didn't do it in the end. Today I'm in bed with a cold but if he asks me for water again he'll get salt with it. So there. And I don't like him because he tells me lies, not because he tells me the truth.

5th April 1939

The solicitor from England has written to say that he can take Lieselotte as well as me, instead of the sixteen-year-old girl. Isn't that wonderful? He didn't realise I had an older sister.

I've bought a new diary, complete with lock, and I shall keep it for England. It cost four Reichsmark. I shan't forget *you*, of course. You're coming too. So be happy, and love me.

17

Conversation with Feldmann:

I: I'd rather have an elephant than a tapeworm in my intestines. Worms are revolting.

F: How silly you are! An elephant is much too big to have in your intestines.

I: It was just a joke! I meant, if an elephant was tiny I'd prefer it.

F: My, you're a cheeky girl. You always have an answer, don't you?

I was so cross I said nothing further. As I write this he is sitting opposite me - imagine it! I don't care if he does see what I'm writing about him.

He told Mummy I was cheeky and of course she scolded me. When Mummy scolds me I always sneak off to the lavatory and cry. I think to myself: "Much as I value life, how nice it would be to die now. How sorry everyone would be then for having been unjust and unkind. Or if I could run away like Tom Sawyer or Huckleberry Finn." But I don't believe in childish impossibilities. When I'm specially sad - and I only confide this in you, dearest diary - then I think of Otto Seifert. I think of him and I wait for the night, when I can quietly cry for him. But not a word to anyone about this!

Do you think every child has worries like mine sometimes?

7th April 1939

Today I had my first English lesson with Lieselotte.

Last night I dreamt that I went on an excursion with the Findlers and Ruth's brother Hans was there and he made a heart out of my signature.

Give me your advice, diary, tell me what to do. I'm in despair about Feldmann. We keep fighting and making it up and fighting again. Blanka, his daughter, who is rather silly, slept at our flat for two nights, but it didn't help matters. She is going to England on a children's transport tonight. I must do some hard thinking and will let you know if I come to any decision.

When I was walking home from school the other day a boy on the Wollzeile stared at me and then followed me all the way home, right up to my front door. It felt really uncanny and yet

18

thrilling. I wish I had a really best friend to whom I could tell all these things.

Yesterday, Sunday, I was at Ruth's. When I went downstairs I slipped, fell and sprained my wrist. It still hurts and I have to write with my left hand, hence the terrible writing. Ouch!

I love hearing the song *Deep Longing*. I feel at one with the singer who, like me, yearns for a loved one far away. Will we see each other again?

8th April 1939

I'm writing in red ink because, firstly, I can't find my fountain pen, and secondly, I have something important to say. Listen: My uncle Fritz and Aunt Anna and their cat have moved in with us. The SS smashed everything in their flat.

One evening Feldmann was sitting with us as usual and we were all chatting in a pleasant way when he suddenly turned to me and said: "I bet you don't know, *'I'*, that cats' eyes are luminous in the night." I was outraged that he should think I - a twelve year old girl - has to be told that, and I answered pertly:

"Do you really think I don't know that?"

He said, "My, you're impertinent."

Mummy scolded me and once again it was all his fault. I also can't bear to see him eat, which he does like a pig, in a disgusting way. Oh, how I dislike that man!

9th April 1939

I'm writing in red ink again. Beloved diary, I have so much to tell you! Listen carefully: Feldmann wants to get married! I don't know if I told you that he has a lady friend whom he loves more than his life. Once when she was late coming he was in such a state that I thought any minute he would drop dead. When she finally arrived he was as happy to see her as if she had been his emigration visa. I don't think she loves him all that much. Anyway, he wants to marry this lady friend but I don't know if he has proposed to her yet. I know he has read *Ariane* and is now reading *Marriage Inn*, probably to be able to explain to her what happens when one gets married. Ruth and Susi Roth have read *Ariane* too, but I haven't. Nor has Lieselotte.

Feldmann is sitting with us again. Just now I took you from the cupboard and he followed me with his eyes, to see if I had 'The Book' - oh, heavens I haven't told you that yet, either - in my hand. I mean the book published by Ullstein called *Ladies' Taylor Goldschmidt* which Ruth and I are reading secretly, and which he once caught us reading.

27th April 1939

I've had another letter from Eva; it was about nothing much. Isn't it strange how different all the girls I know are from each other? Some are babyish, others exaggeratedly grown up, some are very nice, others are horrible, some always tell lies and others can be trusted. What a job, to choose a real friend out of this lot!

4th May 1939

A few days ago Mummy was very late home from shopping and I was frantic. I thought she might have been rounded up and taken to prison. When she finally arrived I cried because I was so happy to see her. Did you know that one can cry when one is happy as well as when one is sad?

My bosom is getting really big - but still no period.

Feldmann keeps kissing me! He always wants me to kiss him back but he can wait long for that! A horrible man. How different it was with Otto! How I loved his kisses and with what rapture I kissed him back! I've written a poem about him. It's too long to copy out in here.

There's not much evidence of Ruth's treacherous character any more but yesterday we almost fell out again. We were going for a walk as usual. For a joke I pulled her hankie out of her pocket; she was annoyed and hit me. I hit her back which annoyed her even more and she said 'goodbye' and walked off. I said goodbye too but, ever anxious to keep the peace, walked after her. This shows we're not so childish any more.

I have some strange dreams. The other night I dreamt I was walking along the school corridor with Lotte Lustig and we couldn't find our classroom. Then Professor Ernst, our teacher, came along and she showed us the way. When we entered the classroom we saw that there were boys as well as girls there. I looked at Lotte to see what her reaction to this was - and she had turned into a boy! I thought this very strange as she still had her black pigtails.

Because I am Twelve Years Old
(Written by me!)

When I see a handsome boy,
I blush a lot.
I stop and look.
Why not?

Once I saw a special one.
Who was he?
I fell in love with him.
That's me.

Loved him like no other,
Just for a time.
That's how I am.
Is it a crime?

Will it always be
Like this?
Will love come and go?
Hit and miss?

Love is for grown-ups.
I know it myself.
It's not for me.
I'm only twelve.

29th May 1939

Ruth and I go for a walk every afternoon, mostly in the town. Jewish people are not allowed into cinemas and other places, and so we go for walks, and window shopping, or to other friends' houses.

7th June 1939

Today, Wednesday, our visas to England arrived, Lieselotte's and mine! We are very excited. Aunt Anna brought them to our room first thing in the morning because she sees the post first. Before our departure we have to have a medical examination.

9th June 1939

Heavens, who would have thought that modest 'I' would parade stark naked in front of a hundred other children and three male doctors? It was horrible. I did as I was told but it was like a bad dream. My mother says that doctors don't count as men, but they looked like ordinary men to me, and I was naked in front of them! I hope I never have to have a medical again.

I'm still in beautiful Vienna, but soon I must leave it. Ruth and I visit all our favourite haunts - Kärtner Strasse, Rotenturm Strasse, Wollzeile, the Prater . . . Now that I must leave it all seems so beautiful . . .

Life has become one round of goodbyes. Tomorrow it is Aunt Ida and Uncle Adolph's turn, where we always get delicious ice-cream. We have already said goodbye to Uncle Berthold and Aunt Wilma, the Rezeks, our dressmaker and my beloved Frau Professor Ernst, who kissed me and cried, and asked me to write to her. She's the nicest teacher I ever had.

18th June 1939

On Tuesday our journey begins. Lieselotte and I are going to England on a children's transport. I'm terribly excited. Yesterday I had my last walk with Ruth.

19th June 1939

We had our customs examination today.

We said goodbye to the Bielitzs and the Engels and I can't remember who else, but the worst parting of all was from Ruth.

Dearest diary, I herewith take my leave of you. In England I shall start my new diary with the lock, so no one will read it. I have not been writing very regularly but I can't express in words how much I have loved you and how well you have served me. To you I told everything and I hope you loved me, too. We were good friends, weren't we? I know you wish me all the best for the future, and you won't forget me, will you? We'll be faithful to each other until death.

As I have a few pages left I will tell you two stories I wrote when I was ten and eleven years old, so we are not parting on a sad note.

1. Elsbeth is Sent Away

A widow who was very poor had ten children. They lived deep in a forest. The youngest child, who was called Elsbeth, was dreadfully naughty. Every day she did something different and had to be scolded. Sometimes she promised her mother to reform, but never kept her promise. As no punishment worked the mother looked around for another remedy, but she didn't know what. One night she went to bed deeply worried. She spoke to her dead husband in heaven: "Help me, what shall I do, no punishment can cure Elsbeth of her wickedness and she gets naughtier from day to day," she said. Where upon the dead soul said to his wife: "I will give you some good advice. Send Elsbeth away from home and don't let her return for a few years. By that time she will be good." Before the woman had time to say thank you the soul vanished. The next morning the mother said to Elsbeth; "Next time you are naughty I will turn you out of the house." Elsbeth took that very much to heart. 'I shall be turned out of my home and I don't want that,' she thought to herself. 'I had better be good from now on.'

The next evening Elsbeth went to bed very tired. But suddenly she got up and went to the door bell. She pressed it hard and it resounded deafeningly through the house, waking everybody up. The mother got up and without scolding told Elsbeth to pack her things and leave.

Elsbeth left her home with a heavy heart. In the dark forest she sat down on a tree stump. Suddenly she heard a voice:

"Elsbeth, what have you done?"

First Elsbeth didn't know whose voice it was but then she recognised her father. She confessed everything to him (which he already knew) and he was a bit cross. Then he said kindly, "Will you promise me never to be naughty again?"

"Oh yes," said Elsbeth, "and can I come and visit you?"

"All right," said her father, and immediately a golden ladder descended. Elsbeth climbed up and in no time she was with her father and fell into his arms. They talked for a long time. Then Elsbeth asked:

"I like it so much here. Can I stay with you?"

"You'll have to ask St. Peter," replied her father.

So she went to see St. Peter and he said that it wasn't possible, she could visit her father often, but she couldn't stay. Elsbeth was quite satisfied with that.

"Now you must leave," her father said, "it's almost one o'clock."

"Oh, what a pity. But where am I to go?" asked Elsbeth.

"To Bethlehem," her father answered. "Perhaps from there you will be allowed home again."

Once again the golden ladder descended and Elsbeth began to climb down. The next moment she lost her footing and fell to earth.

She opened her eyes. Where was she? At home in bed! How happy she was. Her mother was sitting beside her. Elsbeth told her everything and asked if it was really true. "No," replied her mother. Elsbeth promised to be good from now on. "That's good," said her mother, and kissed her on the forehead.

This dream completely cured Elsbeth of her naughtiness.

The End.

2. Little Evi Wants Blonde Hair

A poor carpenter by the name of Feldner lived with his wife and his little six-year-old daughter somewhere near Berlin. Little Evi, a sweet dark curly-headed creature, had started attending the local village school four days ago, and she enjoyed each day better than the last. She already had a little friend there called Louise Bergel. One afternoon, little Evi was invited to Louise's house for tea. She arrived just as Mrs Bergel was combing her daughter's hair. "Oh, what lovely blonde hair! I wish mine was like that," little Evi said, admiringly. When the hairdressing was over the children went to play. But in time they grew bored with Ludo and Monopoly and cards and wondered what to do next. They romped and raced about for a bit and finally came to a halt in front of the full length mirror on the wall. Here the vain little girls stopped and looked at themselves. Little Evi said: "Just look how your golden hair is glistening in the sunlight."

"Yours too," said Louise.

"Oh, no, mine is only brown. I'd so much like to have blonde hair."

Louise thought for a moment and then she said: "That's quite easy. I'll fetch my paintbox and a brush and you can paint your hair yellow."

"What a good idea," said little Evi happily. Louise went to fetch the paintbox when her friend held her back.

"I've just had a much better idea," she said. "I'll cut all my hair off and when it grows again it is sure to be blonde."

This was agreed on and the scissors were fetched. Snip, snap, snip, snap, snip, snap - only a few brown hairs were left and in another few minutes none at all. At the sight of her bald head little Evi got a bit anxious. Suddenly an awful thought struck her and she exclaimed in despair: "Heavens, Louise, what am I going to do when my Mummy sees me like this?" And she burst into tears. Louise, to whom the sight of her bald friend was already eerie, muttered some words of comfort, but as that didn't help, she began to cry too. Hearing the cats' chorus Mrs Bergel came rushing in and nearly rushed out again. Paralysed by the horror she beheld, she exclaimed:

"For heaven's sake, little Evi, what have you done to yourself?"

"I . . . I . . . I wanted to have blonde hair like Louise, and . . . and . . . and we cut my hair off . . . because . . . because . . . so that it will grow blonde next time . . . and . . . and . . . oh, when Mummy sees me like this...oh, what shall I do?" she stammered and wept.

25

b

"What's done is done," said Mrs Bergel. "Don't cry, little Evi. We'll put a nice white bandage on your head so your mother won't notice anything, shall we?" she consoled.

"Oh, yes please," rejoiced little Evi, and dried her tears. A large bandage was wound round and round her head and little Evi cheerfully put on her coat as the downstairs bell was heard to announce the maid who had come to fetch her home. But then she suddenly said: "Couldn't I stay here until my hair has grown back?"

"Oh, little Evi, you would have to stay a year," laughed Mrs Bergel.

"Whaaat?" cried little Evi in dismay. "I thought by tomorrow my hair would have grown back and Mummy and Daddy would have been so pleased about my new blonde hair." She began to cry again, but when the doorbell rang a second time she wiped away her tears and said goodbye. Erna, the maid, was flabbergasted.

"Whatever have you done to yourself?" she cried.

"I . . . I . . . I had such a bad toothache and so . . . and so Mrs Bergel put this bandage on," stuttered little Evi.

"Where does it hurt? Open your mouth wide and let me see," said Erna. Little Evi opened her mouth and after much probing she pointed to the third tooth on top. On arrival home her teeth were thoroughly examined and nobody believed her, whereupon little Evi cried again and told the truth. The cane was quickly fetched and Mr Feldner gave his daughter a sound spanking.

Half a year passed before little Evi saw a new growth of hair on her head, and - what a shock - the hair was brown again! But the next minute it didn't matter any more. She was so happy to have hair once more instead of a hideous bald head that she forgot all about wanting to be blonde and only reluctantly did she ever afterwards think back to her foolishness.

The End

[Pages 27-46 cover the 'diary with the lock'. Thereafter the diary continues, until 1968, on pieces of scrap paper kept in a cardboard cover, and in small pocket diaries containing brief daily entries.]

Falmouth 1939-1944

30th June 1939

I am twelve-year-old *I.P.* and you are my darling diary to whom I'll tell everything and you'll of course keep it all to yourself. I hope you won't be too shocked if I complain too much.

I'm in England! In Falmouth, Cornwall, to be precise, at the house of Mr and Mrs Robins. The house is large and very nice and the journey was quite good but something travelled with me, something I didn't want and which here too is my constant companion. It is homesickness. Not a pleasant feeling. Do you know it? No, of course you don't. We have a private tutor (like in books!). She teaches us English among other things. She told Mr Robins that I don't work hard enough. I do try, but everything is so strange here. It seems to me that I have been torn out of my own warm nest, and it hurts terribly. But nobody knows this, only you and I. And do you know who is the cause of all this? Hitler! He has ruined my youth, but I am sure some good will come out of it and Hitler will one day get his just deserts.

I'm tortured by homesickness. If only I could be back in Vienna, going for walks on Sunday mornings with my parents. I wish Austria could be a monarchy and that Hitler didn't exist. Dreams! Childish wishful dreams. Everything is destroyed. But I must keep telling myself that everything will be all right in the end.

Now I must explain to you the meaning of the word 'melan-

27

choly.' It is when one doesn't feel like doing anything any more and believes that nothing will ever make one happy again. It is wanting to cry all the time. It is looking forward to nothing and suffering from homesickness and memories of the past. But then it passes - I hear music or eat something nice - and, hey presto, I'm cheerful again. Or perhaps I hear you comforting me and telling me that everything will be all right in the end.

2nd July 1939

I'm waiting for the breakfast bell and will tell you a few things in the meantime. The 'Miss' still thinks I'm lazy. I'm still homesick but I tell myself that everything that happens here is only a fleeting dream, and then I feel better. I don't like Mrs Robins but Mr Robins is nice. Yesterday we had a picnic on Maenporth beach with two other refugee children, Lisl Gutfreund and Georg Müller. It was lovely to hear German again. Here's the gong.

3rd July 1939

I'm in a foreign country and no longer at home. If someone corrects me I immediately think the worst: they want to annoy me, they hate me. Then I tell myself: "These people are strangers. What have they got to do with you? This is not your country. You weren't born here and consequently you don't belong here." But then I feel a bit guilty and ungrateful. After all, the Robins' have done a wonderful deed, taking two strange children in. If you are miserable you see everything in a bad light.

How I envy English children! They are able to live at home with their parents. I'm sure there are many in Austria who envy *me*, but they needn't. Homesickness is terrible. Last night in bed I remembered how I used to pray and pray and long and long, in my bed at night in Vienna, for my visa to come to England. My wish was granted. Now I'm lying here in bed and pray and long to be back in Vienna. When I am bored and don't know what to do, horrible thoughts go round in my head. To think I may be here for months, years! I feel I shall die of misery. But then I fetch you out, darling diary, and tell you everything. If Mummy had the slightest suspicion, how upset and unhappy she'd be. She must never, never know! It hurts me to lie to her in my letters, but one

28

mustn't only think of oneself, must one? Nobody knows how unhappy I am here, only you.

Daddy wrote from Paris to say if anything is wrong we can write to him or to Uncle Hans. Shall I? Dare I? Better not.

How I long for freedom from homesickness!

4th July 1939

Mr R. is much nicer than Mrs R. (not because he's a man - honestly not). He's charming. Otherwise I've nothing much to tell you. This afternoon we're invited out to tea at friends of the Robins' and I'm very nervous. Are you surprised that I've so many moods and am sometimes like this and sometimes like that? I can't explain it myself.

5th July 1939

Last night Lieselotte and I had a serious discussion. She doesn't believe in God. She's quite the opposite of me in every way. She tells her best friend Muschi Redlich everything, but I couldn't tell everything to another *person*. That's why I have you. We were very worried because Mummy's letter was three days late. I thought she might have been taken to Dachau, but then her letter came. I cried with relief.

6th July 1939

Again something unpleasant has happened. This morning, during our ten minute break from lessons, we went up to our room, Lieselotte and I, and who is standing in our room? Mrs Robins. She shouts at us that we didn't do our room properly this morning, commands me in an awful tone to go and fetch the broom, accompanied by an incessant "quick, quick, quick" and Lieselotte to fetch the mop. I could have strangled her. Lieselotte must sweep the carpet, I the floor, then she accuses us of scratching the furniture (not true) and then tells me I must open the door for her and always let her go first. I thank you, Mrs Robins, for trying to replace my mother. Am I to be grateful to you for this? It makes me laugh. Only I can't laugh. I cry instead. Mrs Robins has got worse and worse. Poor Mummy, you know nothing of

29

how unhappy your darling child is, and I feel for you so because you worry about us and you may suspect. But I won't tell you, I won't be an egoist. One day everything will come to light.

I feel as if I were in chains, and cannot free myself.

7th July 1939

Today Mr R. said he'd send me away if I don't learn to speak English. Lieselotte and I mustn't talk German together. They listen at our door.

I have become indifferent to everything here and just keep thinking of the future and longing for my mother to join my father in Paris, so that we can all be together again. It must happen soon. I'm no longer an optimist of course, but I won't be a pessimist and so I've become a fatalist.

Why does Mrs R. ask Lieselotte to clear the table, when there are two maids in the house? Is she to be the third one? Is everything really so terrible, or does it only seem like it to me, consumed as I am with longing for my family and home? Lieselotte says I mustn't keep thinking of home.

8th July 1939

Mr Robins has written to Mummy saying I should try and learn English soon. I'm so happy he didn't say anything worse about me!

Mrs Robins was in a very bad mood yesterday. She always asks me where my handkerchief is and she keeps correcting my English in front of other people. But she's only a hated inhabitant of a hated place, there will never be any room for her in my heart, and so I remain cool and uncaring. Only hope sustains me, hope that I shall soon be united with my family. The fact that I am envied by the thousands of Jews who so long to be out of Austria and Germany is really ironic. It's so sad that the Jews are being driven out of their beloved homeland. English people rave about their fatherland. Lucky people! They can rave. We can't. We're rejected by our fatherland. I only know now what that really means. When I return to my beloved Vienna in better times I'll love it properly and be a good Austrian.

11th July 1939

I have such strange thoughts and feelings that I never had before. For instance, I've been thinking about one's mother tongue, and how beautiful it sounds when one hasn't heard it for a long time. So evocative. English hurts my ears. When I am in the Robins' car driving along and think about such things, tears come to my eyes. I don't think I can bear my homesickness much longer. When I die I want written on my tombstone: 'Here lies a child who perished miserably from homesickness.' And you, darling diary, shall be buried with me. I've no pleasure in anything. I've lost my sense of humour. I've no interest in learning or entertainments. I just want to go home. What worries did I have when I lived at home? What did I think about? School, friends, dolls, films, food, boys. That's all I knew. I've lost my youth now. And who's to blame? **Hitler!** Mr Robins took me to the doctor's because of my blocked nose. The doctor prescribed something. Perhaps the Robins' do care about us and just can't show it?

12th July 1939

I often think: Why did I leave Vienna, when so many other poor Jews are still there? If they can stand it, so could I. After all, I'm not free here, either. On the other hand perhaps I'm doing them some good; the more depart, the better for those remaining.

What shall I look forward to? Nothing. Do you know how I feel today? I feel like lying on the floor in some dark corner where nobody can find me and staying there till this ghastly period ends.

I can't stand Mr Robins any more either.

15th July 1939

I have a new and terrible fear: that I may be here for years and years, that I may have to finish school here, that I won't see my parents for a long, long time. Please God, don't let that happen! I could not bear it. I have no wishes or desires left, only to be with my parents again.

During lunch yesterday, there was some beautiful music on the radio and I suddenly began to cry. No one noticed. Anyway they didn't say anything if they did.

31

There's a chance that my father may come to visit us from Paris. I can hardly believe it. To tell you a secret - a dead secret which nobody in the world knows - I love my mother better than my father! Now you must forget this secret.

The Robins' keep on about my blocked nose. I must try and breathe through my nose and not through my mouth. " 'I', your mouth is open!" Mrs Robins says to me the whole time. I have to take some medicine. I'm beginning to believe my body is as sick as my soul, but I know that the doctor, the medicine, breathing cures, the Robins' good intentions are all useless. And why will nothing help me? BECAUSE I AM UNHAPPY!

Can you hate somebody, and yet be a little in love with them? Well, I have another confession to make to you - that's how it is with me and Mr Robins!

16th July 1939

The Robins' say I can't take my entrance exam to the High School until next summer. Next summer! Another year! What do they think? That I'll have my great-grandchildren here? Oh, why did you snatch me away from my home, Mr and Mrs Robins, why didn't you leave me where I was? You just wait, one more year and you'll have a sickly child on your hands, not a fresh and healthy one, with only a blocked nose.

Mr Robins can be so charming. Yes, I can see your shocked and amazed face. I can't help it. But - imagine it - Mrs R. has discovered that I have YOU! I've no idea how. I'm glad she can't read German. I think both Mr and Mrs R. prefer Lieselotte to me. She's a much less naughty girl than I am.

17th July 1939

Last night I dreamt that my dearest wish had come true - I was together with my parents and grandmother again. But of course, this dream was too lovely to be true. What do English children think or worry about? Is there anything more wonderful for a child than living in their own country with their own family? I too had that happiness once, but I didn't value it. I must remember that for the future. Annemarie Breuer is homesick too, and she's in England with her parents! I think my longing for home has gone to my head. I'm going mad.

I didn't tell you that Mr Robins was annoyed with us because we made a noise in the evening, firstly because at that time I didn't love him yet and so didn't much care, and secondly because Lieselotte hadn't yet told me the terrible thing he said to her. Listen carefully. This is what Mr Robins said: "Even the dogs know that there is only one master in the house whom they must obey, and I hope I won't have to show it to you in the way I did to them." As Lieselotte spoke these words they seemed to pierce my heart. True, he regretted them afterwards, as Mrs R. told Lieselotte, but I can never forgive him for them. The hole these sharp and cruel words made in my heart will not heal so long as I remain here, and many pleasurable things will slip through it without affecting it. Only one joy will heal it, and that will be my reunion with my family.

If Mummy knew this!

Yesterday we spoke about Hitler and Germany with the Robins'. Mr R. asked Lieselotte: "Didn't you have anything to eat any more?"

Lieselotte: "Oh, it wasn't as bad as that. Only no butter, no meat, no fruit and not very good milk. But enough to live on."

Mr R: "Then why did you come to England?" This might have been interpreted as a reproach, but he said it unsuspectingly and of course he meant all Jews.

Lieselotte: "But we couldn't live there - haven't you heard about the 10th of November? (I'll tell you about the 10th of November some other time). We couldn't go into a park, a theatre, or use a tram. In the street, anybody could do what they liked to us, the men were being imprisoned, we were thrown out of our homes . . ."

Mr R: "Oh, I see." He found it impossible to understand, but looked sad, and seemed to sympathise with us. I must say I don't blame him, I wouldn't understand or believe it either, if I hadn't experienced it.

Mr R. again: "I expected to find you very nervous. My wife and I were surprised that you weren't." I must say he's at times a little tactless. Lieselotte was furious afterwards and she hates him now, but loves Mrs Robins - exactly the opposite from me! She says she has lost her faith in human nature, and that the British are only Hitler's enemy because they are afraid for themselves, not because of the Jews. Very sad, if true. We couldn't sleep that night.

19th July 1939

Oh my goodness! Every day brings something new that's terrible. I can hardly keep up with telling you about it.

Over breakfast today Mr R. told us that they are going away for three weeks - and we are staying here! Not in this house with the maids, but at someone else's house, with a lady who teaches English and who takes children in for holidays. It was the last thing Lieselotte and I expected. We are very upset. My heart may now be of stone, but these torments can bore painful holes even into this hard texture.

Last Sunday we went to the Lizard with the Robins' in their car, and Mr R. bought me a little glass duck. I sleep with it every night, and of course I kiss it often. It won't disappoint me as people do. How can two such different people as Mr and Mrs Robins love each other? She's hardly ever nice to me, and keeps correcting my English (even though it is really much better now) and never praises my progress. Yesterday she got it into her head that I have a cold, but I haven't. Then there are all the rules we must obey: half an hour every morning Lieselotte and I must play quoits in a particular part of the garden, once with the left hand and once with the right (no idea why); for ten minutes we must play with a large ball and for ten minutes with a small one. It must be thrown with both hands. Now we must go to the lavatory. Now we must sit on this chair, not on that one. I must breathe with my mouth closed. I must do breathing exercises in front of the open window for five minutes every morning. I must always open the door for her ladyship. I must, I mustn't. Isn't that too much for anyone?

22nd July 1939

Who will change with me? I'd love to be someone else. I was so happy once, laughing and playing in my parents' home. Now I'm in CHAINS. And those chains hurt. In moments of my greatest despair I'd prefer to be a prisoner. At least prisoners know when they'll be free.

A few days ago we went for a walk with Mr Robins. I may not have mentioned it before but he has a very bad posture. Imagine my astonishment when he suddenly said to me; "'I', walk with your head up, not down, so that you get some fresh air into your lungs. Shoulders back, hold yourself straight." What do you think of that? I said before that a prisoner is better off than I. At least he can walk as he chooses. Soon the Robins' will sit at my grave and tell me which way to turn! And if they accompany my coffin they will think: "So that's all we get for our goodness in saving her from Hitler." I have no more to write now but tomorrow I'll tell you about Tommy Muller.

23rd July 1939

Well, yesterday we were invited to the house of Tommy Muller's guardian for tea. It was wonderful! Two other refugee children were there. We played games and spoke German as much as we wanted, and I felt quite at home. Tommy told us that he doesn't like his foster parents either. Poor Tommy. How I felt for him. When I saw Mrs R. again after that lovely afternoon I got a real fright.

On the 1st of August Ruth, my best friend, is coming to England on a children's transport!

24th July 1939

Today I must say goodbye to you, because we're going to Miss Davis' for three weeks. I think it's disgraceful to take in two children and then dump them on somebody else, especially without a word to the parents. But the time will pass, and you and I will be together again. I won't have time to write there, but I'm taking the key so no one can interfere with you, and I'll keep praying, to relieve my feelings.

14th August 1939

I'm back. I enjoyed myself very much at Miss Davis'. She wasn't nearly as strict as the Robins' and there was a happy-go-lucky atmosphere. While there, I promised God that I wouldn't be so unkind about the Robins' any more and I hope to keep that promise. Mr R. was going to visit us between Friday and Sunday but he didn't come. On Monday he came and fetched us back to 'Penhale'. My fleeting love for him has disappeared, though sometimes, when I look at him, it comes flooding back, for a moment. When he is not here for meals I hardly say a word, but when he is I chatter away all the time (in English of course). On the whole, both of them are much nicer to us since our return.

Sometimes when I look out of the window into the far distance and see nothing but fields and sea and a few houses, and nowhere where I belong, I lose courage, and inside me I scream: "Aren't you coming to fetch me home? Your child longs for you, she's wretched and lonely here, have you forgotten her?" No reply. All in vain.

17th August 1939

Today I must tell you another secret which nobody but you must know (unthinkable for me to tell secrets to a *person*, not even to Ruth, as Lieselotte does to her friend Muschi). I'm very ashamed of something I've done. Listen. When we were alone at home with the cook today I saw an open letter from Mummy to Mr Robins lying on the table. What did I do? I read it! Just as well really. I shall never love Mr Robins again now, never, never! I read the following: 'Dear Sir, I am very glad that my children are well and happy with you. They write such glowing letters. I am pleased that you like Lieselotte so much and I hope this will soon be the case with *'I'*. too. She is an affectionate, bright and cheerful child and usually very popular.'

So now I know. How could Mr Robins write to my mother saying he didn't like me, or not as much as Lieselotte? It must have hurt her terribly. And why is it so? Am I such a bad specimen of humanity? I never knew it and nobody told me. Am I so bad, Mr and Mrs Robins, that you can't love me? Of course, you wouldn't understand how a refugee child feels, away from home in a strange country. I remember some incidents which perhaps should have told me how you disliked me:

1. I put the spoon back wrongly into the honeypot at teatime. Mr R., to me: "Didn't you see how it should be done properly?" (very crossly).

36

2. Mrs R. to Lieselotte: "I'm cross with 'I'. She's been in England three weeks and what does she know? And she always makes a mess of my newspapers."
3. Mrs R. to Lieselotte (before we went to Miss Davis'): "I'm afraid that when you go swimming in the sea 'I' will swim far out and Miss Davis will call her and she won't come."
4. Mr R. to Lieselotte: "If 'I' doesn't speak English soon we'll send her away."
5. Mr R. to me: "You speak so much German that I think you've forgotten what English is."
6. Lieselotte always sits in the front when we go out in the car, if Mrs R. is not with us.

It seems I can't do anything right. But today Mrs R. actually said that I've begun to speak English very well. I hope she'll write and tell Mummy, and that it will make them like me better.

My heart is so heavy that it feels as if a gigantic stone was attached to it, weighing 1000 kilos. All my sorrows are in that stone: will I ever see my parents again, will I pass the entrance exam to the High School, shall I ever speak English properly, will the Robins' ever like me? Sometimes these fears and worries feel as if a million worms were gnawing away in my stomach.

19th August 1939

Mr R. can be very nice. For instance, yesterday Mrs R. said something about the stone age. I'd never heard this word before and asked innocently: "Did you say 'sausage'?" They all burst out laughing. The one person who politely declined to join in was - Mr Robins. He only smiled sweetly and said: "It is very bad manners to laugh if somebody makes a mistake." And he explained to me what stone age means.

Relations of theirs were here for a week. The lady gave us 6d each and Lieselotte asked Mrs R. if we could accept it. She said: "Of course. You are her adopted nieces." That means we are the Robins' adopted children. It's very nice of you, Mr and Mrs Robins, but please never say that again, never. You can think it but don't say it, because it hurts me nearly as much as if you said: "We hate these children." WE ARE NOT YOUR CHILDREN. We belong to our parents, and they won't give us to you, not ever.

20th August 1939

I have very bad manners. I am spoilt. I am lazy. These are the only observations I have to make today. We're going to the beach now and anyway it's so hot that my thoughts have all melted away.

21st August 1939

The present is a luminous ball. Behind it - the past; in front of it - the future. The whole soars in total darkness and reels to and fro, now gently, now vigorously. Below there is an abyss, above vapour. It is pitch dark. Either the ball crashes, then all is lost, or it glides into the future and that means hope. Which way is it going? We mortals are helpless and can't influence it. We await our fate.

All the Robins' ever think about is dogs, garden, weather, entertainments. Think of it - a twelve-year-old girl has more worries than a grown-up man and woman! When I was at home Mummy always kissed and comforted me if I had something on my mind (what on earth could I have had on my mind?) but now there is nobody. Perhaps it's good for me to be hardened. Perhaps the second half of my life will be easier to bear, if I ever reach it. If a person is unhappy from morning till night, day after day, they may not live long.

22nd August 1939

My Journey to England (told belatedly):

I'm now going to describe to you, belatedly, the journey from Vienna to England on the Children's Transport on which Lieselotte and I came on the 20th June.

On the evening of our departure I couldn't eat anything except a piece of apple. I was terribly excited. Everything seemed like a dream - saying goodbye to Gromi, going through our flat for (presumably) the last time, driving to the station in the taxi for the last time along the beautiful Ring, the Stephansplatz, the Opera, with Mummy and Aunt Anna. On the station we were each given a cardboard number on a string, to hang round our necks. As I lay in Mummy's arms, saying goodbye to her for heaven knows how long, I still didn't realise what was happening. We were told to join a queue with hundreds of other children, and stood about for

A commemorative plaque at Harwich
International Port, 1989.

a very long time. Then suddenly we were on the train and waved goodbye to Mummy and Aunt Anna until the train took us out of sight. I looked at the other children near us and they were all talking and shouting and running about. Naturally we couldn't sleep much that night. We sang Viennese songs and some of the children cried. The train left at 11pm and it was now past midnight. A few children unpacked the food we had all brought, to last us the whole journey, and started eating it. Lieselotte tried to disown me for most of the time and teamed up with the older children. Boys and girls were in separate compartments. A lady was in charge of us who put in an appearance from time to time and told us to go to sleep. When we crossed the border into Holland and freedom a great cheer went up. Some Dutch people handed each child a bar of Nestles milk chocolate through the train windows. On the boat crossing over to Harwich, Lieselotte offered to look after a little girl aged six and shared a cabin with her, instead of with me, which upset and annoyed me. I shared a cabin with another strange girl. In the night I felt seasick and got up to go to the lavatory but ended up in a sort of linen cupboard and was sick there. We arrived in Liverpool Street Station on Thursday 22nd June. The Müllers met us and we stayed the night with them. For breakfast I had toast for the first time and I thought it was burnt bread. Lieselotte must have done too, because she took the only piece that didn't look burnt. The Breuers called to see us later. I still felt giddy from the ship and thought I must be dreaming everything. In the afternoon we were taken to Hyde Park, and I heard English spoken all around me for the first time, even by children, which seemed very strange. The next day we were put on a train to Exeter and there Mr and Mrs Robins were to meet us. They were late and I was in a panic. I couldn't speak a word of English, and when a taxi driver asked us if we needed a taxi while we stood waiting for the Robins', I thought he wanted to abduct us! Lieselotte knew better because she understood some English. The Robins' arrived about fifteen minutes late.

"Are you Lieselotte and *I.P*?" they asked us. We got into their large white car and drove to Falmouth, which took many hours. I was still in a dream. At last we arrived at 'Penhale'. The two maids were at the window. They had probably been waiting there with great curiosity to see what the Robins' were bringing home. The dogs ran out, barking. And that was the beginning of my new life. Little did I know what was ahead of me.

23rd August 1939

Mrs R. has a new unpleasant habit. If I don't understand something and ask for it to be repeated she says crossly: "Why don't you listen? I've just said that." Or: "This was explained to you yesterday, you don't pay attention." But all this is nothing when compared to my new huge worry - namely WAR! Everyone is talking of war. Hitler, that rotter, has made a non-aggression pact with Russia and is demanding Danzig. And he calls himself 'angel of peace!' Why does he want more land? Why do people fight? Please, God, let there not be war. I go to bed with old worries and get up with new ones.

Mr and Mrs R. asked me if I don't like them, because I don't join them in the drawing room after lunch.

I haven't told you much about the political situation in Austria. Jews were forbidden to go into certain shops, into cinemas, theatres, the Opera, parks; were taken in their thousands to Dachau, of whom only 1% came out alive. The rest had their ashes sent to their families, usually with a letter saying something like: 'We regret that your husband (or father or son) slipped on a banana skin, and died.' They were treated and addressed with utter contempt, in the 'Du' form, by the Nazis. They were made to stare into blinding light for six hours, they were made to do heavy work regardless of age, and often shot as they walked in the street. I was afraid of the Hitler Youth boys because they often teased me. We were even afraid to go to places that *were* allowed to us. At any moment someone might exclaim "It stinks of Jews in here," and you might be killed, anywhere, at any time. A Christian dog, if there is such a thing, was more valuable than a Jewish person. Swastikas hung from every window. All conversation among Jews centred around emigration. "Well, have you got your visa yet?" "Where are you going?" "Will we get out before there is a war?" "My wife is domestic help in England." "Yesterday I was at the *Kultusgemeinde, tomorrow I'm going to the Passport office." And so on. Quite small Jewish children played at emigrating.

The worst day of all was the 10th of November. A Jew in Paris killed a German official, out of anger against Hitler. Hitler

*A Jewish organisation.

41

revenged this deed by punishing all Jews with renewed intensity. In the morning of that day Mummy, Lieselotte and I went to the dress-maker's. We saw crowds in the streets and knew something was up. We went home quickly. In the afternoon I went to bed with a bad cold and a temperature. By then thousands of Jews were being fetched out of their houses or rounded up in the streets and taken away. Occasionally also women. At about 8pm our doorbell rang. We heard men's voices. Mummy said: "Here they are. They've come," and went to open the door. I wanted to jump out of bed but lay frozen and rigid with fear, unable to move. A few minutes later Mummy returned. "They only wanted to know about the business," she said. "I told them that Daddy was in France, and they left." We all relaxed, although none of us slept that night. Granny said to me later: "It was your mother's charm. Even those brutes couldn't resist it. Otherwise they would have taken her." Many of our friends were taken to prison. It is now 10pm and I'm dead tired. I'm going to sleep now, to dream of being at home again in Vienna, with my parents, in better times. But first I'll pray for a letter from Mummy tomorrow. Goodnight, my darling diary.

25th August 1939

Mrs R. again told us off for not doing our room properly. "We give you a home," she shouted, "but you must keep it tidy." And if not you'll throw us out, I suppose. I think it's Alice, the less nice maid, who tells tales about us. We sometimes go for a walk with her, but I don't trust her. Mary is much nicer.

I can be justly proud of what I've experienced at only twelve years old, I think, and all the other Jewish children, too. I'm sure we've all become more mature, sensible and clever. Unfortunately also sadder. Sometimes, when I chat and laugh at meal times, I suddenly stop and ask myself: "What reason have you to laugh? Your situation is much too terrible for you to laugh. So STOP!"

Just imagine, Lieselotte has become homesick! No wonder. She is missing parental love and our home. She says she has had enough of living in strangers' houses, riding in their cars and taking their charity. The further the good old days slip back into the past, the more vivid their memory becomes.

Yesterday, in a shop, the shop assistant asked me how I was getting on with my English. Before I could reply, Mrs Robins said: "She's a bit lazy." This really hurt me, because it was so unfair. Everyone else says how well I speak English now. She's so unjust. I hate her.

I'm still in love with Mr Robins - but not all the time.

28th August 1939

MRS ROBINS (A character description):

I'm afraid I've more bad than good things to say about her. She's terribly moody, unjust, strict and usually scolds me for things I'm not guilty of. She has no feelings whatever for refugee children and probably no deeper feelings about anything. She has the nasty habit of criticising everybody she sees in the street, never saying anything nice about them. Sometimes she's quite funny and tells jokes, but that's all I can say in her favour. My last sentence is and remains: I hate her.

MR ROBINS (A character description):

Mr Robins is the exact opposite of his wife - and yet they love each other! He's sometimes not nice, but never as nasty as she is. It's quite obvious that they have no children of their own. He seems to care more about us, sometimes even in an exaggerated way. He's strict too, but he's fun. As you know, often I'm really in love with him. As my feelings for him are not consistent I can't really judge him properly.

2nd September 1939

Germany and Poland are at war. It can't be long now until England and France join in. I'm sure you're thinking, how can I write that down so calmly? Well, I'm *not* calm. I'm in a terrible state. But my imagination fails me for once. What will war be like? If there is really a war, will I ever see my parents again?

Hitler, I hate you even more than I hate Mrs Robins!

3rd September 1939

It's Sunday morning. Lieselotte told me that Mrs R. told her a secret which only she and Mr and Mrs R. know. She says I'll find out what it is in a few months. She swears that it is nothing to do with me, and she had to swear to Mrs R. not to tell me. I think it was really horrible of Mrs R. to come between me and my sister. But God has punished her a little, because her favourite little dog died a few days ago.

Later. Heaven help us! My eyes are full of tears and my heart is pounding. It is WAR! It has come at last, the spectre of horrors I feared so long. Mummy, Daddy, shall I see you again, and when? Up to three quarters of an hour ago I was still hopeful. Now all hope has gone. I should like to die for all the innocent people who will be shedding their blood who have so much more to live for than I. I know that thousands of children are suffering the same fate, but it doesn't help me.

4th September 1939

I was too upset to write more yesterday. This is what happened: Lieselotte was downstairs listening to the news on the radio in the morning. I was upstairs in our bedroom. Then I too went downstairs, and met Lieselotte running up to our room.

"Do you understand what has happened?" Mr Robins asked me as I came into the drawing room.

"No," I said.

"War has been declared," he said. I ran out of the room. In the bedroom Lieselotte is lying on the bed crying hysterically.

"It's war, isn't it?" I cry. No answer. "Isn't it?" I repeat. I begin to cry too. At last we both stop.

"Crying is no use, is it?" I say, and she agrees. Then we talk for a long, long time, and we both look at the photograph of our parents with the same thought in our heads: Shall we ever see them again? Then I go to the calendar and look at the date. Sunday, 3rd of September. The first day of war. At 11am it was declared and at 11.45am I was informed of it. I mark the date with a black ring round and ask myself when I shall be marking the last day of the war?

6th September 1939

First days of war. No sign of it here yet, except that we get no letters from home. I don't know what has happened to my parents in Vienna and Paris. If I am unoccupied for long the wildest thoughts oppress me and I get headaches and stomach cramps. I think the same thoughts over and over again, but too much philosophising is not good for you.

8th September 1939

The old woman (you know who I mean) is cross with me again. Mr R. has also been very moody and unpleasant. I usually bring him the ashtray in the evening but last night I didn't. Served him right.

Because the Robins' are such loving foster parents and so concerned about us, they took us to the optician's yesterday. (They'll have our behinds examined next.) Lieselotte has to wear glasses and I have to see a specialist because there might be something wrong with my eye muscles. Mr R. says it's my fault because I don't move my eye muscles enough and always turn my head to look around instead of my eyes. To think that a forty-year-old man can talk such nonsense. I am sure you are laughing and I almost hear you say: "Well, even '*I*' wouldn't say anything so stupid." Am I right?

14th September 1939

Lieselotte started at the High School today. She passed her entrance exam in the summer. My turn next, but I'm sure I'll fail. Darling diary, I've nearly come to the end of you - only two pages left. We must say goodbye. I'm sorry I had to begin and end in such an unhappy mood.

17th September 1939

Apparently I don't pronounce the word 'toast' well, so Mr Robins decided to make me ask for it every morning instead of passing it to me. I wouldn't do this, so for three days I've gone without toast. Better starve than give in, I told myself. On Sunday, this is today, I was prepared to go without again and was curious to see what would happen. And do you know what did happen? He passed me the toast! Then we had a long chat and he was quite nice to me again. The funny thing is, each time he is especially nasty to me my love for him returns more vigorously.

I'm starting school at Miss Davis' on the 25th. She's going to coach me for the entrance exam to the High School, so I won't have much time to write. Lieselotte has decided only to speak English from now on. The war goes on but there is no sign of it here. Sometimes we hear aeroplanes overhead, that's all.

Now I've reached the last page we really must say goodbye. I don't know when I shall continue writing, but one day I will. I've loved you very much and I'm sorry I had so many sad things to relate. I kiss you goodbye now. Goodbye, my darling diary. Then I shall lock you up and put you away where nobody can ever find you.

[The 'Diary with a lock' now finishes.]

11th October 1939

The autumn leaves are a brilliant gold in the morning sunshine but there is a raw wind blowing and the sun scarcely warms. I see no glorious autumn morning, however, I smell no fresh morning air and hear no birds sing. I see only blackness and darkness. I hear only thunder, gunfire and shooting which I know is going on somewhere in the world. I feel icy cold. That is how I see the world now.

I need happiness, but where can I find it? Does God know I am here? I have one aim in life - just one, to leave England and return to Vienna. Why couldn't I foresee how it would be here? Why didn't I have an inkling that I was going to people who would hate me and whom I would hate?

On the 30th of September, the Robins' discovered that we are not happy here. We told them honestly and openly. I don't suppose it will make any difference.

14th October 1939

I attend classes at St. Joseph's School every morning and afternoon. A boy called Robin, who is the same age as I am, is also a pupil here. He always wants to kiss me and says he loves me. He asked me if I have other boyfriends. Lisl Gutfreund said to me: "You're in love with Robin, aren't you?" "Of course not," I replied. I quite like him, though.

I'm wonderfully happy today, and do you know why? Mummy's first letter since the war has arrived! She writes: 'My darlings, since Ruth's last message that you are well I have heard nothing from you. I am constantly with you in my thoughts. May God grant that you are both well and happy. How happy I should be if I could hear from you - and better still see you. Gromi and I are well and busy all day long, which is a good thing because it stops us from thinking too much. Our whole flat is let and everyone is so kind to us. Findlers, Lambergs, Engls etc. all send you greetings. We often see them. Please write to them. Unfortunately we have heard nothing from Uncle Fritz. Uncle Hans and Aunt Lea are in America. I long and long to be with you and pray that God may soon grant my wish.

'I embrace you, kiss you and love you. Your loving Mummy.'

And Granny added: 'My dearest ones in the whole world, I send you many thousand kisses and live only for our reunion. Your ever loving Gromi.'

26th November 1939

The war goes on, but here in our region everything is quiet and peaceful. And yet it seems to me as if bombs were falling on this house because everything is destroyed for me. What a sad time we are going through. When will it get better? May God protect my family, wherever they all are.

Last week Lieselotte and I and Gerti and Lisl Gutfreund went to the cinema to see Fred Astaire and Ginger Rogers. I've had my eyes tested and have to wear glasses! Terrible! The optician is called Dr Joles.

Ruth and I write regularly to each other and she is still my best friend.

Lieselotte has been in a bad mood. We had a scene in Mr Robins' office and she cried. Afterwards Mr Robins was very nice to her. She's a funny girl, my sister, and gets upset by things I don't care about. Also, she only seems to be able to fall in love with females, and then carries on as if they were boys. She used to be in love with Greta Garbo, and went scarlet whenever her name was mentioned.

1st December 1939

I feel restless and can't settle to anything. Nowhere feels right. I want to go home but of course I can't. Something happened last night, something I saw coming a long time ago: I had an attack of crying. It was ghastly. Then I pulled myself together and considered my situation. Was I really in England? In an English house miles away from my home? I look around the room with weepy red eyes. Am I in my own nursery, my own beloved nursery in Vienna? No! A small pink frilly room meets my gaze. This is not my own room in Vienna. But wait - perhaps the room has changed, as rooms do in dreams, perhaps this is all only a dream? I almost say this aloud. To convince myself I go towards the window to see if the Wipplingerstrasse is out there. I hear no cars or trams, only a gentle swishing sound. I am soon to know what this sound is. Now I am at the window - and start back in horror. What do I see? Blackout curtains meet my gaze. Of course, I remember now, there's a war on - a WAR, ein KRIEG, une GUERRE! Now everything is clear to me. This is no dream. I do not need to look out of the window. I know what is out there - the garden, with its tall wind-blown trees, and beyond it the sea, whose swish I had heard. Everything is alien, unfamiliar and hostile. I want my mother and Vienna but they are far, far away. Nobody hears my crying. I make up my mind there and then to go back to Vienna and to my mother as soon as I can.

13th December 1939

My poor dear grandfather died on 27th of November (in Czechoslovakia). The news came in Mummy's last letter. Tomorrow is his birthday.

Guess what I heard from Gerti Gutfreund today! Mrs Robins is expecting a baby! I've thought of nothing else all day. I wonder what it feels like to be pregnant? Would I like it? Yes and no. Perhaps having a baby is not as nice as I thought after all, or perhaps again it is even nicer. Maybe I shall soon know - no, not very soon, I don't think!

A Week From My War Diary:

Thursday, 14th December 1939
German Pocket Battleship *Admiral Graf Spee* badly damaged.

Friday, 15th December 1939
Prime Minister went to France to visit B.E.F.

Monday, 18th December 1939
Captain and some of the *Graf Spee* landed at Buenos Aires.

Tuesday, 19th December 1939
Helsinki bombed by Russian bombers.

Wednesday, 20th December 1939
Reported that Captain Langsdorf, new commander of *Graf Spee*, committed suicide on Tuesday night.

Sunday, 24th December 1939
After blazing for a week the hull of the *Graf Spee* burnt out.

Monday, 25th December 1939
The King broadcast a Christmas message to the people of the Empire.

20th December 1939

Today is the last day of school, and then the Christmas holidays begin. Tomorrow we are moving to St. Josephs again, thank goodness. Miss Davis is very nice, and takes us on lots of outings. In the summer she often took us to the beach and for picnics and out to tea, and once even to an open air performance of Shakespeare in the park, though I couldn't understand it. The Robins' can't have us any more because of the coming baby.

25th December 1939

Today is Christmas day. In the morning I went for a walk with

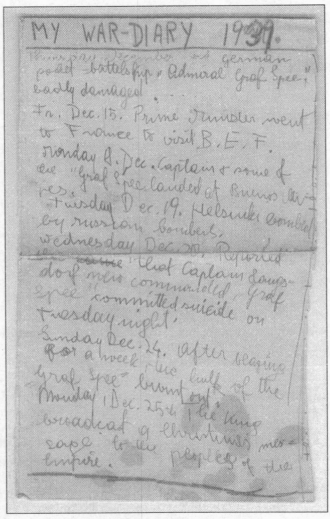

MY WAR-DIARY 1939.

...ship aeroplane ... German
pocket battleship "Admiral Graf Spee"
badly damaged ....

Fri. Dec. 15. Prime Minister went
to France to visit B. E. F.
Monday 8. Dec. Captain & some of
res. "Graf Spee" landed at Buenos Aires.
Tuesday Dec. 19. Helsinki bombed
by russian bombers.
Wednesday Dec. 20. Reported
that Captain Langs-
dorf who commanded "Graf
Spee" committed suicide on
Tuesday night.
Sunday Dec. 24. After blazing
for a week the hulk of the
"Graf Spee" burnt out.
Monday 1 Dec. 25th. The King
broadcast a christmas mes-
sage to the peoples of the
Empire.

A page from my War Diary.

50

Gerti and Alan Tothill, who is a nephew of Agnes and Kitty Davis and is staying here. In the afternoon we had a celebration! There were crowds of people and everyone had presents. It was lovely. The day before, which was Sunday, we spent at the Robins' and they gave us our Christmas presents. I had a black dog - a pyjama case really - and a book from the Rotary Club called *Black Beauty*. Robin also gave me a book, *The Oxford Song Book*. Tomorrow is Boxing Day and there is to be a party here. The priests from the Catholic church across the road will come, too. St. Joseph's is a very large old house. It used to be a convent and has a cross on top.

1st January 1940

The year is over. I loved you, my little red and white spotted diary. Please, God, help to make next year a better one. We had a wonderful New Year's party here last night. We played 'Murder' and 'Black Magic' and 'Charades' and various guessing games and got to bed *very late*. This morning I went for a walk with Lieselotte, Gerti and Barbara Wilson, who also lives here. Unfortunately there is blancmange for pudding today, which I hate. On Thursday we are all going to a party at Wendy Cooper's house. I've been to a lot of parties during the Christmas holidays. (Wendy Cooper is a pupil at St. Joseph's).

I have four shillings and ten pence.

3rd January 1940

We went to the cinema yesterday, to an evening performance. My favourite film stars, besides Shirley Temple, are Allan Jones, Freddie Bartholomew and John Boles. I used to want to be a film star but now I'd rather be a fashion designer or a poet. I love reading, and I like listening to the radio - but how much I'd like to hear again - "Halloh, halloh, hier Radio Wien." It makes me cry to think of it. Because there is no electricity at St. Joseph's the radio is run on a huge battery which has to be refilled with sulphuric acid once a week.

People born in March are Pisceans, love nature and life, are friendly and cheerful and very attached to their families. That is what I read in the newspaper. My lucky number is eleven, my lucky day is Monday and my lucky stone is chrysolite. And we often fall in love! I have to admit that is true. Of course it's mainly masculine people that I fall in love with; when I love feminine ones it shouldn't really be called 'in love'. One can be in love with pretend people, too. Ruth and I used to pretend that we knew a charming boy called Erich whom we loved and who loved us, but it wasn't true at all.

My favourite subject at school is drawing. I always have to help the other children.

4th January 1940

I forgot to tell you about Gerti and the turkey feet. On Christmas Eve we put the raw turkey feet in Gerti's bed. Gerti always gets teased. She screamed when she found them. But she's a good sport and laughed about it when we ate turkey for lunch on Christmas Day. It was not the last she had seen of them, however. It was Miss Kitty's idea to wrap them in pretty Christmas paper and put them on the Christmas tree, with Gerti's name on. Gerti was very excited when she received her present, and as she opened it all eyes were on her. Next thing, the turkey legs were flying across the room and Gerti was in hysterics. So were we, only with laughter. Poor Gerti. I can still hear her screams.

All the girls here love Alan Tothill, the Davis' seventeen-year-old nephew, especially Barbara, who is eighteen and whom I don't like as she is very bossy. He's very handsome and talented. He can play the piano and draw, both of which we often do together, and he can play the flute and sail. We spend many happy hours together on icy cold winter days, sitting round the fire, playing rummy, chatting or drawing. One day he offered me a cigarette. I didn't want it at first but finally he persuaded me. I shared a cigarette with him - and then we shared a second one. It tasted terrible. I did it for a joke. The other girls told him that I was too young to smoke, "Why shouldn't she? I don't see why she shouldn't," he kept saying. He's very natural and unaffected and doesn't care in the least about girls. In fact I think he was quite pleased that he wasn't the only boy at the New Year's party; a young soldier was here too, called Lawrence.

After Alan had gone away it was very dull. I hope he comes again soon. Miss Davis and Miss Kitty are also always pleased to have him here, even when, like last time, he just sent a telegram the day before which said: "Please find room, coming tomorrow."

13th January 1940

Mr Robins was here and said some really mean and nasty things about us. Lieselotte cried. I did not. I'm so glad that we don't live with them any more.

We had a school party here, for the day pupils.

This is my very first 'Pocket Diary' from England. But I'm writing in German. Diaries understand all languages, don't they? You see, German is my own, my native language. This curious circumstance of my writing in German into an English diary has been brought about by Hitler, who has deprived me, and I don't know how many others, of my country. Dearest little diary, do you perhaps know if the coming year will be a better one?

I'm ashamed to confess that I had a look at Barbara and Gerti's diaries! They were left lying around, but I know it was wrong. I discovered that Gerti has had a quarrel with a boyfriend and has suffered from an inferiority complex ever since, and Barbara is in love with Alan, which I knew; also that Alan's sister is expecting a baby.

Just imagine, I've told Lisl the facts of life! She's a year older than I am. She lives here too now because the husband in the family who 'adopted' her has been called up. I told her as delicately as I could. I said: "The man does to the woman what he normally does in the lavatory," and she understood at once.

We've been to Connie's party. She is the niece of the Misses Davis and my age. She lives down the road. The day after tomorrow we are going to see a Tarzan film with Johnny Weissmuller.

18th January 1940

School started today at St. Joseph's. I did a lot of homework in the afternoon and then I fetched Lisl from the High School. She has already passed her entrance exam and has been going to the High School for a term. I shall be taking the exam in March. Lieselotte also goes to the High School.

22nd January 1940

I'm so happy today because Alan is back. God is always doing little good deeds for me: a letter from Mummy, a party, no more visits to Dr Joles, and now Alan's unexpected visit. Do you think He can do big deeds too, like reuniting us with our family and ending the war?

There are a lot of books for little children about the place here, and the other day I came across *Snow White*. I thought: "How I would love to be kissed awake by a prince and be happy ever after!" Because I'm sure the life I am living now is only a dream from which I'll wake sooner or later. The awful things that have happened are the stuff of nightmares, and can't be true. I'm freezing. The rooms are awfully cold here.

4th February 1940

Yesterday Mrs Robins had her baby - a boy. She wanted a girl. I wonder if it is as fat and ugly as its mother? We are going to 'Penhale' to see it, probably next week.

Lieselotte, Lisl and I have been to the pictures and seen a silly film called: *Three Smart Girls Grow Up*.

Mummy has written to say that one of her lodgers who knows English well thought our last English letter to her very good. There were no mistakes in Lieselotte's at all. I always call Mummy various tasty nicknames, and she said: 'First I was a potato, now I am a *Gugelhupf! You're making a whole menu out of me! I wonder what I'll be next time?' I do so long for her.

29th February 1940

I have German Measles and I am in bed. Lieselotte got it first, but it's quite mild and I don't feel ill at all. A lovely birthday letter from Mummy cheered me up completely. She sent me a tiny calendar and a lucky clover.

9th March 1940

My first birthday away from home. All the same, it was a nice day. Everyone gave me presents. Connie and her seventeen-year-old sister Monica came to tea and Miss Davis had made nice

*A cake.

54

things to eat, including a beautiful sponge cake. I have made up my mind not to think of the past any more.

We found a bird in Kimberley Park. It was sick or injured so we took it back to St. Joseph's. It was a jack-daw. Miss Davis put it in a shopping basket with a hot water bottle. I was very sad when, two days later, it was dead.

24th March 1940

Easter Sunday today. We went picking primroses in the morning and in the afternoon Lieselotte and I went to tea at the Robins'. Tomorrow I have to stay at home and do arithmetic and other school work as I take my entrance examination to the Falmouth Girls' High School on Saturday. Help!

4th April 1940

Yesterday school finished at St. Joseph's until the 1st May, and we went back to live at 'Penhale' with Mr and Mrs Robins, unfortunately. I had to help out with the baby today and take the dogs for a walk. The baby is called Francis. He is to be christened at the Parish Church on Saturday and afterwards there will be a big party.

Tomorrow we are going to Plymouth by car with Mr Robins for the whole day.

Before leaving St. Joseph's I found a little chocolate cake on my bedside table, with this note from Robin: *[see overleaf]*

I had told him about eating a nasty bun I didn't like. Wasn't it nice of him?

14th April 1940

Today I am going to tell you something about each member of my family. There is nothing much else to tell you as all we do is take the dogs for walks or help with the baby or go to the beach, except yesterday, when I had to go to the dentist in Falmouth and then had tea with Miss Davis. So I'll start with:

Before leaving St. Joseph's I four on my bedside table, with this note f told him about eating a nasty bun of him?

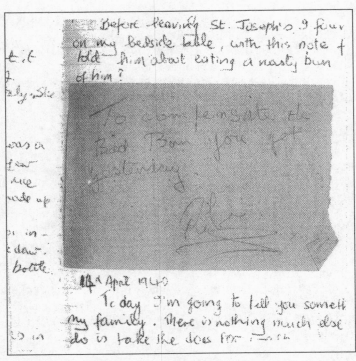

To compensate the Bad Bun you got yesterday.

14th April 1940
Today I'm going to tell you somett my family. There is nothing much else do is take the does for

Note from Robin as placed within original diary.

56

My Father

I'll be perfectly honest and write exactly what I think. Well, he's very, very selfish and in some ways awfully funny. I don't know whether I've told you yet - but my parents were never happy together. They quarrelled each day, hour, minute of their lives. My father avoided coming home as much as possible. The reasons for their quarrels were always silly ones, and they were always supposed to be my mother's fault. I think my father once kicked my mother - but I never saw him kiss her.

He's quite intelligent and has read a lot and he's rather popular. Of course, I love him, but I don't think he loves me as much as Lieselotte because he wanted me to be a boy. Many of my parents' quarrels were about me. My father considered I was spoilt by my mother and neither of them would reason. I was quite small when I first heard these arguments but my heart understood. I always envied my friends who had kind gentle fathers who came home in the evenings; mine hardly ever did. To avoid quarrels, I suppose. I think he played cards in the Café Louvre most evenings. There were days when my father hardly spoke to my mother and that was awful. The best days were when he was in a good mood and made up funny stories for us or told us jokes.

I can never, never understand why my parents married.

My Mother

My mother is the kindest and best person I have ever known. She is a real mother and would do anything for her children. For us, she gladly gave up her own pleasures. Unfortunately she spoilt us in her complete devotion to us, which is a great pity. The one thing she could not do was keep her temper (like me), and probably the quarrels were as much her fault as my father's. I can't tell. She was often rude to her mother, Gromi, because she in her turn had been spoilt as a child. She was very popular and had a lot of friends. When she was a young girl the Mayor of Vienna once kissed her - she was so pretty. Once, about two or three years ago, when I had been very naughty, she said something terrible to me in a temper which I shall never forget. She later said the words just slipped out of her mouth and I was to forget them, and I wish I could.

My mother is not as clever as my father but much better with people. She likes everybody but most of all her children, with whom she is over-concerned. Now, in her letters, when she tells us to put on warm clothes and do our hair nicely and be polite and always brush our teeth in front of the mirror and things like that, I can actually hear her say them.

I always took my mother's part against everybody else. Now that I am older I understand that in a quarrel, both parties are to blame. But whatever her faults, my mother is the most marvellous mother I know, and I can't wait till we're together again.

My Sister

I have waited a long time to tell you about my sister and I am glad I did too, for now I know quite a lot more. Since we came to England we've begun to understand each other, and although there are times when we don't get on too well, on the whole we are true friends now. We even promised to tell each other all secrets - excluding our innermost feelings, that is. I have come to like her so much that I miss her when I'm not with her. But, like everyone else, she has faults, and some rather bad ones in my opinion. For one thing - I won't say she lies but she doesn't always speak the truth. She twists things around until they are unbelievable and then she won't admit it. This is her worst habit. Next, she's immensely indolent. You could say to her: "The world is coming to an end tomorrow!" And she would reply: "Is it?" If you ask her anything she usually replies: "Don't know." This drives me mad. She is also very untidy - so much so that one adjective is not enough to describe this trait. If I didn't put things away they would stay in the wrong places for months on end. She's forgetful, a bit unfriendly and has no common sense at all, but she's very intellectual. She has a temper but not as bad as mine, and she can be unjust. Now for her good points - well, she's intellectual as I've just said; she's good, helpful (though not particularly capable) and popular at school. When she likes people she's very, very nice to them . . . She's good at sport, she is much better behaved than I am, and never seems to get into so much trouble, partly I suspect on account of her indolence. This was true in Vienna, too. She's not a flirt like most girls of her age

58

- in fact she doesn't seem to care about men at all. I often wonder if she will marry. I think she will, but not too early, and probably very happily.

That's all I can think of for the time except to repeat that I have come to like her very much and could not do without her. I hope I shall never be separated from her.

Myself

There is little and yet a lot to say about myself. Where shall I start? With my bad points first, I think. I used to bite my nails. I am cheeky, rude and always want to be right. I have a bad temper. I'm very argumentative and - so I'm told - always want to have the last word. I'm supposed to be thoughtless - but I consider I've plenty of thoughts! Now, some good points; I'm kind-hearted (but haven't much brain, which goes with kind-heartedness); I like to please people. I like food and fun and boys; am usually cheerful and friendly. I'm quite good at art - in fact it's the best thing I do, because it doesn't require much brain! I sometimes have good ideas, and would definitely be the brightest person there if ever I was put into the Bodmin Lunatic Asylum! I adore music, which goes with love. Music can always make me happy. I hate injustice and I'm quite strong-willed - although sometimes I think I must be weak, because my happiness depends so much on other people, for other people arrange my life and make me sad or glad.

That's enough about me.

20th April 1940

Hurrah! Hurrah! I've passed the entrance examination. Next week I'm getting the school uniform; a navy blue tunic, a white square necked shirt, a hat, a blue blazer with a badge, and navy blue thick knickers.

Lieselotte and I are sent out on walks every day. Sometimes we lose our way, like the time we went to Durgan. We've also been to Helford, Port Navas and Pennance Point. We take picnics.

On the 30th I have to meet Miss Frost, the Headmistress of the High School, and school starts on the 1st of May.

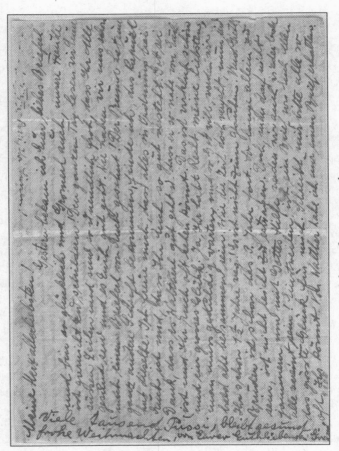

A letter from my mother.

6th May 1940

School is wonderful. I am in form 3b. Best of all it means that I'm not at 'Penhale' all day, with horrid Mrs Robins. I had my first science lesson today. After school Lieselotte and I go to Mr Robins' office in Market Street and he takes us back in the car.

24th May 1940

Today is Lieselotte's birthday. She had a watch from the Robins', and other presents, and a birthday cake for tea. Tomorrow she has to register with the police because she is now sixteen years old - and an alien. She may have to leave Falmouth as it is a protected area. I'm too afraid to think about it.

I had a letter from Ruth. She has to work in the jeweller's shop which belongs to the family who 'adopted' her in Portsmouth. We write each other long letters, sometimes on lavatory paper. Daddy has sent me a bracelet from France, for passing the entrance exam.

29th May 1940

Lisl is going to the pictures with Robin. Shall I tell you a secret which no one must know? Yes, I shall: I'm a bit jealous! But why should I be? How could I go when I'm stuck out here in 'Penhale', Maenporth?

Everyone is talking about an invasion. There is barbed wire along the beaches and stacks of sandbags everywhere. If Hitler comes to England, what will happen to us?

We are not allowed to have all our things out of our trunk, but on Saturday we can have our summer clothes out. Wonderful. I'm longing to wear my summer dresses.

7th June 1940

On Sunday we are moving to St. Joseph's again!

Lisl didn't go to the cinema with Robin after all. She says he is stupid.

We had a medical at school today. While we were waiting in the cloakroom to see the doctor, some of the girls were singing:

> "Whistle while you work,
> Hitler is a twerp,
> Mussolini's barmy
> So's his army,
> Whistle while you work."

13th June 1940

It's Mummy's birthday today. I've been thinking about her all day. How is she and what is she doing? We don't get so many letters now.

We are having very hot weather but the sea is still cold. Last Tuesday we had Speech Day at school. Some sixth form girls performed a scene from King Lear.

Yesterday I was just coming out of the school room at St. Joseph's, having played the piano (not that I can really play) and was about to enter the kitchen when I heard, through the slightly open kitchen door, Miss Kitty say to Miss Davis: "In my opinion, they make allowances for the refugee children, otherwise how is it that they all pass? Poor Monica and Connie didn't. It isn't fair." My heart stood still. I didn't want to hear any more and so I went straight into the kitchen and pretended that nothing had happened. But of course it had, and now I know that they are jealous of us.

 22nd June 1940

Daddy is in Plymouth! The Germans have invaded France, where he was living (in Paris) and he got away on the last boat to leave the country, leaving all his possessions behind. It is the third time he has escaped from the Nazis - first from Vienna, then from Italy and now from France. We shall probably go to visit him soon, or he'll visit us here. He came to England with the B.E.F. We haven't seen him for two years.

When Connie and I arrived at the Odeon today, to our amazement there was no film on and it was closed. The reason: it was full of French refugees who were put up there until other accommodation can be found for them. We got talking to a French couple who, like my father, had arrived without any possessions. I gave them a bar of chocolate for their little boy which I had just bought for myself, and they were very grateful.

"Merci beaucoup, Mademoiselle, merci beaucoup," they kept saying. I like to think that this good deed of mine shows my gratitude to God for saving my father.

There's a French refugee boy coming to live at St. Joseph's tomorrow, and Ilse Rosendorf, another German Jewish refugee child who goes to the High School is coming to tea. The French boy doesn't know where his parents are. Next week I must start revising for school exams.

Lieselotte doesn't have to leave Falmouth! Mr Robins arranged it. Thank God.

5th July 1940

Today Falmouth had its first air-raid of the war. I was at school.

10th July 1940

We've had five air-raids now. One caught me in the street. I ran into a house and a lady sheltered me until it was over. The worst and longest raid was on Sunday.

We play ping-pong every evening, in the garden shed. Denzil Lovell and David MacFarlane, whom Miss Davis knows from the Church, come over and we play the whole evening. It's great fun. Denzil is seventeen and David is eighteen. Sometimes they stay for supper. Once or twice some soldiers who were billeted nearby joined us but they weren't very good.

27th July 1940

Daddy has enlisted in the British Army! He was pleased with the parcel we sent him, which contained: 4 white handkerchiefs, a hairbrush and comb, a pair of socks and some cigarettes because he has no money for such things.

We broke up on the 15th July but didn't get a report - thank goodness! I go to school to play tennis occasionally, weather permitting. The weather has been very bad most of the time, with rain nearly every day.

On the 19th July we had our first *night* raid. Miss Kitty has asked some of the soldiers who are billeted nearby to dig a trench for us in the garden. It is going to be long and deep, and a flower-bed will have to make way for it. That's war! But it will keep us safe in an air-raid.

The day before yesterday it was Barbara's nineteenth birthday. She had a party and we had a ping-pong competition which David won. He's much the best player among us.

Lieselotte and I have been to tea with some girls called Mary and Ann Gibbs who go to the High School. Their mother asked us what it was like living surrounded by so much water. We didn't know what she meant until she said she has always wanted to see Venice. We told her we came from Vienna, not Venice. We all laughed heartily, but I secretly thought that she should have known the difference between Vienna and Venice. People don't understand why we are here or anything about our background.

Lisl, Lieselotte and I have been to see *The Hunchback of Notre Dame*, with Charles Laughton. A marvellous film.

When it isn't raining - and sometimes even when it is - we all, Miss Davis, Miss Kitty and all the boarders here, go to the beach and take a picnic, usually Cornish pasties which are delicious. We always go to different beaches. I like Swanpool best.

7th August 1940

I was sick today for the first time since I came to England. Miss Davis and Miss Kitty have lots of visitors - there's someone here for tea or supper almost every day, and we also often go visiting with them. Tomorrow we are all invited to spend the day at Barbara's sister's in Mawnan Smith. And on Friday Daddy is coming to visit us. So Friday 9th August will be the day of our reunion.

12th August 1940

Well, my father has been and gone. On Friday we went to the station to meet him at 3.49pm, Miss Davis, Lieselotte and I. You can imagine how excited we were. The train arrived - but he wasn't on it! Completely bewildered, we went home again, speculating what could have happened all the way home. Miss Davis was very sympathetic and tried to cheer us up. About half an hour after we returned home, the large green gate at the bottom of the garden opened, and there was my father, in soldiers' uniform. It

From left to right: Denzil, Barbara, David, Miss Davis,
Christine (standing). Lieselotte and I (sitting).

was a very strange reunion. What had happened was that we had gone to Penmere Halt and he had travelled on to Falmouth station.

"How could I have known that I had to get out at Penmere Halt?" he asked us. So the first words he spoke to us after two years were angry ones. Miss Davis was very apologetic. Presently she left us alone with him in the hall, where we sat in the armchairs and spoke German again, which felt very strange. He admired the house and I was very glad because I had been afraid he wouldn't like it. The next afternoon we had tea at the Robins'. I forgot to say that we had found him a room in the house of a blind lady; when we took him there in the evening we left him at the wrong house, so he came back to St. Joseph's again and this time he was even more displeased with us. The second time Miss Davis took him. On Sunday we were invited to the Robins' again, this time for lunch, and then we had tea at St. Joseph's. On Monday, Daddy took us to a restaurant in town and then he returned to Plymouth.

14th August 1940

Father Millerick, the Catholic Priest, came to supper today. He said he thanked God on our behalf for reuniting us with our father. We haven't been exactly ungrateful ourselves, even though we saw him only for a short time and there were some mishaps. He hopes to visit us again in three months time.

28th August 1940

Today was a very sad day. We said goodbye to Lisl, who is going to Shanghai with Gerti to join their parents there. I am sure it is goodbye forever and that we shall never see them again, even if they arrive there safely, which is doubtful because of the mines in the sea. It is a very dangerous journey. Everyone was very fond of Lisl, in particular Denzil, and David always wanted her for a partner in ping-pong.

31st August 1940

Hurrah! We had another ping-pong competition and David and I won the doubles and got the prize. Afterwards David and I were alone together for a long time in the shed, talking. He's a medical student and only comes home in the holidays.

Denzil brought his brother Roy to St. Joseph's for the first time. He's twenty-three, in the army, tall and *very* good looking.

After a long time of getting on really well together Lieselotte and I had a terrific row. This is what happened: she was reading but I wanted to tell her something. She didn't listen. I asked her a question. She didn't answer. Suddenly my patience snapped and I did everything I could think of to annoy her: I whistled, I looked at myself in the mirror (which always infuriates her) and I threw everything I could find of hers on the floor. This roused her, she put her book down and threw everything of mine she could find on the floor. I laughed, and said, with a Yiddish accent, which she hates, "I don't care how many of my things you throw on the floor. I can easily pick them up again." Her anger was great and her face was scarlet. When there was nothing left to throw on the floor the storm abated but we didn't speak to each other for the rest of the day. Well, sisters have to quarrel from time to time. We were soon friends again, with me, as usual, as the peacemaker.

8th September 1940

Already a year has passed since the outbreak of war. Today is a Day of Praying for Peace and I went to church with Miss Davis (I know God understands, as there is no synagogue here). After church, Denzil came home with us for lunch. Last night he and I went for a walk alone in the dark!

9th September 1940

A letter from Mummy today! She received our letter telling her about Daddy's visit. She complains that we didn't go into enough details, such as what he looked like and said, how he got on with the Robins', where he stayed etc. She and Gromi and the lodgers are all well, including Feldmann who is still there. She says everything is bearable except her longing for us. When I read that I cried. And she can't understand why we are not living at the Robins' any more. How to explain that without upsetting her?

Mr Jack Davis, a brother of Kitty and Agnes Davis, has come

67

on a three day visit. He's an elderly bachelor and loves brown toast for breakfast.

School starts on Thursday, and on Saturday Lieselotte is going to go collecting for sailors.

9th October 1940

I have just escaped death by a hair's breadth. This is what happened: Connie and I were going for a walk as usual after homework. We felt a bit hungry and were going to buy a penny worth of chips. We were just passing the Wesleyan chapel on the Moor when we heard sssssssss, the unmistakable whistle of a bomb. There had been no air-raid warning. We heard no bang. But suddenly all around us there was rubble and people were screaming and belatedly diving for shelter. One woman and her little girl under an umbrella came running towards us and seemed hysterical. We didn't know where the bomb had dropped until someone shouted, "It's the Chapel!" Then we saw that it was in ruins - and we were not a stone's throw from it. How had the bomb missed us? One minute we were exactly in front of the chapel, the next we were ten steps away, and in that split second the bomb fell. Thank you, God, for saving my life. But the ginger haired son of our air-raid warden, who had been inside the chapel, was killed.

We were too excited not to tell Miss Davis and Miss Kitty what had happened although we never tell them when we've been to town in the evening as I'm not allowed there then, because of the sailors and soldiers. Connie's mother doesn't mind - she's more broad minded. At first no one believed us. Then Miss Davis said: "What were you doing in town at that time?"

"I was nearly killed, Miss Davis!" I cried.

"You shouldn't have been in town. You see what happens when you disobey," she said.

I still think God meant to save me, not punish me.

[To this point the diary was written in German. It now continues in English.]

16th October 1940

I'm so sick of everything! You don't believe me, do you? But I mean it. All the people here and everywhere are awful, horrid. They hate me and I hate them. I haven't been really happy for two years. I want a home. Shall I ever have one again, or shall I be killed by one of Hitler's bombs first? Sometimes, like today, I'd like to run away, but where to? My father is in the army in Cirencester. My mother is far away in an enemy country. And I'm among strangers. I've quite changed since I left Vienna. Do you know what I was in Vienna? A little nothing. I was a spoilt, rude child, empty headed and silly. And I didn't care about school and never paid attention. But now I'm a different person. I want to learn and be clever. I want to be more than just a silly refugee child. I want to read books and more books - but I've so much homework . . .

I don't think my father understands me any better than all the strangers around me. And how about my mother? I have forgotten. I remember nothing. It was too long ago.

31st October 1940

Oh, unhappiness, unhappiness, will you never leave me? My troubles have increased because Mr Robins hasn't sent us any pocket money and I miss things. Miss Davis can't give us any. I haven't even got any money to buy a stamp.

The other day I took little Christine, one of the boarders here, to the park. As I was gently pushing her on the swing, I had a vision of a peaceful, sunny little lane, far removed from the war, with birds singing and beautiful flowers all around. I walked along this lane, my parents, my sister and grandparents at my side, and we were all so happy and united. No troubles, no sad thoughts. What I mean by happy is really very simple: my own home with my own family, especially my own dear, sweet mother.

13th Birthday

13th November 1940

I don't know if it is because it is the 13th today, but it has been an awful day. I'll tell you about it. I came home from school. I found a letter from Daddy. Oh, what did I read! He said that Mr Robins and Miss Davis wrote to him and Miss D. praises us, but that beast Mr Robins complained that we are disobedient and untruthful children and our clothes are always dirty and unmended. Lies, all lies. Even Lieselotte talks of running away now. Perhaps the Rotary Club could help? My father writes: 'Be brave, children, I'm on your side and know that you are being treated unjustly.' Poor Daddy. Do you think I'm sorry for myself? Not a bit. I'm sorry for Daddy. He has so many worries. But the Robins' guaranteed for us until we are eighteen and can't get out of this now, however much they threaten. I'm sure that Mrs R. is behind it all although there's an awful change in him, too. My poor parents.

28th November 1940

This evening I played Monopoly for the first time in England, with Barbara, Denzil and Janet Tressider. Janet came last week. On Saturday we had a wonderful evening: Denzil played the piano and we had a sing-song. He plays beautifully. His favourite composer is Handel but the piece in my opinion that he plays best is Paderewski's Minuet.

Next Saturday Lieselotte and I are going window shopping for presents.

I came top in the geography test! And another nice thing: I met Roy Lovell in the street! He was in soldiers' uniform, and gave me a lovely smile.

7th December 1940

In the evening Lieselotte and I went to the pictures with Miss Kitty and saw a film called *Convoy*. Miss. K. had forgotten to bring her torch so we had to stumble back groping our way in the blackout. I fell over somebody's doorstep in Killigrew Street. When we arrived home, what a surprise awaited us! Guess what - Alan, my marvellous Alan, was there! He has come to stay for a few days.

We play Monopoly nearly every evening. The other day we were joined by Gladys E., the daughter of friends of the Davis', who is about nineteen and half Mauritian, half Cornish, and Father Milligan. Gladys is a very unusual girl.

Alan is about the only person I know who has no faults.

70

Evening: (In bed, where I usually write).

'The White Cat Day.' You'll hear in a minute why I call it that. It was an ordinary Sunday. Connie and I went for a walk in the morning, and again in the afternoon when her younger brother Tony came with us. There are usually visitors here for tea on Sundays, and today was no exception: there were Connie and Tony and Denzil and a lady called Miss Hankins. We played Monopoly and ping-pong. In the evening, when I was in my bedroom ready to undress by the light of the little oil lamp, I suddenly felt very sad and unhappy. I cried, and prayed to God to help me. It seemed to me that there was meanness all around me and that nobody really loved me except my mother. Suddenly I heard a low miaow. I looked round and in came Heather, the little white cat. My first thought was that she was bringing me a message from those who still love me. She was very affectionate, which she isn't usually, in fact she once tried to scratch me. She rubbed against my legs and licked my face - I'm sure animals know when one is unhappy. And do you know, the cat wouldn't leave me. Wasn't that strange? And all the time I had the feeling that she was bringing me a message from home and telling me to be hopeful and not to forget that there are still some people who love me.

On Tuesday we are being inoculated against diphtheria at school and then we can go home.

18th December 1940

Didn't I always believe that when the worst troubles have come upon you, God steps in and helps? I've noticed it over and over again. And here's proof once more. Do you remember when I complained that I had not a penny of pocket money? Now Christmas is coming and of course I had no money for presents. I cried, and begged God to help me out of this situation. And He did - He sent us 10 shillings through Mr Robins! How happy it made me! My first thought was: thank you, God. Now it is evening and after having talked a little with Lieselotte I shall thank God properly. Can you tell me a really good way to please Him?

20th December 1940

Yesterday was the last day of school. We had a Christmas party and a show. Today, the first day of the holidays, I did something fantastic. Listen. When I had no pocket money I thought hard of how I could earn some, and determined that somehow I would. AND I DID! I had an idea. I told Connie about it. This is what we did: we searched our possessions for some we could spare and between us we found a comb, a pair of red shoelaces, a box of matches, some handkerchiefs, three painted shells, two ribbons, a few pencils, a rubber, a belt, a few sweets, and some picture books for small children. We wrapped them up in Christmas paper and put them in a big bag. To the bag we attached a piece of paper on which was written: 'Lucky Dip, 2d Each'. Then off we marched to the town and stood outside the Post Office. We did not have to wait long for customers. One little girl even returned for a second go. By the time we had to go home for tea our bag was empty and we had made 1/4d each! I was immensely proud and even Connie, who hadn't really wanted to come, couldn't believe our success and had enjoyed herself. We stood giggling together by St. Joseph's gate for a long time before parting. At teatime I related my experience. They were all amazed and full of admiration. But then Uncle Jack, Miss Davis and Kitty's brother who has come to stay for Christmas, said: "Do you know that what you did was illegal? You need a licence to sell things." That was a shock.

"No, I didn't know. Nor did Connie," I said.

"I expect the police will be round presently," said Barbara.

Well, they haven't been round yet. Barbara always likes to say something nasty.

29th December 1940

I had a lovely Christmas. For Christmas dinner we were joined by two soldiers, Father Millerick and another priest. I got the silver sixpence in the Christmas pudding. On Boxing Day we had the most wonderful party I've ever been to. It lasted from 7pm till 3.45 in the morning. Denzil, David, Miss Luard, Gladys and Father Millerick were here. We played 'Murder' and Lieselotte had her first kiss! It was from David, in the dark. The following day Lieselotte and I were invited to tea at Betty and Mary

Crothers who go to our school, and next week we are going to see _Rebecca_ with them at the Grand. It's my favourite book. There is to be another party here on New Year's Night, and on the 1st we are all going to a concert at the Princess Pavilion. Then, on Friday 3rd January Daddy is coming to see us. He has a week's leave.

Well, another year is nearly over. Goodbye, little diary. All's well that ends well.

2nd January 1941

Now I'm the only one of the older girls here who hasn't been kissed; both Lieselotte and Barbara have. I'm longing to be sixteen or seventeen, but I want to be that age now, because there are so many nice young men here and I may never have such an opportunity again. Denzil kissed me once, but only as a friend. He sent me a Christmas card.

I'll tell you now how the greatest of all games, 'Murder', is played: Everyone assembles in the drawing room, which in term time is a school room but in the holidays is completely transformed, with armchairs in flowery covers arranged round an open fire, the school desks being stored away in the garden shed. The person who draws the ace of spades from a pack of cards is the murderer, but keeps it a secret, of course. A policeman is chosen. The rest of us then run upstairs. It is pitch dark everywhere. Confusion reigns. You hear whispering and giggling but can't even see who is next to you. I and others are rolling on the floor, grabbing people's legs. Once I recognised Father Millerick by his shiny trousers; he's quite a flirt, though he certainly shouldn't be. Sometimes you lie on the couch and suddenly feel a man's head near you, and then you fight and laugh. The object is to avoid being murdered. You know the murderer has struck when you feel hands gripping your throat, and then you have to scream loud and long. Immediately the policeman comes running, carrying a torch or oil lamp. Everyone then returns to the drawing room, the 'corpse' being carried there. Now the questioning starts. You are allowed to tell one lie. If the policeman finds the culprit he gets a prize. And then we start all over again. A wonderful game.

d

13th January 1941

School has started again, my father has been and gone, and David
has gone back, too. He said goodbye yesterday. Last night we had
a bad air-raid again, after a long time. Coats, wellingtons and
woollies are always ready to be grabbed as soon as the siren goes
in the night, and we all troop out into the garden and down into
the trench, which is damp and cold and smells of earth. There we
sit until the All Clear goes, sometimes for hours. Everyone takes
something with them - Miss Davis and Miss Kitty their valuables,
the younger children their toys and I my diary! Oh, and Timothy
the dog comes too, of course. He's a Dandy Dinmont and bites,
so always has to be on a lead.

16th January 1941

Just imagine - Denzil's full name is Gordon Denzil Francis
Dominic Lovell! He told us that Roy was supposed to be coming
for Christmas but then his leave was postponed till now. I was
very glad that he didn't have his leave at the same time as my
father! Roy is coming this weekend. I can't wait. Alan didn't
come for Christmas. When he said goodbye to me the last time he
was here he said: "Well, goodbye *'I'*. I *might* see you at Christmas
- or I *might* at Easter - or I *might* never again." What did he mean?
He's the nicest, cleverest person I know and he's very popular,
(I'm not popular, I know that). Sometimes I feel sorry for Alan
because he has no home, like me. His parents live abroad. On
Alan's last evening Denzil happened to be here, as usual, and
when he left he called Alan out and then I heard them shut the
porch door and talk in low voices. I really was surprised. They've
only seen each other a few times, and already they are such close
friends that they have secrets? The next time I saw Denzil I said
to him: "What were you and Alan whispering about in the porch
the other night? Are you spies?"

"Yes, we're spies!" he said and laughed. But then he said:
"After the war Alan and I are going to live in a caravan and play
Handel all day. We shan't ever marry." I was too surprised to
make a reply. Boys always make out they can do without girls;
it's not so the other way round.

Yesterday was the most exciting day I've had in England! I marked the day with a red ring in my pocket diary. This is what happened: Roy, Denzil, Barbara and I went to the canteen at the back of the church for a social. Lieselotte didn't come because of a bad foot. We had a gorgeous time. Roy was sweet to me. Then something happened that I shall never forget. We were going home, Denzil opened the door of the canteen, I stepped out into the pitch dark, stumbled over the step and fell into the arms of Roy, who was just behind me. He held me - it seemed for ever - and his chin was touching my hair. Then he took my hand and we walked home like that, with Denzil and Barbara in front. Oh, it was lovely, lovely, lovely! But that's not the end of the evening. I wish I had the time, paper and patience to describe every detail of events to you over and over again! Anyway, soon after we returned I had to go to bed - Miss Davis is quite strict about bed time, though not about much else. When I was washed and undressed (in pyjamas and dressing gown) I began to write my diary. I was just going to tell you all about Roy holding me in his arms when Denzil came rushing in, tickled me and cried: "Give me Roy's hat!" I had hidden it. I often hide their things for a joke. I wouldn't go downstairs with him because I had my dressing gown on, and besides I had fooled about so much with Denzil that I nearly lost my pyjama trousers. Suddenly Roy appeared in my bedroom. Before I could take that in, Denzil snatched my diary and ran downstairs with it - and I at once after him. I gave him Roy's hat and he returned my diary and then I went back to my room as quickly as possible knowing Roy was there, with you, my beloved diary, safely in my arms. *I could not open the door!* Someone was holding it. At last I forced it open even though Roy and Lieselotte were behind it together - and it is said defence is easier than attack! They didn't want me to see what Barbara was doing and so Roy held me tight and I was once again pressed against his delightful body. In fact Barbara was making me an apple pie bed. I freed myself form Roy to try and stop her, and then we were all in a heap, romping and fighting and then darling Roy helped me to make my bed up again and afterwards I kissed each sheet and blanket because he had touched them. At last he said "Goodnight, *'I'*," and I replied, "Goodnight, Roy," although

I wanted to say "Goodnight, Roy, my dearest darling, my heart's desire," and everyone departed. January the 23rd was truly the nicest day I've had in England.

Today, in a more sober mood, I'm sure I'm truly in love with Roy Lovell. But I nearly cried because I thought myself so stupid. I looked in the mirror and was shocked. I saw an ugly full moon face, untidy brown hair, round pop eyes, thick lips, crooked yellow teeth - and glasses! Ugh! How could such a fat ugly school girl, with no home and no family, and a religion that no one has ever heard of here, dare to love such a marvellous young man who has everything in life? How dare I be in love when I have so many troubles and worries?

10th February 1941

'Oh, where oh where has my handsome Roy gone?
Oh, where oh where is he?
He's gone to Plymouth to join the army,
Oh, there oh there is he!'

And will I ever see him again? The other day Denzil, Lieselotte, Janet (who is staying here again) and I went for a walk. We approached a large white gate on which I remembered I had written 'I love R.L.' when walking here with Connie. At that moment there was a roar, and aeroplanes appeared overhead. Everyone looked up, wondering whether they were British or German, and I hoped my scribble would go unnoticed. I was wrong. As we came level with the gate Denzil saw it and exclaimed: "Look at this! 'I love R.L.' R.L. - Roy Lovell. You wrote that, didn't you *'I'*?" Up to now Denzil had only teased me indirectly about his brother Roy.

"Of course I didn't," I cried. My face felt red hot and must have been the colour of my blood.

"But you are not looking me straight in the face, are you?" he said with a sarcastic smile.

"Aren't I?" I said, and did so. I had to deny my secret, and the necessity made me brave. Now my face felt stone cold and pure white. No more was said and I was very quiet for the rest of the walk. Love is a secret feeling and must be kept to yourself.

I hope this will do nothing to harm the friendship between

76

Denzil and me. Although he is moody, he is usually very nice to me and sticks up for me, for instance if Miss Davis or Miss Kitty tell me off for something. We are often alone together and have very interesting conversations.

14th February 1941

I've had a Valentine! Who can it be from? I wish it was from Roy, but I know it isn't. I don't know why anyone should send me one because I am neither clever nor pretty and girls are usually one or the other.

You know, I would very much like Lisl to be here still - I miss her and yet I'm glad she isn't. Do you know why? Because she was my rival. The boys took far more notice of her than of me. Now I have no rival because the other girls are much older than myself. David MacFarlane in particular was very fond of her for a partner in ping-pong. Do you remember when he and I won the competition? He had really wanted to play with Lisl but it didn't work out like that. He was quite kind and shook my hand and said: "Thank you," after the game but he didn't want to accept his prize, which was a torch, (I did of course - it was scent). He wanted to give it to Lisl but she wouldn't take it. When the time came for him to say goodbye to Lisl he said to her: "Well, thanks awfully for everything, and whenever I put my torch on in the dark I'll think of you, and I'll call it Lisl." She blushed red as an apple. Well, you can't make people like you and there's no point in being jealous. Miss Kitty always says: "You die if you worry, and you die if you don't worry, so why worry?"

17th February 1941

Today is a half term holiday. When I don't have much to do I play the piano, which I adore. I've never learned to play but I've taught myself a little. And of course, just because I love it, it is spoilt for me, because everyone shouts: "Oh, do stop that awful row!" That really hurts. Five minutes ago I was chased away from the piano and went upstairs and cried and talked to you. How do people expect me to play when I never learnt? Like Mozart and Beethoven? Miss Davis (who plays well herself) is not like that. She is the kindest of all this strange lot of English

77

people around me.

Now I've told you two of my worries I feel less gloomy. You are only plain paper but you understand much better than any people ever could.

There's a verse at the bottom of each page of my pocket diary. For this week it says: "Be modest in victory and cheerful in defeat."

20th February 1941

A few days ago we had a terrible gale. It was almost as frightening as an air-raid, with bombs falling. I wonder when the war will end? Sometimes I feel proud that I have gone through so much, and would by no means want to change places with an English girl. Most have never been more than a few miles from Falmouth, and they have never learnt to value parents and home. Anyway, I had better get on with what I really wanted to say. Lieselotte, Barbara and David were in the garden shed after dark the other Sunday. They were joking and saying stupid things. They called each other 'little boy' and 'little girl'. David was saying that little girls of eight shouldn't sit on a bench with little boys of eleven. All this time I was standing not very far away from them, but it was obvious that they didn't want me because I'm too young for them. After a bit they started talking about more sensible things. Then I had an idea. I went into the house and told Miss Davis about the beautiful scene in the garden shed - a boy and two girls sitting on a bench in the dark. I asked her to creep up on them and suddenly frighten them to death. As Miss Davis is always ready for a joke she did it! She tip-toed out to the garden shed carrying a large pillow. I watched her from the house. Unfortunately things didn't work out as intended because when Miss Davis arrived at the shed and threw the pillow at David's head they weren't a bit startled - they said they had heard her coming but, thinking it was me, had taken no notice.

I hope you enjoyed this story even though it went wrong in the end.

Barbara has a boyfriend called John Tuffin who's a naval officer. She met him in the bank where she works.

1st March 1941

My father has been to visit us again. We went for walks and had meals in the canteen. While he was here I didn't go to school in the afternoons. Exams are over so it didn't matter too much but I missed an art lesson. One evening we went to the pictures and Miss Davis and Denzil came too. My father doesn't know about English table manners and passes his cup without the saucer when his tea is being poured! Miss Kitty laughed about it.

A girl called Moira McLeod is staying here. She is two years younger than I but very grown up and we've made friends. Little Christine is sleeping in Lieselotte's and my room for a week as her room is required for Moira.

10th March 1941

I had a lovely birthday yesterday. My 14th. Denzil, Connie and John Tuffin came for tea. Afterwards we played rummy and Happy Families. The following gave me presents: Miss Davis, Miss Kitty, Lieselotte, Daddy, Denzil, Moira, Christine, and John, Mary and Maureen Skinner (three children living here).

Next Thursday our school is performing *Joan of Arc* at the Parish Hall.

I keep thinking of Roy and the lovely times we had together. When we all played ping-pong he always said: "We won't toss for partners, I'll play with '*T*'." Above all I remember the 23rd of January. Did I tell you that, on that evening, he paid for my supper at the canteen? Imagine how I felt when Denzil told me the other day Roy has a girlfriend! Was I only a child to him then? Can a child love like that?

Barbara told me that David kissed her. I always thought that when a man kisses a girl it means they're engaged, but he can't be engaged to both her and Lieselotte, can he?

23rd March 1941

War Weapons Week started today. I went to church as it is a National Day of Prayer for Peace. In the afternoon Denzil, Moira and I went for a long walk to Pennance Point. Yesterday we went to see the War Weapons Parade on Western Terrace.

Last Monday, St. Patrick's Day, I didn't go to school because of a bad cold. We went to visit Moira's aunt, Miss Carpenter, and she gave us a glass of milk, three biscuits and 3d each. In the evening Moira, Connie and I bought 1d worth of chips and then we went for a bicycle ride. I learnt to ride on Janet's bicycle. I wish I had my own. Janet has a job now; she works and lives at Addison's Café. Her mother is French and lives in France and her parents are divorced. St. Joseph's boarders almost all have a sad tale to tell.

25th March 1941

Something About School

I was furious! It was only a little thing but it caused me to be in a terrible temper.

During an English lesson Miss Clift, our English mistress, asked me a question to which I knew the answer as well as I know my own name but I couldn't get it out. She had called my name so suddenly and all the girls had their hands up and were shouting and I just couldn't get a word out. Later she asked another question and I put up my hand (I don't usually because of my foreign accent) but she ignored me. From then on I closed my ears for the rest of the lesson and paid no more attention. The next lesson was my favourite one - Art. I'm the best at that, and belong to the sketch club. But even that I couldn't enjoy, not even when the mistress said: "What a beautiful piece of work!" on seeing my painting. The day was spoilt for me.

There's a nice girl called Pam Bath in my form who I think is going to be my friend, but there is also a horrible one called Melvyn Ralph who doesn't like me and whom I avoid as much as I can. Although smaller and thinner than I she is a bully and very bossy. I hate her.

27th March 1941

I have a sprained ankle and stayed home from school today. I spent the day tidying drawers and things, and reading *Lorna Doone*, which is a beautiful love story. It must be wonderful to be loved like that, as Lorna is by John Ridd.

We only very rarely get letters from Mummy now. They are

sent via the Red Cross or Uncle Erwin P. in Zurich. Our relationship has to be concealed and she signs her letters Emmy and calls Daddy Waltherl. It sounds very strange. She tells us all about our friends and relations who are still in Vienna, which makes me feel very homesick, and she asks us to pray that we may soon be united, which I do every night. I have not had a letter from Ruth for ages and pray for her too, because Portsmouth gets far worse air-raids than Falmouth. If I never hear from her again it will mean I have lost the best friend I ever had.

3rd April 1941

Today we broke up for the Easter holidays - hurrah! After tea Moira and I went for a walk with Denzil and he wanted to give us 1d each but we refused it. He shared his bar of chocolate with us instead. David is home for the holidays. He has been here to tea with his mother, who is a tiny woman who lisps and speaks Scottish instead of proper English.

I have joined the public library.

Tomorrow my father is coming to visit us again.

One day when it was raining Connie, Moira and I went to the museum. We thought the exhibits rather dull. Suddenly I had an idea: there was an old chair standing there, for people to sit down in case they felt tired. "Let's make people think this old chair is an exhibit, too," I said to Connie and Moira.

"How?" asked Moira.

"It hasn't got a label," said Connie. I took a piece of paper and a pencil, which I always carry with me, from my pocket, and I wrote on it in large capital letters:

THIS CHAIR WAS USED BY JUDGE JEFFREYS AT THE
BLOODY ASSIZES.

We put the piece of paper on the chair and left the museum. We were laughing so much that people were looking at us as we sneaked out.

The next time we visited the museum the piece of paper - and the chair - had gone.

5th April 1941

Last night was a dreadful night. Poor Miss Davis had a terrible accident. I don't know what time it was when I was woken by a scream. So were the others. We ran downstairs, several of us with torches, and there stood Miss Davis in the hall at the bottom of the stairs. We didn't know what had happened and why she was standing there without moving. "Quick, come and help me!" she cried. Then we saw that the wire hook from an old gong which hangs in the hall was caught in her eye. There was blood on her face. One move and - oh, I can't even bear to think about it. Lieselotte rushed to hold her, and Miss Kitty fetched the oil lamp which I held for her while she tried in vain to remove the hook. Then Barbara was sent to fetch Dr Johnson who lives about twenty minutes walk away. Hours seemed to pass while we waited. The children went back to bed and Lieselotte and I took it in turns to hold Miss Davis, who was very brave. We also had to prevent Timothy the dog from jumping at her. Miss Kitty finally managed to shut him into the kitchen without being bitten. Apparently Miss D. had come downstairs in the night because she had forgotten to get the children's things ready for the trench in case there was an air-raid and had caught her eye on the hook in the dark. This old gong was used by the nuns when St. Joseph's was a convent. The doctor came at last and removed the hook, and now Miss Davis' eye is bandaged but her sight is saved. The gong, of course, has been taken away. Today Lieselotte is taking Miss D. to the doctor's.

My father arrived yesterday and we fetched him from the station. It's the first time I've seen him in civilian clothes since we lived in Vienna. He has been invalided out of the army on account of his sciatica. Now he has to look for work, which is not easy as an alien. Poor Daddy, what a lot of troubles he has in this troubled and not-worth-living-in world. I'm sure if it wasn't for Lieselotte and me and our mother he would follow in the footsteps of his father (my grandfather in Czechoslovakia) and commit suicide.

10th April 1941

Denzil is very changeable. I can't decide whether he likes me or not. When Janet is here he always seems changed towards me. Yet, the other day, I found an envelope with my name on it on the hall table inside which was a piece of paper with a heart and an arrow through it and some scribble in German (wrong German), asking me to marry whoever wrote it and telling me he loved me - unsigned, of course. I couldn't make it out but suspected Denzil. Then Moira told me he left the note and told her not to tell. Next time I saw him I tackled him.

"I know nothing about it," he said. "Probably some little Grammar School boy is in love with you and is too shy to tell you." I just smiled and didn't say anything more. It often seems to me that there is a chain linking Denzil and me, and however much we quarrel or hardly talk to each other, it won't break. I suppose he must like me a bit because he is always teasing me, and you don't tease people you don't like, do you? I also know that he read some of my diary on the occasion he stole it from me. It makes me blush with shame just to think about it.

On Sunday Daddy, Lieselotte and I wrote a letter to my mother. On Tuesday Daddy went to the police station to register his stay in Falmouth, and to the British Legion. Then we had tea at 'Penhale' with Mr And Mrs Robins. On Saturday we are going there again and shall collect some of our spring clothes. Mr Robins has told Daddy that he might be able to find him a job in Truro.

15th April 1941

Oh, foolish, foolish, foolish creature, oh what an idiot I am. I don't know what to say except that I feel sorry for myself for, though I'm only fourteen, I've already experienced unhappy love. Fancy loving a man who never, never thinks of me or cares about anything I do or where I am. That man is of course Roy. I ask myself why I love him but love has no reason or explanation. I get no answer from my heart in reply to my question. My heart only says - come, come, come Roy, and hold me again as you did on the 23rd of January. But Roy doesn't come. He has nicer days to remember than 23rd of January - a walk in a moonlit garden perhaps with a beautiful girl or a kiss in the dark.

Spring has come, the sun is shining, the sea is blue, but seasons make no difference to me.

"You think too much about boys and love," Lieselotte said to me. Should I instead think about my sad fate and the home and mother I can't have? What's the use?

I have started eating less today, as I'm too fat. I gave some of my jam ration to Lieselotte.

21st April 1941

Moira left today. I shall miss her. Last week she had chickenpox and I thought she might not be well enough to go, but she was.

My father didn't get the job in Truro; he's working in Falmouth at the Green Bank Hotel as a fire watcher, on night duty. His bedroom is a servant's room in the basement, small and dark. He hates it. It must be terrible, remembering the comfortable life he used to lead and being reduced to this. After we have been for a walk with him he usually goes back to his room to sleep.

The little verse at the bottom of the page for this week in my pocket diary says: 'It is easier to offer objections than to get busy.'

25th April 1941

On Daddy's birthday he, Lieselotte, Denzil and I went for a long evening walk. Denzil walked in front with Lieselotte, I behind with Daddy. That night when we went to bed I asked Lieselotte what they were talking about.

"About you," she said.

"What?" I cried. She then told me that Denzil said I am thoughtless, always want to be right, make silly jokes and start quarrels. I didn't want to hear any more so I said I was tired and wanted to go to sleep. Instead of sleeping though I cried. If a person says what Denzil said about me they can't like you. And yet I can hardly believe what I am writing. Hasn't he shown me often enough that he likes me? Only a few days ago we were frolicking and boxing each other in fun until it hurt, and laughing all the while. And what about all the times he confided in me, and even told me about Betty King, the secretary at the Architect's office where he works, whom he liked until he met a nicer girl (looking at me). Oh, I don't understand anything. I hope he comes tomorrow so that I shall have the opportunity to ignore him.

I wish I knew who my Valentine was from. Sorry about my awful writing today. I usually write late at night, standing at the mantelpiece as I have no table, by the light of the little oil lamp which is very faint tonight, or else in bed.

Well, well, well, three holes in the ground. Yesterday afternoon Denzil and I were at home alone. First we played ping-pong and then we began to talk. The talk was triggered off by a quarrel! I touched his bicycle and said, joking of course: "Now I'm going to ride away on it."

"You'll do no such thing," he said, and grabbed the bike. "You shouldn't touch other people's things," he added.

"Oh," I cried, "and who touches my things every day? Who touched my diary - and did more than touch it?"

"This diary of yours," he said, with one of his meaningful smiles, and probably with no idea of how what he was about to say would wound me, "shouldn't be in England. You should have left it in Austria. It's a dirty, filthy country, anyway." Now I flared up. Not in a noisy way, but saying all the things that I thought would hurt him most. When I'd finished my face was red hot and my eyes were fixed on my fingers because I didn't know where to look. When I dared to look at Denzil's face I thought he seemed ashamed and he was staring at the ground. Presently he put the ping-pong bat he still held in his hand down and came towards me. He said quietly and seriously: " '*I*', you shouldn't get in such a state. I know you're very sensitive, but you know I didn't mean what I said, don't you?"

"Well," I replied, becoming less furious by the minute, "in future will you please only say things that you do mean. You know it hurts me when you say something against my own country."

"But you often hurt me too with what you say, and you know I'm sensitive too."

"But I never knew I hurt you. I never meant to."

"And nor did I mean to hurt you."

"Not even with what you said just now about Austria?"

"One often says things one doesn't mean," said Denzil. We then talked about Miss Davis and Miss Kitty and decided they don't understand us. Then we wrote a letter to Lisl in Shanghai and he said he could have fallen in love with Lisl. I said: "Why didn't you then?" He knows Lisl was my rival. He said because he wasn't the sort of person to fall in love with anybody. He contradicted himself, and he admitted it! There was something else I wanted to say to him and now was my opportunity.

"Will you tell me something?" I asked.

"Try me," he answered.

"Did you read my diary when you took it?" After a long time he said:

"Only one page."

Oh, horrors! Which one?

I can't write any more now. Goodbye, dearest diary, goodbye, goodbye, and forgive me please for having been so careless with you as to let you be stolen.

2nd May 1941

Lieselotte is studying hard for the school certificate. School started again yesterday. A pity. I saw two good films in the holidays: *The Thief of Baghdad* and *Spring Parade*. Next week I'm starting tennis lessons at school. Dad has got friendly with the Holdichs, Tommy Müller's guardians, and we've been visiting them several times. I think he would prefer us to be living still with our guardians, the Robins'. Not me! I have discovered that Roy's full name is - ROYDON PIERCE LOVELL. How lovely it sounds. According to Denzil, Roy's the brainiest of all the family. He's tall, he's handsome, he's clever. What good taste I have. I wonder if I would love him if he were short, ugly and stupid? Lieselotte says that I only imagine I love him. How little she knows.

6th May 1941

A few days ago, Denzil, Lieselotte and I went for a walk, and a young girl, terribly made up - scarlet lipstick, rouged cheeks, dyed hair, very flashy clothes - passed by. Denzil and I looked at each other and smiled because we had seen a similar girl the day before.

"That one is a little prettier than the one we saw yesterday," I said.

"'I' loves these made-up creatures, you know - she's going to look like that herself one day," he said to Lieselotte, although he knows I hate these types. I wasn't quite sure whether he was joking or not so I said: "You know I hate girls who look like that, you soppy thing." At that he flared up and said a lot of mean

86

things. I walked away. When we arrived home Denzil and Lieselotte sat in the garden and I went upstairs to do my hair. Through the open window I could hear their conversation, and when I heard my name mentioned I listened. I heard nothing but bad things about myself. I threw myself on my bed and cried bitterly. I hated Denzil. I couldn't very well hate Lieselotte as she is my sister and I love her, but I didn't feel any love then. When I stopped crying I threw everything I saw on the floor to relieve my feelings, picked everything up again, and then went downstairs and out into the garden quite calmly, carrying two books Denzil had lent me.

"Thank you for the books," I said icily, and handed them to him.

"I didn't ask you to bring them down here into the garden," said Denzil.

"Never put off till tomorrow what you can do today," I replied, quoting a verse from my pocket diary, and holding on to my temper.

"And you could say thank you," said Denzil.

"I did!" I cried. "Wash your ears out and don't try and start a quarrel every time!" We didn't speak to each other for the rest of the evening. When I had gone to bed and was nearly undressed I suddenly heard Denzil's voice outside: "Inky Dinky Doo, where are you?" (his name for me when we are friends). I still didn't in the least want to talk to him and at first kept silent. Then I said briefly:

"Here."

"Where?" he called back, though he must have known perfectly well.

"In my bedroom, of course," I called back. There came a knock on my door.

"May I come in? It's me, Denzil. What are you doing?"

My heart began to soften and the terrible bitterness and hate I had felt all evening gradually left me. I said: "I - I am in my dressing gown. Yes, come in." He came in, came towards me and held out his right hand. He was smiling. I said nothing, didn't smile and didn't extend my hand.

"Surely you won't refuse my hand," he said, still holding his out.

"No," I said and gave him my hand.

87

"Thank you," he muttered, and went towards the door.

"How do you like my latest picture?" I asked him, when he was nearly outside. He came back, looked at my painting (he's an artist and an amateur architect himself) and thought it very sweet. As a matter of fact he never thinks my pictures 'sweet' but it seemed to me that he would do and say anything just then to soften my heart. I said: "What did you actually come here for? You don't usually come into my bedroom in the evenings, do you?" (Except to pinch my diary, I thought.)

"No," said Denzil, "but I just came upstairs and I thought of you." We then said goodnight and he left the room. Of course, I knew why he had come. I was extremely glad about this visit and now didn't need to cry in bed as I had intended. At least I know now that he's as upset when I'm mean to him as I am when he is mean to me. Unfortunately, I, being a girl, can't make it up with him afterwards.

I'm going to stop fighting with Denzil because it isn't lady-like or even girl-like.

8th May 1941

Something else about Denzil! It happened yesterday and it's about you, my poor darling diary - I saved you! Listen: I brought you downstairs to write because one of the children was sleeping in our room. I didn't know Denzil was there, so I put you under a tray to hide you. We had supper and Denzil left early - much earlier than usual. When bed time came I went to get you from under the tray - AND YOU WERE GONE! I knew your fate at once. I wasted no time looking for you, put on my coat and ran to Denzil's house although it was ten o'clock at night, but still quite light. Everyone said I shouldn't go but I paid no attention. I soon found myself ringing the bell of Denzil's front door. Luckily he came to the door himself and not one of his sisters. I said neither 'halloh' nor 'good evening' but simply: "Give me my diary at once!" At first he denied having you but I persisted and in the end he had to own up and brought you back to me. I answered neither his good night nor said thank you and dashed back. It was ten-thirty and quite dark by the time I reached home but I had you back.

Denzil had promised me faithfully never to touch you again

and he broke his promise. I haven't seen him since. When I do I'll tell him what I think of him, and it will be a great deal! I'm sure he read you again and knows more of my secrets now. Lieselotte thinks it was very mean of him too - of course the women here say it was my fault. They always stick up for young men rather than girls. The next bone I pick with Denzil will be a big one!

11th May 1941

I've discovered who my Valentine was from. Lieselotte knew and she finally told me - it was Miss Kitty! Oh, how disappointed I was.

The Robins' have sent us some of our summer clothes, which has cheered me up a bit. We had our first meal in the garden - we always eat in the garden shed throughout the summer - and then we sat on deck chairs. Denzil helped with my maths homework, probably to make up for his wicked deed and broken promise.

By the way, everyone still hates me.

13th May 1941

Today I have something unbelievable and terrible to tell you. Last night we had a dreadful blitz. Bombs were falling for ages and quite close to us, the noise was terrifying and we shivered and trembled in the trench. One bomb fell on the Moor again. The bombs were meant for the docks but missed mostly. I was quite tired when I arrived at school the next morning. As soon as I opened the door of my classroom several girls rushed up to me and said: "Melvyn Ralph is dead!" She and all her family were killed in last night's raid.

I simply couldn't believe it. I still don't. I thought about her the whole day. I kept looking at her empty place. How often I had wished that Melvyn wasn't in my form, but not like this. What should be one's proper feelings when one's enemy is killed? I hardly know what mine are. They are all topsy turvy. Much as I hated her when she was alive, I would like to see her back at her desk today with all my heart. Several of us are going to buy flowers for Melvyn's funeral with Miss Wright, our form mistress, but only Miss Wright will go to the funeral.

19th May 1941

Today we started our monthly marmalade ration. One day I dropped my whole week's butter ration into my cup of tea, and had to eat horrible margarine for the rest of the week. It's Lieselotte's birthday on Saturday - her seventeenth - and we are going to the pictures and then there is to be a birthday party here - Dad is invited too, of course. He has been travelling about quite a bit lately, to Plymouth, Truro, St. Austell etc., trying to start up in business again. Soon after he got his job at the Green Bank Hotel (which he hates) and earned some money, he gave us back the few handkerchiefs we bought him when he first arrived, as he said they were ladies' hankies, not gents'. We didn't especially want them but I embroidered a different design in one corner of each handkerchief- a flower, an umbrella, a treble clef and a bell - so now they are no longer plain white, and a pleasure to use - so long as you haven't got a bad cold.

25th May 1941

Your Great Adventure

My darling diary, this time it is you who has an adventure and not me! And what an adventure! Please don't be too surprised when I say you are in Portsmouth - this very minute - but I am not - I am here. What do you think of that? And how is it that I am still writing and telling you everything? Simple: I'm writing on pieces of paper and when you return, which I hope will be soon, the pages will just be added. Well, I suspect you are longing to hear the story so I had better start. On Wednesday 21st May a nice young man who happens to be called Allan too visited Miss Davis. He used to live with our neighbours and when the war broke out he went to Portsmouth where he works on a dockyard. I didn't remember him but he knew my name and who I was. Miss Davis suggested that I give Allan something to take to my friend in Portsmouth when he returns on Saturday. Allan said he would come again on Friday to say goodbye and fetch the parcel. So then I thought and thought what I could send to Ruth, and at last I had an idea! I knew she would be more pleased with it than anything and I knew you would enjoy a little holiday - for I had decided to send you for her to read. "What?" you are saying, or

90

would if you could, "I thought I contain all your secrets that no one else must know?" Yes, but you must understand that Ruth is my very best friend and she understands me nearly as well as you do, and it will be so nice to know what another person thinks of my thoughts. My secrets will be safe with Ruth. Allan came on Friday as promised and so by now you are already in Portsmouth after, I hope, an enjoyable journey with such a kind and handsome young man. Little did he know what a valuable item his parcel contained.

1st June 1941

Roy's name and mine have been mentioned outright at last at the table. I think Denzil has drawn the conclusion that I love Roy. Barbara knows because I told her but Miss Kitty only laughs about it and teases me. Denzil said he always sends my love to Roy when he writes to him and that Roy returns it. I don't believe it but said nothing. Denzil has been paying a lot of attention to Barbara lately.

Miss Hankin, a friend of Miss Davis and Miss Kitty from the church, sleeps here now as she lives alone and is afraid of the air-raids. She has a bed in a niche in the hall outside the kitchen, with a screen round it. The first time I met her - I was alone in the house when she came - I thought she was a spy because her face was almost hidden behind a thick scarf and under a large hat. We've called her the spy ever since.

I'm very worried because I've had no word from Ruth yet. Oh, what should I do if I never saw you again? You who are so valuable to me? I never knew I could love and miss a simple blue file of papers so much. Perhaps it was a bit risky to send you off on such an adventure, away from your safe home in a dusty, smelly drawer. What if Allan left you on the train? What if Ruth mixes up all your pages? What if you get bombed? All these are possibilities but I'm not going to think about them any more.

6th June 1941

Mr Davis - Uncle Jack - Miss Davis and Kitty's brother, has come to stay. We always play rummy in the evenings when he is here. The other evening during a game, while I was waiting for my

91

turn, Tinker, my favourite of the three cats here, came in. I always hug and cuddle him, and I picked him up and put him on my lap. When Uncle Jack saw me with the cat instead of concentrating on the game he said sternly: "'*I*', kiss the cat once and put it down!" We've laughed about it ever since, and whenever I fondle Tinker everyone says in unison: "Kiss the cat once and put it down!" He's a tabby cat.

On the 4th June we had a letter from my darling mother.

9th June 1941

You have safely arrived at Ruth's! I'm so relieved. Now I anxiously await your return.

Lieselotte and I spent the weekend at Gladys Eggins' house. She has a gramophone and we spent hours listening to records, especially Liszt's *2nd Hungarian Rhapsody* and Richard Tauber singing *Wien, Wien, nur du allein*, both of which I heard over and over again. Richard Tauber is my favourite singer. Gladys played the piano some of the time, and on Saturday afternoon we went to Flushing by boat. On Sunday there were visitors for tea, among them my form mistress, Miss Wright. We played forfeits and Miss Wright's forfeit was to kiss the person she liked best - she kissed me! She teaches Latin which I don't do and nor does Lieselotte, because it was thought we would have enough on coping with English. If I did, I would probably be as bad at it as I am at most subjects and Miss Wright wouldn't like me.

The other evening, as Connie and I were walking in town eating chips (forbidden!) we passed the public library (to which I belong) and I had an idea - out came my pencil and a piece of paper from my notebook and I wrote:

    Underneath the spreading chestnut tree,
    William Shakespeare said to me:
    If you want to write good plays like me,
    Go and join the library!

We then fixed the piece of paper to the library door with Connie's chewing gum. I wonder if the library will appreciate my effort to supply them with more borrowers?

12th June 1941

You are back! You came yesterday with the afternoon post. Oh, if only *you* could talk to *me* instead, and tell me everything you've seen! You've done so much more than I have - been held in Allan's arms, been to Portsmouth, seen Ruth whom I haven't seen for over two years, and travelled on an English train. Lucky you. Now I shall keep you for the rest of my life and never part with you again. Here is what Ruth wrote: [over page] I must run off to school now.

18th June 1941

Today I had a very nice letter from Allan. He apologised for not delivering the parcel straight away as he could not get away from work. His other name is Newman. I'd been hoping to hear from him and God granted my wish.

Monday was a half term holiday. I accompanied Daddy to the station; he was going to Penzance on business. In the afternoon Gladys came for tea and we went for a walk. She can't go for long walks as she says it gives her a sore throat.

My sister gave me an autograph book for my fourteenth birthday, and this is what Denzil wrote in it:

'When boys you meet so full of fun
Just think of Denzil the quiet one!'

And with it is a beautiful pen and ink drawing of a church in a wood.

21st June 1941

A Terrible Impression

I had arranged with a school-friend to go to the beach today. This friend is the only other Jewish girl in my form, and an evacuee from London. Her name is Mary and she is very nice. When I went to her house to fetch her she wasn't at home yet and so I had to wait. I was taken into a dark, small, dirty room in which I was offered a chair and sat down, but I hated it, because everything seemed so filthy. Mary has three little sisters and I don't know which of them was the worst. They spat, they fought, they

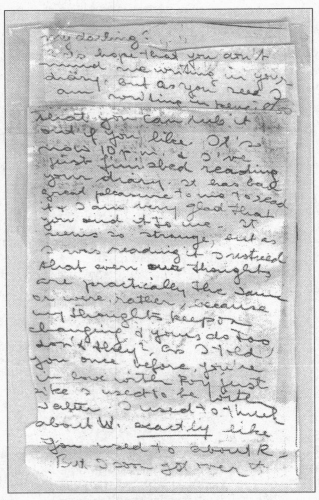

The letter from Ruth.

spoke rudely to their mother and hit her. Their manners were disgusting - in fact they hadn't any. The floor was covered with crumbs and torn papers and dirt and the carpet was coming to bits. However badly the children behaved, the mother, kind woman, just ignored them or called them darling. I was disgusted, and sorry at the same time that the first Jewish house I've been to in England should be like this. At last Mary came and the whole family had tea. They drank their tea out of saucers and licked it off the table if they spilled it. By this time I was feeling quite sick and could not have drunk the cup of tea they offered me to save my life. Then we all went to the beach. I had no idea that the whole family was going and had the shock of my life. I didn't want to be seen in the street with such a disreputable lot of people and sincerely hoped I wouldn't meet anyone I knew. On the whole I think I would like to forget this experience.

23rd June 1941

Yesterday, Sunday, we were having breakfast in the garden shed when Uncle Jack who had been to early Mass, came up the path excitedly waving a newspaper. "Wonderful news!" he cried. "The Germans have attacked Russia!" I couldn't see at first why this should be good news but Uncle Jack explained that now England had another ally and the war would be over in a year. That certainly is good news.

Denzil is in one of his moods again. He is altogether different - and talks only to Barbara. To think that he always said he didn't like her or her silly boyfriend John, and often used vulgar and abusive language about her!

Oh, Denzil, what game are you playing? You always had a special place in my heart, but now you are out of my heart forever. What a false creature you are. He invited Janet and Barbara to the pictures and to his house for supper, but not us. It is beyond me what he thinks he is doing - I don't understand it. I am heartbroken. Ruth behaved like this to me when we were small, and wasn't she punished for it? Her situation is worse than mine because both her parents are left behind in Vienna, her brother and sister are in Palestine and her guardians make her work in their shop. And if God wishes it Denzil will be punished for his behaviour as well. I'm going to tell Barbara everything he

95

said about her. Denzil, you better look out if you think the lamb is as tame as it looks! Your Inky Dinky Doo can hit back.

27th June 1941

Miss Davis noticed how Denzil has been ignoring everyone except Barbara and asked us why it was. We said we didn't know. Miss Davis said she wasn't going to have such things going on in her house, and that Denzil was very rude. I agreed with her (for once) and so she talked to Denzil the next time he was here. I saw them talking from the window and Denzil seemed very upset. The next day Miss D. told us what he said. It is not worth repeating because it is all rubbish and lies. Perhaps if I give you one example you can imagine the rest. According to him, when Daddy is here, which he is most days after school, we take no notice of Denzil and exclude him from our conversation. Absolutely untrue! Miss Davis was very cross with him and Barbara, and entirely on our side. Well, the end of all this muddle and quarrel was that Miss D. had a letter from Denzil saying that he would stop coming to St. Joseph's. Miss D. was very annoyed at that. Can it really end like this, after all the happy times we've had together?

3rd July 1941

Uncle Jack left on the 30th. On Sunday I went swimming for the first time and next Saturday I'm going to buy a new bathing costume.

Denzil has been here to say that he was very stupid to have written that letter to Miss Davis, and now he comes again, but not so often and not for long. I know why - because he hasn't made peace with Lieselotte and me and I doubt if he will soon. I say that because I've had quarrels like that before and usually guessed the end of them. But I have so many happy memories of Denzil that I say to myself: "Oh, for heaven's sake, let it all be my fault, but let's be friends again." Isn't there enough fighting going on in the world?

Lieselotte doesn't often go out now as she's studying hard for her school certificate which starts next week. My end of term exams start on the 10th.

Late evening now - dead tired . . . so I'll only tell you one more small incident: Janet said to me a few days ago: "Why are you so sad?"

"I'm not sad," I replied, but knew what she was getting at. "On the contrary, I'm happy because I had a nice letter from someone, and you can't guess who from."

"But I can - it's from D., isn't it?" She always calls Denzil, "D."

"Ha ha. No, it isn't."

"From Roy, then."

"Of course not." Then I told her about Allan Newman's letter, and she was interested and pleased for me. I had succeeded in luring her away from the trail that leads to Denzil.

By the way, I never told you that your blue 'coat' - the blue file in which you're kept - is from Denzil. He returned you in it after he stole you the first time, in the good old days. I mean the days when he still had a place in my heart, but this will never happen again.

Goodnight, my darling.

9th July 1941

Tommy Tothill, Alan's older brother, has come to stay for a week. He's just as nice as Alan. He has taken us all to the pictures and we've played ping-pong and Monopoly and been swimming. He's good at everything, like Alan.

Dad gave us our first pocket money in England today. I also earned 2s for some stockings I sold for him.

Denzil doesn't come half as often and it's not the same Denzil who comes. When he enters the room he looks white and dull and unpleasant. When he sits down he says nothing and soon departs. Once he was a good friend - but a false one. Men can get away with much more than women. I'd love to be a man, except for one reason - I'd have to marry a woman!

14th July 1941

I'm home from school today. The reason - a cold. The real reason - I didn't want to go because we're having a science exam today. So I have plenty of time to tell you of:

e

A Terrible Happening and a Faint Hope of Being Independent of Mr and Mrs Robins.

One day, when I wasn't at home, my father found you - and read you! He read all about himself and about him and Mummy quarrelling. He didn't mention it to me but Lieselotte did, because we've promised to tell each other every secret. She told me not to write such things and to put you away and lock you up. But isn't that what you are here for - for me to tell you my deepest thoughts and feelings? To say exactly what I think? Shall I just tell you harmless nonsense in case other people read you? Shall I tell you the weather is fine, I won at rummy, I wore my red dress? Shall I tell you my parents never quarrelled and everything is perfect? As for locking you away, that would be impossible because my drawers have no keys. So, if people find you in spite of my taking such care of you, then God willed it and some good will come of it.

Now for 'the faint hope'. There's a slight chance that I may have my own home again, with Daddy and Lieselotte! As soon as Dad has enough money and a good business he intends to set up a home for us and we shall be a family in our own house again, and after the war Mummy will come over and join us in our house which we shall have got ready for her, and then, and then . . . Oh, it will be so lovely.

I sent a story to a magazine for the first time - but the ungrateful editor returned it very soon. Never mind, I'll try my luck with another magazine.

21st July 1941

Today after school I went to Truro with Daddy who had some business there, and then we visited the Cathedral. Tomorrow there's a concert at St. Joseph's school to celebrate the end of term, and I break up on Thursday - hurrah! Lieselotte has her last school certificate exam on Wednesday. On Saturday I'm invited for tea at Robin T.'s for the first time. His parents are very strict and don't often allow Robin or his sister to have friends for tea.

Denzil is with Janet and with Janet only. He has forgotten what good friends we were. All right, Denzil, if that is how you want it, then go, go, go, and never let me see you again. Or perhaps I should say "Oh, Roy, come, come, come and help me out with your brother before it is too late!" I used to like Janet but I hate her now.

My brain has been knocked out of my head and I dare say that the same will happen to you when you hear what I have to say: On Wednesday, when Daddy, Lieselotte and I were out on a walk, we talked about religion. It was to be a very important day in my life because I discovered that *my father doesn't believe in God!* This is a horrible sentence but they are his words. His explanation, as far as I understand it, is as follows: God, my father says, did not make the world. The earth is a splinter of the sun. God did not make people; they came from millions of cells and eventually from apes. Religion started because people didn't know any science, and they invented God to explain what they could not understand. So this invisible, unknown, beloved God whom nobody understands is no more than a figment of people's imagination. Thus says my father.

But I say the world may have started in a scientific manner but there is someone in heaven who decides our fate. For a day, however, I was in a terrible state. I thought of nothing but what my father had told me and wondered if it was true. But then I remembered how everything turns out right in the end, and when you pray how God listens to you, and how much my mother loved God and taught me from babyhood to do likewise. How dare I believe otherwise, I told myself. I talked to Connie about it. She's a Catholic and goes to church every Sunday. To my surprise she replied that she had often thought about this but that she had come to the same conclusion as I.

Lieselotte is going to be converted! She will be baptised in the Parish Church and will become a Protestant. My father would like me to be converted too, but I WON'T. She's not doing it because she believes in Jesus Christ but because my father has convinced her that it is better to be a Christian in England, especially if Hitler should invade. I think this is very wrong of her.

1st August 1941

Oh, 23rd of January, what a delightful day you were! I wish you would come again, but perhaps you don't want to. You would find everything much different and much worse. 23rd of January - the last day I saw my lover - the man I love but who doesn't love me - Roy Lovell - and why should he? Some dates are engraved in my heart and this is one of them.

I have a Post Office Savings Book and Dad put 10s in for me. He, Lieselotte and I go for walks nearly every day but often I would prefer to go for a bicycle ride with Connie. On one of our walks recently we talked about my mother, and he said that she was always to blame for their arguments and quarrels. I was furious, but I said nothing. He has also been criticising Lieselotte and me a great deal lately, saying such things as we have made no useful friends who could help us in any way, just like our mother who frittered away her time. This was such a downright lie that I nearly cried.

Last Tuesday I went to the vet's with Miss Davis because Peter, one of the cats, is ill. Today she went on holiday to Teignmouth and I accompanied her to the station in a taxi. It will be very lonely with just Miss Kitty here.

Tomorrow, Lieselotte is having an interview at a Bank. She has left school and is looking for a job.

4th August 1941 (Bank Holiday)

Miss Kitty is ill. Yesterday was a terrible day. I did some housework and Miss Hankin was here all day helping out. Today a distant cousin of mine, a girl called Inge Rezek came to visit us with her guardians from Penzance. She's eleven years old. Her guardians treat her like their own daughter. My father said afterwards: "What a pity the Robins' weren't as fond of you." It was said reproachfully. I know he believes it was our fault that the Robins' didn't take to us.

David MacFarlane is home and has been to play ping-pong. He's rather friendly with Barbara and my sister (he doesn't like me though). He told Barbara that he and Denzil are not particularly good friends. And all the time I thought they were.

16th August 1941

Thank goodness, Miss Davis is home again, and Miss Kitty got up yesterday for the first time. Miss D. brought a fifteen-year-old girl back, as a companion for me, and because her own holiday fell through. My father says I'm under no obligation to entertain her, but why shouldn't I? We all played ping-pong in the evening.

Last week I went to the pictures with Monica W., who attends St. Joseph's school (she failed the entrance exam to the High School) and lives on a farm outside Falmouth. She wears ringlets and looks so old fashioned that you have to laugh. Another girl I'm friendly with and whom I've not mentioned is Angela Burdett whom Connie and I have christened the Bird, because she even looks like one. Last Tuesday I was supposed to go to a concert with her but we missed each other and everything went wrong and the whole day was messed up. Oh, dear, oh, dear.

Barbara is away on holiday. It's rather nice without her.

22nd August 1941

Hilda, the fifteen-year-old girl who's here on holiday, and I have been playing tennis and taking picnics to Sunny Cove, where the swimming is lovely. On Wednesday Lieselotte and I went to St. Ives by train with Dad. He had business there. Lieselotte didn't get the job at the Bank. On Mondays and Fridays she attends Miss Hoare's Secretarial College in Truro, learning shorthand and typing which my father thinks are very necessary for a girl. She has to apply for permission to work.

Hilda is leaving next Monday and Moira McLeod is coming to stay for a week on Wednesday.

On Saturday Miss Kitty is going on holiday and I'm going flag-selling in town with Connie - for the first time. I hope we make a nice lot of money.

31st August 1941

Tonight I'm going to my first dance! I feel awful because I can't dance and because of the fine clothes I have to wear. Please think of me.

The Eggins family invited Lieselotte and me to go to this dance with them, which is given by Dutch naval officers. At first my father didn't want us to go but when he heard they were officers he changed his mind. Also, he has been to the Eggins' and spoken French with Mrs Eggins (who comes form French Mauritius) and that made everything even more all right.

2nd September 1941

First of all about the dance. Lieselotte and I arrived at the Eggins' house feeling very nervous. Mrs Eggins took us into the garden where she picked a marigold for each of us because that is the Dutch national flower. We pinned it to our dresses. Then we all set off in the Eggins' car and soon arrived at a beautiful country house where the Dutch officers were stationed. A funny little officer took us into the house where we were shown around and then we had a wonderful tea. I knew quite a lot of people there. Then there was a short very good entertainment - and then the dance started. Lieselotte went off first. She danced with the same officer all the time and then they went out into the garden together. Then Gladys danced, and then - a tall, fair, very good-looking young officer came up to me and asked me to dance! But I refused!

"I'm sorry, but I can't dance," I said. He just smiled and went away. I never dreamt that anyone would ask *me*. I certainly must learn how to dance before another such occasion. As I watched the dancers I thought what a sad and serious thing love is, and I shall never joke about it again. The couples looked very romantic.

Tomorrow we shall have had exactly two years of war. Today a priest called Father Francis was here to tea. He said it was a great shame that Lieselotte was being converted to Protestantism and not to Roman Catholicism, and Miss Davis and Miss Kitty agree, of course. Father Francis said that Roman Catholicism is the only true religion. I have my doubts about that.

There's another young man, also a soldier and also called Roy, coming to see Miss Davis. I wonder what he will be like?

11th September 1941

A letter from darling Mum today! We hadn't heard from her for ages and it was such a relief to have news again, even though she can't write what she wants.

School started today after the summer holidays. I'm in form IV B. Lieselotte has passed her school certificate but is sorry to have left school, which I shan't be. The last week of the holidays was very full. Yesterday we all spent the day at St. Mawes from where we walked to St. Just church and saw a fig tree in the garden. I also sold some more stockings for Dad. The day before, Miss

Davis took Lieselotte and me to Grampound to pick blackberries and to visit a priest who lives in a caravan there, in the middle of a blackberry field. It was lovely. I'd never had tea in a caravan before.

Earlier in the week there were new visitors at St. Joseph's - a Russian woman called Mrs Tshertoff and her son, who's about ten. They are refugees from France and now live in Falmouth. Mrs T. speaks five languages. David has also been visiting us - and Denzil has stayed to supper again on several occasions, but is still more serious than he used to be, and our friendship is not what it was.

Lieselotte goes to the Parish church every Sunday, and last Sunday I accompanied her because I like hymns.

When Connie and I were in town last Friday we were followed by some Grammar School boys. She knows quite a number of them because her brother Tony goes to the Grammar School. To escape them we went into Woolworth's and lingered until they were fed up with waiting.

We had a letter from our Aunt Grete who lives in Palestine. She's Dad's sister. The envelope stated 'Written in German' and was sealed with an orange label which said in large letters 'OPENED BY CENSOR.' Tomorrow, Saturday, I'm selling flags again in the morning; I hope I get lots of money!

15th September 1941

My heart is broken - my hope has vanished - all has failed. Why? Because Roy Lovell has been to Falmouth, and has gone again, and didn't come to visit St. Joseph's. He has been here since Denzil's birthday on the 4th. All this time, and he never came, and has probably forgotten all about me. He doesn't understand - nobody does - that at fourteen you can love as deeply as at twenty. He doesn't care that in all these months I have not changed or even tried to change my feelings towards him. Everything else has changed - Denzil and Janet are not the same people any more, my father is no longer a poor soldier, my mother's letters no longer come regularly - but my love for Roy is unchanged. I shall not waste any more paper on my hopeless love. After all, there's a war on.

Today I got my first book out of the school library. Miss Clift thinks my taste in literature is pretty good. I'm not sure if I love books or films better. I adore films. Once upon a time my only wish was to become a film star. That has passed, but I am still very interested in film stars. I'd prefer to be an authoress though. How lovely it must be to see your thoughts in print and your name underneath their title, and to be famous! Most people I know don't care about such things, including Lieselotte. Last week I saw *Lady Hamilton*, with Laurence Olivier and Vivien Leigh. It's the most wonderful film I've ever seen. I lie in bed at night and think about it. I even act some of the scenes from it. For instance, at the end, Emma Hamilton is sitting in an armchair doing her embroidery when Hardy enters and tells her that Nelson is dead. She says nothing. She doesn't move. She continues embroidering. He goes on talking and still she says nothing. After Hardy has gone she gets up slowly, draws the heavy velvet curtains - and falls to the floor. Whenever I act this scene in our bedroom, and draw our thin cotton curtains which hardly meet in the middle, Lieselotte gets furious with me as she can't see to read in the darkened room. She doesn't mind me falling down though, and just says I'm silly.

20th September 1941

On Wednesday my cousin Herta arrived to stay for a week. She's a nurse in a London hospital and nineteen years old. In the afternoon she and Lieselotte fetched me from school. And then, on Thursday evening, Herta left suddenly and unexpectedly. I was very disappointed.

Today the Arnold children arrived. Keith is ten and Sheila is eight. Their father, a Grammar School teacher, is in the air force and their parents are divorced. Their mother is working and unable to look after them. I have often seen Keith and Sheila hanging around in town on their own, in shabby clothes and looking neglected. Gladys has gone to work in London, and Barbara is leaving too - she's going to work in Wales, where she comes from.

Lieselotte has weekly sessions with the Rector, Canon Roxby, reading the New Testament and being prepared for her baptism. What would my mother say?

Now I'm going to surprise you with something. I'm going to

give you a name! It's about time you had one. And I'm going to call you DENZIL! What do you say to that? Not because I like him but because he has been and still is such an important, interesting and mysterious subject contained in these pages. And that is what you are - important, interesting and mysterious. I'm going to put your name on the front page of your blue cover, but now we need a secret code, so no one will know your real name. And this is it:

A=Z; B=Y; C=X; D=W; E=V; F=U; and so on. Get it? In this language your name is WVMARO.

Goodbye for today, dearest Wvmaro.

30th September 1941

I go to the Falmouth Art School every Tuesday evening now. It's lovely. Denzil and his sister Enid go too, and we walk back together after the class. Denzil is his old self again, and we are friends once more. I'm so glad - oh, so happy about that. Lieselotte asked him for an explanation of his behaviour and he said he had had a nervous breakdown and walked in his sleep and didn't know what he was doing most of the time. Poor Denzil.

We have got our winter clothes from 'Penhale', and next week we have to wear our winter uniforms to school again - navy tunic and white blouse - instead of summer dresses. I prefer it. The other girls look nicer in their summer dresses than I, and the tunic hides my big breasts better. There is a trench which runs all along one side of the hockey pitch at school, and every time there's an air-raid during the day the whole school goes down the trench clutching their gas-masks. Occasionally we have to put our gas masks on, just for practice. It's pitch dark in the trench. Each form has its allocated place. Once there, we have to stand in a line and then we start singing, which passes the time and, if loud enough, drowns the All Clear. This has happened once or twice and we missed a whole morning's or afternoon's lessons, much to our delight.

5th October 1941

Denzil continues to be Denzil again, an ordinary young boy who has his good and his bad points and who has yet to learn and to develop. He has gone off Janet, thank goodness. The other day he and I were walking along the road and I met a girl I know and we greeted each other. She's about twenty and she works at the chemist's. Denzil said: "Good heavens, do you know her?" and I said "Why not?" He said: "Well, what a coincidence because my brother used to be very friendly with her." Roy seems to have been friendly with many girls. Oh, how foolish I am to love him. Lately I've reproached myself a lot for loving Roy, for I'm no more to him than a flea is to an elephant.

Dear Wvmaro, your foolish flea is going to sleep now, so goodnight.

22nd October 1941

Lieselotte started work in Truro today, in an office, and yesterday we had a letter from darling Mummy. She hasn't received the photos we sent her. She says she has many funny episodes to tell us about the lodgers but is saving them until we are reunited. If only that day would come!

Mrs Tshertoff and her son and a soldier friend of theirs have been coming in the evenings and we play cards until 11pm! Tomorrow I'm going to the gas mask centre with Keith and Sheila to have our gas masks checked. I hope we never have to wear them. On Sunday Inge Rezek is coming to visit us again from Penzance.

I'm doing a drawing of Ipswich Cathedral at the Art School. It will take me several weeks to finish.

8th November 1941

Mr Arnold is home on leave and came to visit his children, wearing his airforce uniform. He seems a very nervous man, and keeps scratching his behind, but probably doesn't know he is doing it. Keith and Sheila were very upset when he left again, especially Keith, so Miss Davis invited his friend Jim to tea, to cheer Keith up.

Mr Robins has sent us more clothes from our trunks which are kept at 'Penhale'. I wish we could have them here, so that I could wear what I want to at any time. Yesterday was Poppy Day. In the evening I went to visit the Eggins' with Miss Davis. Today, Saturday, I went to the pictures with Dad and we saw *Bitter Sweet*. Monday is a half term holiday. I always hate the thought of going back to school after a holiday - I wish I was old enough to leave. There is a nice girl called Margaret Lawrance in my class and she has invited me to tea at her house on Thursday. We shall probably do our homework together. She's very good at school and gets high marks in every subject. She's left handed, which I've always wanted to be. In Vienna I used to practise writing with my left hand, and I can still do so quite well.

On Friday, 14th November, Lieselotte is going to be baptised and I'm leaving school early - at 3pm - to be at the church. She is taking the name 'Elizabeth'.

26th November 1941

We've had a lot of air-raids again lately and last night was the worst. It was Tuesday evening and I was at the Art School. About ten minutes into the lesson the siren went. Then we heard the roar of aeroplanes and a minute later - bombs. It was awful. We knew they were falling quite close by because of the terrific row. It happened that Denzil was in a bad mood, and although we were all scared stiff he still didn't speak to me or to anybody else. Then he suddenly announced that he was going home to see if his sister was all right, and another student, a boy called Wilfred, aged about sixteen, whom I first met at the church canteen and who once chased me on his bicycle, said he was also going home. Denzil then asked me if I was coming too. I was in such a stew about the bombs that I at once said "Yes." So the three of us left the Art School together, Denzil opening the door and Wilfred standing politely aside to let me pass. Outside there was bright moonlight and it was very cold. We walked quickly, talking of nothing but the bombs, of course. We met two soldiers whom Denzil knew and they walked with us. When we reached Denzil's house he went inside to see his sister, while Wilfred and I waited outside and the soldiers departed. Then Denzil joined us again and we walked to St. Joseph's. As we approached, there were piles of debris everywhere. Nearer still, there was a huge crater ahead of us and Kimberley Place - the street where St. Joseph's is - was closed! Now I was really terrified. Luckily I remembered that Lieselotte was at her night school - but what if a bomb had dropped on St. Joseph's? The police wouldn't let us through at first. Denzil had a short argument with a policeman.

"This young lady lives here, and we are seeing her home," he explained. So then we were allowed through. We stumbled over goodness knows what - broken glass and other bits of buildings - Denzil and Wilfred holding my arm on either side of me. I'm sure I would have fallen without their support. Thank goodness - St. Joseph's was all right except for some broken windows and a hole in the roof, and the garden shed was littered with debris. Apparently the Catholic church opposite had been hit. Wilfred said goodnight and went home, but Denzil came in with me - thank goodness everyone was OK.

It was a terrible night - but also an exciting one! I saw search lights in the sky long after I'd gone to bed.

6th December 1941

Today for the first time I started collecting for the Red Cross. Little Christine came with me; that was in the morning. In the afternoon I went to the pictures with my school friend, Pamela Bath. Pam is a very clever girl - in fact she's top of the form. The only subject that I am better at than she is art. She's not in the sketch club. After the pictures she came to tea at St. Joseph's. And in the evening I walked back to her house with her. She reminds me a little bit of Ruth because she is very tall too, and always seems to be in charge of things.

Janet is living here again, but has been on holiday, and Miss Kitty has been in hospital and came home on Tuesday. Miss Davis has had a letter from Tommy Tothill in which he sent everyone his love including me.

I have long wanted to tell you something but didn't think it was worth writing down. Now something has happened that has given me the push. Darling Wvmaro, can you imagine that anyone except you could like me? Really like me - love me - be in love with me! Well, someone is! Someone who would do anything in the world for me, give me anything I want, give me presents every day. I did not think it possible, and with good reason. I noticed a long time ago that he liked me, and sometimes I even thought that he loved me, but I never thought of telling you till now because it's someone I'm not in the least interested in. I noticed because first of all he made it a rule to put presents like sweets and chocolates, chestnuts, books, papers, ornaments, pictures etc. - with notes attached - into my bedroom. One day I found out that he was writing a novel about me, and to my great surprise found the novel in my bedroom the next day with a note asking me to read it. I read it, and then I knew all I wanted to know. He loves me, he adores me, he wants to marry me. Everything a lover would say, he says in this novel. The next day I returned the novel and thanked him - I think without blushing. He thought I would be furious, but I wasn't. The novel was only proof of what I had long suspected. Robin - for the person is no other than Robin - said: "Of course, it's only a novel. It isn't true."

"Good," I said. But today I got another present from him - a book by P.G. Wodehouse called *Dr Sally* which is very funny. I had read it before, and he knows I liked it, so he bought me this copy.

You don't know how unhappy this makes me, dearest Wvmaro. Perhaps you're surprised that I say this, and it doesn't seem natural, does it? But I'm used to writing 'I love him,' and not 'He loves me!' Aren't boys lucky to be able to tell girls their feelings - girls can't. But apart from all that, I'm simply not interested in Robin. A hundred times a day I've wished it was Roy who loved me and yet ninety nine times I have said to myself: "No! Definitely no. It wouldn't be half so nice." I'm very modest and I'm satisfied with my quiet, unrequited love for Roy. If only I could see him at least once in three months my love would be happy. It seems so very, very strange that for the first time I have to tell you that somebody loves me but I don't love him, and I don't like it.

7th December 1941

I haven't got much paper left and until I can get hold of some more, I must economise.

Denzil wasn't at Art School last week and I had the surprise of my life when Wilfred asked me to go home with him after the class. Of course, I agreed. It was moonlight again, but luckily there was no air-raid this time. We talked about the war, and then he asked me how long I'd been in England. I said two years. Apparently he had known me all this time and knew when I was

109

living at St. Joseph's and when I wasn't. He even knew my nick name - Inky. He certainly knew a lot about me. He took me all the way home (which Denzil never does) and he was very nice. Of course, he's a bit common, and I don't suppose Daddy and Miss Davis and Miss Kitty would approve of him, but nobody can help not belonging to the 'better class'. People are all the same, aren't they? Now I must finish and try and find some more paper.

13th December 1941

This morning, Saturday, I went collecting with Lieselotte, and in the afternoon we had our photographs taken with Dad and then he took us out to tea at Andrews. He likes the ham there but nothing else much. Lieselotte left her job in Truro on Wednesday, which was also the day we had our first ever school party and bazaar. I enjoyed both.

America has joined the war because the Japanese bombed Pearl Harbour in a surprise raid and killed over two thousand people. Now England has another ally.

15th December 1941

He is here! He is here, with turned up collar, no tie and open neck shirt. He, who helps me over my troubles, he who puts all the other boys in the shade bar one, and obscures Denzil totally. My very favourite of all. He came yesterday, and yesterday life began to look more pleasant. He is, of course, Alan Tothill, the person who likes everybody and whom everybody likes, who is always nice and never moody and to whom I shall never be equal. I'm such a little nothing compared to him and yet he treats me as an equal. I have received more kindness, pleasure and knowledge from Alan than anyone I can think of. I'm proud of knowing such an Englishman. Thank you, England, for producing such a person and letting me meet him. I love you for it.

We break up on Thursday - hurrah, hurrah! And on Saturday Pam and I are going Christmas shopping.

15th December 1941

I'm in bed with flu and a temperature. But that is not the only thing that I am trying to recover from - for two days ago I heard the news of Roy's engagement. You and I and no one else know what a terrific blow it was to me. I must have been quite mad to imagine that he would ever marry me. I must still be quite mad because I still adore him. I can't talk about it any more now.

I had a good report - but what is that to me now?

27th December 1941

Another Christmas has been and gone - my third in England. It was wonderful. On Sunday David came and we all decorated the hall. In the evening I went to the pictures with Denzil, Lieselotte and Alan. In the afternoon we went for a walk with Dad and then out to tea. He works in the evenings. On Monday I went Christmas shopping with Sheila and called at Mr Robins' office, and we exchanged presents - ours to him was for the baby. Later that day I helped Dad with packing at the Green Bank Hotel as he's going to London for a week. On Tuesday Alan and I went to town and in the afternoon Pamela and I went for a walk. The next day I went walking with Margaret Lawrance. She's my next best friend to Pam at school.

On Christmas Day Lieselotte, Alan, Sheila and I went to church (the Protestant one) and we all gave each other presents before lunch. Christmas dinner here was a big occasion - Roy Elliot (the soldier), Dad, Connie, Tony and Mr Davis (who's staying over Christmas) were all here. On Boxing Day we had a wonderful party to which all the above came (except my father) including Denzil, David and Gladys. Goodness knows when I got to bed. Today I helped Dad some more with his packing and also went collecting in town. Tomorrow Dad is going to London and Lieselotte and I are going to the station with him. In the evening we shall go to the Christmas Carol Service in church.

3rd January 1942

We got home from Gladys' party on Monday at 1pm and the following morning I stayed in bed till 10.30. Then, on New Year's Eve, we had another marvellous party here; I had three cigarettes and didn't get to bed until 2.30pm.

Last night I was talking to Alan till 1pm. He is so gentle, calm, kind, decent and fair that it makes me feel good just being with him. He's as kind to me as he is to the birds and cats. I'm sure one could not find another young man like this in any other country but England. He will be leaving in a few days. Dreadful. I shall go to the station with him. Why do people one likes always have to go away?

We had a letter from Dad two days after he left Falmouth.

I now want to say something about which I have not talked for a long time, even though it was never far from my thoughts. It's about God. I'm in terrible doubt about whether there is one or not. I discussed it with Alan, and he said that he has been through exactly the same himself, but would not commit himself. I must decide one way or the other. This uncertainty is terrible. There must be a God, mustn't there?

The last verse in my pocket diary for 1941 was 'Kindness forges a bond stronger than steel.'

I've kept the page of doodles Alan did during our long conversation late into the night, and then gave to me.

8th January 1942

We had a 'mock invasion' in Falmouth last Sunday. I'm enjoying the Christmas holidays, which go on for another week, going for walks with Pam or Margaret and having tea with them. On Wednesday Miss Kitty, Sheila and I went to the Princess Pavilion to see Miss Martin's, the St. Joseph's dancing teacher's, performance. We had free tickets. Dad returns on Friday and we shall fetch him from the station.

15th January 1942

School started again yesterday - pity! Art school has also started. Lieselotte and I have been at Dad's hotel to do some mending for him, which we are not very good at. He's going away again next week, this time to Wales. He's building up a business and it takes him all over the country.

I found the following note from Robin in my bedroom: *[opposite page]* I thanked him.

I keep a special pocket diary now into which I write down the

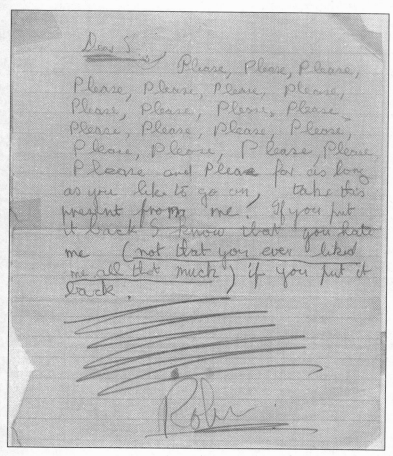

Note from Robin.

113

names of books I have read and films I have seen. My favourite author is Hugh Walpole. I've read nearly all his books.

23rd January 1942

Do you realise what the date is, dearest Wvmaro? DO YOU REALISE IT? Do I? For the first time in my life I am wishing it was one year back. Never, never have I wished time to do anything other than rush on as fast as possible - for me to get older, for the war to be over, to be reunited with my mother. But today I want it to be the 23rd January, 1941 - and then immediately 1942 again. Will I always remember that date? It's 6.30 in the evening now and I distinctly remember how this time last year, or perhaps a bit later, Barbara, Lieselotte and I were talking about whether we would rather be a boy or a girl. Then I heard Miss Davis coming out of the school room and Denzil's voice saying: "Roy is here." Then footsteps, then the door opening, and Denzil coming in . . . and then Roy. My poor heart was behaving most unreasonably. "Look at him - now, now!" it said. Look at him and don't blush. But my face felt hot and scarlet and my knees shook and all I could say was "Halloh," and "Very well thank you." After we had all sat down Barbara told Roy and Denzil about the conversation we'd just had. I asked Roy if he'd rather be a girl and he said his shoe size and finger nails wouldn't quite fit, and we all laughed. I then suggested a game of ping-pong but they said they had decided to go to the canteen. I was sorry - how was I to know what was to follow? They asked me to go with them and I went upstairs to put on my best light brown shoes. Luckily I had no homework. And then we all went to the Catholic church across the road, where the canteen is, and then and then . . . All that happened a year ago, and I remember it better than I remember what happened yesterday. How happy I shall be on the day I am able to say: "I love Roy no longer; it was just a stupid fancy which has passed like a wandering cloud." Oh, show me the girl who is allowed to love Roy, the one who succeeded, show me her, satisfy me, I want to see her. I don't want to love Roy any more, I want to be rid of my terrific feelings for him and be healthy minded once again.

I have some sad news. Denzil is going - for good! Next week. I can't believe it.

What a lot of fuss people make about my art. Oh, isn't it lovely, oh aren't you good. So I went to art school, but now I go no longer. My father said we don't learn much there and the teacher, Mr Seaward, is no good. It's true all we did was copy pictures. Anyway, I don't think I'm very good at art. My father says I must keep on drawing if I want to improve, and then he will pay for me to have piano lessons, which I have wanted ever since I can remember. This would be a reward for my working hard at drawing, because my father can see a future for me in art, but playing the piano is just a luxury.

I long dreadfully for my mother. I love her so, and I miss her love. But when I want to cry about it I force back my tears because she doesn't like me to be sad.

I wish Ruth would write. I don't know what's happened to her and I'm worried and angry. She promised she'd never stop writing. I hope I'm not about to lose my very best friend.

30th January 1942

After having had to stay at school for dinner for some time I have started coming home again, thank goodness.

Denzil has left. He has gone to live in Newport. I will tell you about our goodbye now. He came on Tuesday evening. We talked a little and then he went to play the piano, which he does awfully well. He played all our favourite pieces and at the end the most favourite of all - *The Allegro Moderato* by G.F. Handel. Then he had a glass of wine and offered us each a cigarette. I only had a puff at mine as I wanted to keep it as a souvenir. He said he must go, but lingered on for another half hour. At last the moment came. He kissed Miss Davis first and me last of all. I said goodbye and good luck but I don't think he took it in. His expression seemed far away, his thoughts further still, he looked sad and pale and there was a sad, faint smile on his lips. I felt very queer when he'd gone.

I probably won't write much for a long while for I have noticed that Denzil inspires me more than most other people and events.

19th February 1942

Freedom

There is nothing like it and I haven't got it. How wonderful it must be to be free to do as one likes, not to have to ask: may I go to the pictures? May I go out to tea? May I have a shilling? May I have a biscuit? How wonderful it must be to have your own house with your own husband and children in it. If I don't marry I want to go right away from everybody and live in a beautiful house with my mother. We would be happy together and we wouldn't spoil each other's lives. I've always preferred my mother to all other members of my family. She was the one who always stuck up for me and to her I owe my life (of course I know I wouldn't be here if it wasn't for my father as well but I wasn't sitting in *his* womb for nine painful months!).

I envy you your freedom, Wvmaro. Yes, yours! Your only occupation is to listen to me and have beautiful peace when you don't. I know you never get tired of it - you don't know anything else. Well perhaps it isn't exactly freedom but it is trouble-free. Somebody is dealing out cards and giving some people all the good ones and others all the bad ones. For instance, I am here, among strangers, and only enjoy a small percentage of the happiness that my friends enjoy. They live in their own homes, with their own mothers, someone to go to when they're in trouble and someone who truly loves them. But the biggest injustice of all is, that, though my father should make up for some of the things that I don't have, he binds me! He forbids me things that are a part of other girls' lives and which my friends are free to enjoy. He who ought to understand best understands nothing. When he isn't here I am almost free. The following little incident has taken place: I happened to have been to the pictures a few more times than usual and now I haven't been for over a week, and Margaret asked me to go with her to see our favourite Charles Boyer - but my father won't let me! I don't think that parents ought to allow their children everything but he is taking advantage of the fact that I have only one parent to consult, and also I think he is mean with money. It's a Jewish habit, and he has it. Every time I see him he tells me how much money he's making, and counts his notes before my eyes - but woe betide if I want anything extra. One thing is certain - my father is no English gentleman!

Talking about money, I never mentioned that for some time now I've been collecting for the Penny-a-Week Red Cross Fund - and here's a message from the Duke of Gloucester to prove it.

116

H.R.H. The Duke of Gloucester
wishes to record his grateful thanks to

Miss I. P.

for help so generously being given to the
Penny-a-week Fund for the Red Cross & St. John

117

21st February 1942

Two nuns have been staying here for ten days. They left today. Father Francis and another priest came for supper several times while the nuns were here. I wanted to ask whether it's true that they have no hair and that they mustn't have a bath naked, but of course I didn't. One evening they came into the kitchen, having just returned home, and their hands were blue with cold. I asked them why they didn't wear gloves and they replied that it is forbidden. Well, I've been forbidden some stupid things but this beats them all!

A few days ago Miss McCreight, a friend of Miss Davis and Miss Kitty, was here for lunch and tea and I showed her one of my stories and asked for her opinion. She's an English teacher and I've often had interesting discussions with her. She liked my story but suggested I make some corrections. In the afternoon Connie was here and I dressed as a boy and then Connie, Keith and I went for a walk. It was great fun. We laughed all the way.

27th February 1942

I hate doing gym at school, especially when I've got the curse (to think I once longed for it!), so I go to Miss Frost (our head-mistress) and say I have a headache and get an excuse for gym. But last time Miss Howell (the gym mistress) asked me: "Why do you so often stay away from gym?"

"I get headaches," I replied. The mean woman goes to Miss Frost and complains, otherwise Miss Frost would never have cared whether I do gym or not. So now I have to bring a note from my father if I want to be excused from gym. I hate Miss Howell. Luckily it was half term last Monday, which is a gym day. Miss Davis took me and some of the St. Joseph's children to town, where she treated us all to a cup of cocoa and a bun at a café.

Tomorrow my father goes away again on business.

Some evenings, when Connie and I have no pocket money left for chips, we go 'Gassarding'. You don't know what 'Gassarding' is? I didn't either, until Connie told me. It is something she and her brother Tony used to do. This is what happens: we go out for an evening walk. We choose an area we want to 'do'. We then pick a house at random, one we like the look of, and ring the doorbell. When the door is opened we ask: "Does Mrs Gassard live here?" The answer of course is always "no" because there is no such name. We often have quite a lengthy conversation with the house-holder explaining that Mr Gassard is away in the navy and his wife and twins aged twelve are supposed to be living at this very address, which was given to us by a friend who wishes to get in touch with them. The whole story is an invention but no one ever doubts it, and in this way we get to know interesting people and have several times been invited inside for a cup of tea and a biscuit. It is a very pleasant way of spending an evening.

1st March 1942

Some time ago Dad, Lieselotte and I had a letter from Herta in London. Her dearest wish - to go to university - is about to be fulfilled. She has managed to get a grant but is not allowed to study medicine, only chemistry. Her parents (my Aunt Grete and Uncle Kurt) who live in Palestine have moved to the country because they fear the bombing in the cities. Aunt Grete hates Palestine and is very homesick, but Herta says her mother longs more for the old way of life than for her old home, which was in Hradisch.

Didn't I tell you that there would be nothing much to write about after Denzil left?

2nd March 1942

If ever I have grieved, I cannot understand why now. I grieved about such small things which matter so little in life. Today I had some very sad news. I have been through three miserable years, been unhappier than most English girls or boys of my age have probably ever been. I don't say that during these three years I have known no happiness. I have, generally speaking, come across only kind people apart form Mr and Mrs Robins. I have spent many happy hours at parties or walking with friends and having fun with boys. I don't complain of continuous unhappiness but all this doesn't change the fact that my situation during those years has been sad and miserable and all the little pleasures merely diversions. But today, when the terrible news arrived, I felt all joy had vanished from my life forever and that I would never be able to recover my sense of humour. When I came home from school at dinner time I found a card from my Uncle in Switzerland, informing us that my mother, my darling mother, has been - sent to Poland.

We have feared and feared it. I have dreaded it. Now it has happened. While I was reading the words my face grew very hot and my heart seemed to stand still. Millions of terrible thoughts rushed through my mind which I have not enough paper to write down. I threw myself on my bed and then seemed to turn to stone - but the first word of sympathy from kind Miss Davis made me burst into tears. I had wanted to avoid crying because my mother doesn't like me to be sad, but it was unavoidable. I have so much here to make me happy, but what has she got now? I have always loved life and quite little things have helped to make it happy, and she loves life too but what can make her happy now? When I was about six years old our maid once said to me: "It is always good people who suffer and are unhappy, but they'll be happy in heaven. Bad people are happy on earth but they'll go to hell." Poor comfort, but was she right? If so, that evil Hitler, those wicked Nazis, will one day get their deserts. They are not human - though what are they then?

I cannot bear to see people around me carry on as though nothing had happened. My mind is occupied with only one thought: my mother in Poland. I didn't go to school this afternoon and Miss Kitty took me to Flushing on the ferry. She bought me an ice-cream and told me jokes, but nothing pleased me and I couldn't laugh. I can only console my sister. Oh, if only I could do something to help my poor mother, and my grandmother too. If only I could let them know that we are all well and happy! If only it was in my power! If only . . . if only . . . it had all never happened.

We are all human beings, and yet some human beings' only object is to bring misery on others. WHY?

I must stop now. Everything comes to an end, and so does unhappiness. Some day perhaps I will read these pages and I will say: "I am too happy to remember how that felt."

9th March 1942

Today, my fifteenth birthday, Monica W. was here for tea and so

120

was Mr Arnold, who's on leave. My father returned to Falmouth yesterday and we spent the evening at his hotel with him, Lieselotte and I. Tomorrow he's taking us to the pictures for my birthday treat. My proper birthday tea party was on Saturday; Connie and Mary Gibbs were here.

Miss Davis had her first letter from Denzil on Friday. He sent us all his best wishes. It reminded me how I miss him.

I am reading *Anne of Green Gables* borrowed from the school library, or perhaps I should say I am living in it. I pretend I am on Prince Edward Island with Anne and her friends, where there is no war, and no Denzil or anyone else to disturb my peace of mind. I have also just finished a marvellous book, this one from the public library called *An Unsocial Socialist*. It is by G. Bernard Shaw.

Roy is MARRIED. So that episode is over for me. If I ever see him again he will probably treat me more than ever like a little school girl. You and I know that I loved, loved, loved Roy with all my heart, but I must now forget him. Indeed I have more serious and important things to grieve about. When I swore that I would love Roy to the end I certainly didn't have this particular end in mind.

15th March 1942

Denzil is back! On Thursday he suddenly walked in - it was a complete surprise - and it was like old times again. He played the piano, he tickled me, he joked with me, we talked and we laughed. It seemed as though he had never been away. Denzil has changed my life, although I know that he is only half as nice and faithful as many other people. Still, there is something about him . . . He told us that Roy has only known his wife for three months and his parents didn't want him to marry her and didn't come to the wedding. Poor Roy.

Yesterday I went to the pictures with Anne G. We saw *Lydia* with Merle Oberon but it wasn't very good. Afterwards Lieselotte and I had tea at the G's house and had a really lovely time. We stayed there till 10pm.

Today I was in bed all day with a tummy ache. Dad was here, and Denzil and Connie came to tea.

f

21st March 1942

It's the first day of spring! I used to love spring in Vienna. I can still smell the lilac in the Arenberg Park. I haven't much paper today. I just want to tell you that, as soon as Denzil is here, I am different. My mood depends on his. He is sweet when he is in a good one. He's my old Denzil again - such an old friend and so nice to be with. We were alone for most of the evening today and we played ping-pong and the piano. All the time I knew that, in spite of everything, Denzil's character is bad and he is unmanly - but it doesn't matter! Isn't that funny? I often wonder if he likes me. And then there is the question, do I like him? But I will not answer it yet. The more I see of him the more I puzzle. I know he can't help his bad character, but why do I understand him so little, when I know him better than all other boys? However, he has revealed something which might explain a few things: his father drinks! Apparently there are continual quarrels in his family, none of them are regularly at home and that's why Denzil was here so often and that's why he was sometimes so sad or in a bad mood. And I used to think: "How lucky he is to have a nice home of his own with his family!"

David is here again. He's growing a moustache.

I was at Dad's hotel this morning and had to dust his room. What a way to spend the first day of spring!

I wonder why I am so sad lately? I could cry at every mortal thing. My mother, my mother, how I long for you! And my father doesn't make things better by forbidding me most things I want to do although he can well afford them. I know, because he said so.

If only this war was over.

22nd March 1942

There was a mothers' meeting at school and Miss Davis came. A little while ago my father went to see Miss Frost and she said some nice (undeserved) things about me. And - as I'm talking about school - we had a hockey match against the sixth form - and lost. I only watched. I'm hopeless at hockey, and just as hopeless at gym. I loathe having my period at school and always try to get out of gym then, and spend a lot of time on the lavatory. I'm always afraid of losing my sanitary towel at school, as I once did at St. Joseph's. It was terrible: Miss Kitty was cleaning the stairs and I was running past her upstairs, when the thing dropped and fell down just by her! I snatched it up, feeling terribly embarrassed. She said: "I hope you don't throw these things down the lavatory." That's another problem. I usually wrap them in newspaper and put them in my waste paper basket, but that means that everyone knows I have the curse. It's even worse when I have to borrow money to buy sanitary towels. They cost 1s a dozen. Once I hadn't got any and the curse came. It was the day of a school outing and I could barely walk for fear of losing the hankie I had wedged in my knickers! The whole day was a nightmare.

Connie and I had a shock during our last Gassarding expedition. We went to a house in Marlborough Road that we liked the look of, rang the bell and when a woman came to the door, said as usual: "Does Mrs Gassard live here?"

"That's me," she replied. For a moment we remained speechless.

"Is your husband in the navy and do you have twins?" I then said. She laughed.

"Mercy me, no me dears," she answered. "I never married. What name did you say?"

"Gassard. G A S S A R D," said Connie, and spelt it out for good measure.

"Oh, I thought you said Gasson." I breathed freely again and Connie looked very relieved too. Miss Gasson was very nice and said how hard it must be traipsing about in the blackout looking for somebody, and what brave girls we were, and the best of luck to us. Unfortunately on that occasion we didn't get tea and a biscuit.

In addition to Gassarding we also go 'detectiving' now. This means picking somebody in the street and following them and trying to find out all about them. It means following them on every occasion we see them and noting everything they wear, what shops they enter, whom, if anyone, they meet, etc. I keep a little notebook for this game in which each case is noted and not closed until we discover that person's name.

Mrs Davis - Connie's mother - took Connie, Tony and me to the pictures and paid for me.

23rd March 1942

This evening I went for a walk with Dad on the sea front in the moonlight. He never again mentioned God, thank goodness, though I thought he might tonight.

Last week Keith Arnold sat for us at the sketch club at school and I did quite a good portrait of him - in fact Miss French said it was the best.

Janet, David, Denzil and Father Wiseman have all been here on quite a few evenings and we played cards and Monopoly and asked each other riddles. On Thursday I didn't go to bed until 11.45pm!

Pamela B. is my best friend at school and we go for walks together or to the pictures at weekends. Her father is a bacon cutter at Powells' grocery shop, but she is much cleverer than I am.

Next Sunday is National Prayer Day.

3rd April 1942

Good news! First, I'm going to learn to play the piano! Secondly, I DO believe in God. An oracle decided it and I'm very happy. I've repented my temporary disbelief and I'm sure I've been forgiven. There is an eternal God or some higher being and I must not doubt it again.

The Easter holidays started yesterday - we broke up on Wednesday and I had a not too bad report. Yesterday Pam, Margaret, Joan, Megs (all from my class) and I took our picnic to Maenporth and then we picked primroses and violets - bunches of them. It was lovely.

Lieselotte has a day off today. Perhaps I didn't tell you she works in Mr Cox's office in Penryn? I don't think she likes it much. We went for a walk together. Gladys came in the evening. Denzil played the piano and Miss McCreight was here too.

Tomorrow we put the clocks forward one hour.

9th April 1942

On Easter Eve Lieselotte and I were at Dad's place and had to clean his room in the morning. On Easter Sunday I went to church

124

Portrait of Keith Arnold.

with Lieselotte and in the afternoon she and Connie and I picked primroses. Standing out from the sea of pale yellow were a few beautiful purple ones. Father Wiseman, Father Parkin, Miss Hankin, Denzil and Connie were here to tea. The following day, Easter Monday, Miss Kitty, Connie, Sheila and I went to St. Mawes on the ferry and took our lunch. The sea was very rough. I loved it when the boat rocked violently and there were huge waves. From St. Mawes we walked to St. Just and were caught in the rain and got drenched.

Moira McLeod is in Falmouth for a week but not staying at St. Joseph's. She seems more grown up than ever.

Lieselotte went back to work on Tuesday.

Miss Davis had a slight operation on her injured eye today. She was very brave about it, as usual.

13th April 1942

David has gone back, thank goodness; for the first time without saying goodbye. But Denzil has gone as well. Now things will be dull again. He said goodbye to us on Friday. His mother and sister were here too, which has only happened once or twice before. They chatted with Miss Davis while Denzil, Father Wiseman and I played ping-pong.

Last Saturday I went out collecting for the blind and made quite a lot of money.

17th April 1942

It being the holidays, we can go on outings nearly every day. Today Miss Kitty, Connie, Tony, Sheila and I were on the Stack. Keith ran away for the day but returned in the evening. He does that sometimes. Yesterday we were at Penjerrick for the day and came back over Maenporth Cliffs. We found lots of primroses, and in the evening Connie and I went to see Mrs Eggins to give her some - and bought some chips on the way. On Wednesday Miss Davis took Connie, Keith, Sheila and me to Malpas, near Truro. We took our lunch - pasties as usual - went on a ferry and picked primroses. It was a lovely day. On the way home we visited an old lady called Mrs Bradley and gave her some of the primroses.

Janet and Moira have been to tea several times, and so has Robin T. I don't think he loves me any more.

19th April 1942

I want my mother! I need her! I want someone to love me, advise me, sympathise with me. I cry for her nearly every day. "Can you hear me calling while my tears are falling?" I whisper to her. If only I knew where she was, knew she was safe, had a letter from her - but she is as good as buried alive for us. Oh, God, God, hear me and save her, let her live to see us all together again, comfort her, tell her the family is happy except for her absence! What must she be feeling like in Poland? Oh, how I miss her, but how much more wretched she must be than I. Please God, answer my prayer, and let me just have a line from her.

29th April 1942

School started again today, worse luck. Last Saturday I helped Anne G. collect for lifeboats, and Miss Tomkin treated us to coffee and buns to give us a bit of a break. In the afternoon I went to a wedding at the Catholic Church with Connie. In the evening we went detecting, stalking a man we think is called Clay. We saw him in Woolworth's at 3.15pm. He wore the same clothes as before, he was alone, we followed him through the town and through Arwenack Avenue but retreated and hid when he stopped to chat with an elderly lady in a grey coat and a mauve hat (or the other way round) - and found him gone when we re-emerged.

Miss Hankin lent me a book called *What a young Girl ought to Know* which I started and finished on the same day. There was nothing of interest in it. But I love *Little Women* by L.M.Alcott and can't read it without crying.

I earned 5s for selling some old clothes to the second hand shop in Killigrew Street. I spent some of it as follows:

    $2\frac{1}{2}$d - chocolate
    $2\frac{1}{2}$d - flag
     2d - chips
    2/6d - pictures
    $2\frac{1}{2}$d - stamps
    $4\frac{1}{4}$d - battery for torch.

6th May 1942

The King and Queen came to Falmouth today! The whole school was lined up outside the school gate in Western Terrace and saw them drive past. It was the first time I'd seen them. They waved and smiled at us. I was very excited.

10th May 1942

Well, here I am in my new home. I told you we were going to live together, my father, Lieselotte and I, didn't I, dear Wvmaro? I was glad to come but very sorry to leave Miss Davis. We moved here yesterday, and on Thursday Connie helped me bring some of my things. We gave Miss Davis and Miss Kitty a visitors' book for a farewell present, and Miss Davis treated us to the pictures (1/6d seats) and gave me some lilac - my favourite flowers - from the garden. I shall go to see her often.

It is really very nice here. We live in a boarding-house run by an elderly couple called Mr and Mrs Tamblyn, only five minutes walk away from St. Joseph's, in 47 Kimberley Park Road which overlooks Kimberley Park. We have three bedrooms, a drawing room and an empty room, and pretty well the whole house to ourselves when there are no visitors staying. The rooms and food are lovely. If only my mother was here!

Last Sunday Connie and I were walking in the town and as we passed the Odeon we caught a free glimpse of Tyrone Power through the open door - on the screen, of course. When I got home I did a drawing of him, with Rita Hayworth.

19th May 1942

On the 14th of this month I washed my hair myself for the first time. Previously I have always been to the hairdressers', and so has Lieselotte.

Our cabin trunks arrived today! At last I have all my things with me, and can wear what I want. It was like meeting old friends again.

Tomorrow I am going to see Miss Rogers with Miss Davis, to arrange my piano lessons. Miss Rogers also teaches music at St. Joseph's School, besides giving private lessons at her house. Dad is going away on business for a few days tomorrow. Next Sunday,

128

Drawing of Tyrone Power and Rita Hayworth.

on her 18th birthday, Lieselotte is going to be confirmed at the Parish Church.

Really nothing worth telling you has happened since moving to this place. There are no boys here - very dull. Except that I haven't said yet that I'm not talking to that lousy little Robin T. ever again because he insulted me by saying something about my religion which I didn't like.

23rd May 1942

I once saw a film about a madman. And cross my heart, last night I believed my father to be that same madman. You will too, when you hear this: I was a little too long in the bathroom (I always am) and that was the cause of it all. I was innocently washing myself when someone tried the door and, on finding it locked, gave an enormous knock and shouted: "Open the door!" It was my father. "I can't! I've nothing on!" I called back. He went to the lavatory. When he came out I was nearly ready. He tried the door again and, finding it still locked, knocked so hard that I thought he would break the door down. I was perplexed. Had something happened? Had an incendiary bomb dropped and water was needed in a hurry? He shouted that it was 10 o'clock and I was to open the door immediately. But I was still wet. At last I was ready. To the continuing noise of knocking and shouting I turned the key - and the door simply flew open, nearly pushed me down, and my father rushed in, his face looking - well, mad. He raised his hand to hit me and screamed something about how dare I keep him waiting so long. I tried to explain, and then my eyes met his and - they looked MAD! I had never seen such eyes: two huge, round, goggling, dark, flaring things, one on either side of his dilated nostrils, staring back at me. I made haste, went to bed and prayed that I would never become like this. I'm used to people telling me quietly "Please hurry up, '*I*'" - this was something quite new and terrifying.

Don't be surprised if I don't say much about Dad any more. He is so changeable - five minutes loving, twenty minutes angry, three days in a bad mood. I can't keep up with it.

31st May 1942

Today came the sad news of poor Connie's father's death. He was an engineer in Rangoon. When the Japanese were approaching he fled to Mandalay and was killed in an air-raid there. Connie and her family have been very worried about him since the Japanese invaded Burma in February. He was one of Miss Davis' and Miss Kitty's many brothers.

I got some new shoes on Thursday. My father paid for them. They replace my beloved blue ones from Vienna, which got bombed in Plymouth when sent there for repair by Lennards.

7th June 1942

We've had a terrific heat wave this week. Instead of walking, Connie and I have been going to Kimberley Park and sitting on a bench - and talking to a group of Grammar School boys who lie in wait for us. One of them is called Ben C. He looks like Bob Hope and his stock phrase is "Maybe, maybe not." They all have bikes. One day they had two smaller boys with them, both with brand new bikes.

"It was a present for passing the entrance exam to the Grammar," one of them told us.

"Yours too?" Connie asked the other boy.

"No, I failed it," he answered. "It was a present for taking it."

He was dead serious, but Connie and I laughed out loud. Ben and his friends seem to enjoy flirting with us, but they are a bit common.

Last Friday was Keith Arnold's birthday and I had tea at St. Joseph's. I took some coupons to Miss Davis and gave them to her. On Saturday Connie and I went to the Grammar School Sports Day. Tony had a bicycle accident and so couldn't take part.

Life is very monotonous now that we don't live at St. Joseph's any more. Next Thursday Dad goes away again on a business journey.

14th June 1942

Today is United Nations Day and I attended a service on the Recreation Ground with the school.

Ben C. and company are certainly quite different society than I've been used to. Once, a long time ago, he put a note in my shopping basket in Woolworth's, asking if he could see me home.

131

He's of Wilfred P's type only much nicer and not so dense. He has left the Grammar School now and works in the Penryn docks office and, according to Connie, he's well known in Falmouth, especially by girls. Last time in the park he wanted to know all about me and I bet him a farthing he wouldn't find out. His friend, Pop R. said, "You bet he will!" Ben would come with all the information the following evening. I would be there? Yes!

I don't want to tell my father about meeting Ben in the evenings as he would disapprove, although in one of the last letters I had from my darling mother before she was taken to Poland she asked us always to tell Dad everything. But I can't.

Yesterday was my mother's birthday.

25th June 1942

I had my first music lesson last week. I've had three lessons in all now and I LOVED THEM. There's a piano here and I practise at least half an hour a day, usually longer. The piano is a very good one and it belongs to Mrs Kent, Mrs Tamblyn's daughter, who comes to stay occasionally with her son.

We had a half term holiday on Monday and I was at St. Joseph's. Father Oddy is staying there again, and he has brought one of his boys, called John, of about my age. Father Oddy runs some kind of a home for Catholic boys in London. I played ping-pong with John. Alan and Tommy Tothill are joining the Navy! I hope they'll come down before. They are the best boys I know. I want to talk to Alan again. I've also been thinking a lot about Denzil lately.

Do you think I'm a flirt?

5th July 1942

We had exams all last week and I've done nothing but revise. We also had a tennis tournament and I won through to the third round, when Mary Crothers (a year older than me and very good at all sports) beat me. Pity!

I'm *still* in an uncertainty. About God, I mean. I wish Alan was here to talk to. Oh, if only you knew what a terrible feeling this uncertainty is! I want my mother so badly. I know she would put me out of my misery. I have prayed to God for three long years to let me see her again but God has not fulfilled my wish.

This is the end of my paper so I can't write any more today.

14th July 1942

We have fire fighting lessons at school. I attended my first one last Wednesday. We learnt to use a stirrup pump. Our next fire-fighting lesson is at The Quarry, in a smoke hut. I'm not looking forward to it.

On Thursday my father returned from his business trip, bringing with him a mannequin called Jane Marston. She is staying here for a bit. Lieselotte and I went to Truro with them on Sunday and were treated to tea at the Royal Hotel. Next week my father goes to Plymouth.

Connie and I have only seen Ben and his friends once since the last occasion I mentioned - and they ignored us! I hate that sort of thing. Anyway, they are not my type.

16th July 1942

The following looks mysterious but you and I understand it and nobody else is meant to.

My mind is made up. What I am about to disclose has been brewing for a long time and I've at last given in. Don't be surprised. And don't think I'm complaining. I'm simply stating a fact. It is this: I loathe ------. That's all. Most people love their ------ and it ought to be quite difficult to hate ------ but ------ has made it easy. Briefly, it really started since ------ returned from one of --- longer journeys. I never missed ------ when -- was away and was always sorry when -- returned. I know that ------ doesn't like me either and hates to see me happy. If I had been a boy everything would have been different. I'm really very glad I've confessed to you. It is much better to be honest with oneself. In my heart of hearts I knew that I never cared for ------ in Vienna but made myself believe I did. Some of the trouble may be my fault as well but as ------ gets worse so it makes me worse. I can honestly say that there is no one except Hitler and Mrs Robins whom I hate more than ------. Isn't it sad that I'm together with ------ whom I loathe and separated from my mother, whom I love?

On Saturday Lieselotte is going for a week's holiday to St. Ives

133

with her friend Betty Crothers.

2nd August 1942

What strangers you and I are becoming, but I have so little to tell you.

We broke up on the 29th. Hurrah!

Today Lieselotte and I had our first swim of the summer - and then got caught in a thunderstorm.

I hope to play a lot of tennis with Margaret and Pamela during the summer holidays.

6th August 1942

I've got a bicycle! It's a Hercules and cost £8. It's all black because there's no chromium available in wartime, but I love it despite its plain appearance. I've been on my first long ride on it with Connie - it was wonderful!

We have chocolate rationing and I usually buy mine on Saturdays. It's gone long before the next lot is due.

Denzil is home again. I met him in the street. He looked very pale but otherwise unchanged. He's leaving again in a week.

Miss Kitty told me she's sure she saw Allan Newman. Well, if he was here he could at least have looked me up and given me news of Ruth.

I don't think I ever told you that Pamela sometimes taunts me by repeating over and over again: "You're from Austria! You're from Austria!" One day I couldn't take it and, hot with stupid anger, I hit her with my school satchel. She doubled up with pain. I thought for a moment I might have done her some serious injury, and was quite frightened, but she soon recovered - and has never taunted me again.

On Saturday the clocks go back one hour. This is to postpone the 'blackout'.

13th August 1942

Connie and I were going to cycle to Redruth today - but cancelled it because of rain. In the afternoon we took our tea to the seafront and ate it in a shelter. Later we were followed by Ben and company, but ignored them.

I had a long letter from Moira McLeod. She says she's coming to Falmouth next week and thought she better write so she will not be met with reproaches from me. She has just come back from Oxford where she had a spiffing holiday. She went to see the Colleges, walked in the Gardens and took a boat and went on the river. She saw the picture *Thunderbirds* and thought it top hole. On one day she went riding but it was murky and rather disagreed with the horses. If you wanted them to canter they just wouldn't, and it took her all her energy to make hers trot. She certainly leads a much more interesting life than I do, and writes interesting letters.

19th August 1942

My cousin Herta has come to stay for a week's holiday. On the whole I don't like having holiday visitors, for the simple reason that you're bound to them and can't do anything but entertain them. But it didn't matter. Yesterday afternoon I thought to myself: "I like her. If I were a man I might consider falling in love with her." I could see how charming men must find her. It's been fun going about with her. We've been to town and to the pictures - she treated us and bought us an ice cream - and to the Museum, and she has had a ride on my bicycle. But the occasion I want to tell you about is last night, when Herta, Lieselotte and I went to St. Joseph's to play ping-pong. (Herta is nearly 21, by the way). Lieselotte and Herta played first, then Herta and I. Our game led to a ridiculous little incident: I went wrong in the score somewhere by adding my mistake on to my score (she was losing as it was). She blurted out: "That was your mistake, but never mind, carry on." Her sarcasm vexed me but I said with some self-control: "Oh, sorry - my mistake," and corrected the score. But she was suddenly a different person. She would not speak, she would not laugh, she snapped at me, she didn't even try to play properly and she lost every game as if to show she didn't care. Well, I mustn't trust or like people too soon, I know that now. What good is charm, if it can suddenly change to nastiness? I consider moodiness a kind of dishonesty. People like that immediately go down in my estimation. Another silly thing happened the next morning, when I was walking back from the town with

135

Herta. It was sunny, and I said: "What is on top of a sunbeam?" this being the name of a song. "Do you know?"

"The sun of course," she replied, quite seriously.

Later Lieselotte told me Herta thinks I'm not only a bit of a cheat but I ask stupid questions like what's on top of a sunbeam. Lieselotte explained to her it was a song.

"A song! I never knew that," said Herta. Perhaps she thinks me less stupid now, but I don't care.

22nd August 1942

Herta went back to London today, and Lieselotte went with her for a week's holiday.

Angela Bird had breakfast with me this morning after going to 8am Mass, as she lives some miles outside Falmouth, and then we spent the day together. We went to the Museum, of which I know the exhibits by heart now, because it was raining again. Connie came to tea.

Herta doesn't believe in God. I told her (before we had our silly arguments) I was in doubt, and envied people who can believe. "So don't envy me," she said; earlier I had told her I envied her her life in London. Really, I'm in a most hopeless state. I wouldn't mind talking to a high priest, if I could find one. I just want to be brought back and believe blindly again - it was so much better. If my mother knew! I wonder if she ever had any doubts? I don't want to find out the truth. I just want to believe.

30th August 1942

Lieselotte came back from London today. I fetched her from the station. The train was three hours late! We sat up till midnight, talking.

I go cycling with Connie or Pam nearly every day. On Thursday we cycled to Perranwell and visited Angela. She gave us apples from her orchard. From there we cycled to Truro and went to the Truro Museum.

Next Thursday, September 3rd will be the third anniversary of the outbreak of war. There's no end in sight.

The other night I went to St. Joseph's, and Denzil and Joseph, the Irish sailor, were there. Joseph is a friend of Connie's sister Monica and I've met him once or twice before. I seem to have made friends with him because we laughed and joked together a lot of the time and he was calling me his little girl. He's 23 (Roy's age). Then he said something which quite embarrassed me. You see, he's a little deaf in one ear, and I couldn't understand his Irish accent easily, so we made a fine pair! "Well," said Jo, "it wouldn't do for us to get married, would it, little girl? If I asked for an egg I'd get a shoe . . ." He said that about three times and at last I said, "Well, it's out of the question, anyway." Denzil played the piano and Jo sang and we played cards and ping-pong. We had difficulty convincing Jo that, in ping-pong, the loser always starts serving in the next game. He was usually the loser.

Denzil was his old self again. He still fights with me but in good fun.

Now I must tell you about last night. *I went to a dance!* Anne Gibbs (15), Miss Davis, Lieselotte and Denzil went too. I didn't dance because I still can't, although I was twice asked to. Anne didn't either and so she and I didn't have to pay. Soon after we arrived at the Princess Pavilion we went to the refreshment room, except Lieselotte - she wanted to dance. The priest who was with us paid for our grub. When Anne and I went back to the dance hall the fun started. We were surrounded by a crowd of vulgar, tipsy, rowdy sailors who flirted with us and asked silly questions. They wanted to dance but we wouldn't. The best looking one sat on the arm of my chair, held his face so close to mine that I could smell his beery breath, and put his arm round me. I told him not to do that as it was too hot. He asked me if I objected to him talking to me. I said nothing. He was very insistent. I got up and went to talk to Denzil, and the sailor hooked Anne. We could not get rid of them but all the same I had a glorious time and lots of fun. We went home in a taxi for which one of Miss Davis' friends paid. When we were in bed Lieselotte told me of her experiences at the dance. She met an airforce chap who bought her refreshments and danced the whole evening with her. He took her out into the garden and - I ask you - he kissed her there, after only knowing her for an hour or so! He took her home and at the gate he kissed her again. I don't think anyone should kiss you unless they love you. Lieselotte says he asked her first and seemed a nice fellow, but all the same I think she did wrong.

We're having a Mock Invasion this weekend. Just in case we forget there's a war on, as we haven't had any air-raids for some time.

18th September 1942

I talked to a blind man the other day whom I'd often seen about. I asked him if I could help him across the road. He took my hand and we crossed together. Then he kept me talking. First he asked me to look at my watch and see what time it was, and he bet me that he would tell sooner than I could, by feeling his special braille watch. He did, too. Then he became very vulgar, and talked about men and women naked, and the bed business. He took my hand and put it on his private thing, but I quickly snatched it away, and left him. I'll never offer to help a blind man across the road again! When I got back Mrs Tamblyn said she saw me talking to the blind man from the window for a long time, and what were we talking about for so long? I said he was a disgusting man and I would never speak to him again. But I didn't tell her what had taken place.

If the weather is fine I cycle to school every day. On Thursdays I cycle to Penryn as we have Cookery lessons there. I'm hopeless at Cookery and always the last to finish. We have to bring our own ingredients, which I often can't as I don't like to ask Miss Davis for them.

Janet has a tall, dark, lanky sailor boyfriend called George, who's very nice, has been all over the world in pre-war days, including Vienna, speaks German and is very clever. She met him at a dance and I think they'll soon get engaged. She's small and fat, so they look funny together. He played ping-pong with me.

Connie and I have been pursued by Grammar Sows (as the Grammar School boys are nicknamed), have made the acquaintance of two cheeky errand boys and - misery of miseries - I dropped my chips in the street.

That's all for now. Goodnight.

All About Everything in Short

If there is no God, why don't scientists proclaim it? And if there is one, why doesn't God let me know? Can anyone go through life without ever doubting, I wonder?

I imagine nearly every night that I have a boyfriend called Gary Romney Demarney who is tall, dark and handsome. I'm 18, he's 22. We're in love, and I imagine thrilling bits - things that THRILL me right through, often very sad ones. Sometimes we're married (but no children yet). These fantasies belong to my Inner World. My other world is the one which contains all my favourite belongings like you, dearest Wvmaro, my bike, my watch, my fountain pen. They're alive to me, and give me much comfort. I need this world too, but how humdrum it would be without the other; nothing but home, school, home, school and waiting for the end of the war, which never comes.

How could anybody reading this diary explain (for I can't myself) my love of life and human beings, my cheerfulness, my trust in the future, in spite of all that has happened? But it is so. I want to do some good in the world, I want to harden my character, I want to be agreeable, popular, uncomplicated, intelligent, quiet and reserved, and have a sense of humour. And I want to be famous!

Because today I am concerned with the good things in my life I have to admit that there are quite a number of these: I have plenty of nice friends (even though I'm different from the other girls), I quite like school, I learn music and am quite good at it, I get post, I like Falmouth, I have many pleasures by way of outings and invitations, we don't see much of the war here (even though it once nearly killed me!), I can write stories (though not nearly as well as I'd like to) and my essays are always read out in class. I have a 'home', - although a funny one, because it's so different from other girls', and the Disagreeable Person in it is fortunately often away. I love England and English people. I am in good health. And most of the time I'M ABLE TO KEEP MY TROUBLES AT ARM'S LENGTH AND NOT THINK OF THEM. On the whole I manage the monotony of life well, I think, don't you?

I must stop now. It's late and very cold and if I go on writing much longer my hands will be blue like those of the poor Little Sisters of Nazareth who are not allowed to wear gloves.

28th September 1942

In Vienna, if anyone did not like me, if other children teased me, if a teacher scolded me at school, shortly, if anyone upset me, I felt that they didn't only upset me, but my mother too. In such a case I always felt very sorry for her and avoided telling her. I read the same thing in a book today, that's what made me think of it.

I believe I have forgotten what it is to have a mother. When I had her I couldn't imagine life without her. Now that I haven't seen her for over three years and heard nothing for over one year, I've almost forgotten what motherly love is. I've learnt to do without it. The fact is I don't know whether she is dead or alive. Oh, to see her again! If only I could!

When I read a good book I forget everything. I am reading H.G. Wells: *The Country of the Blind and Other Stories*, from the school library now. It's wonderful! I met Miss Clift, our English mistress, in the school library the other day. We started talking, and I told her I liked writing and should like some day to be a writer. She asked me to let her see one of my stories, and seemed really interested.

Miss Davis has been here for tea. She told me that they now have a gardener who's a religious maniac. When they see him kneeling in the vegetable bed he's not weeding or planting, but praying. Apparently he doesn't believe in digging for victory but in praying for it!

Instead of going to school today I was in bed with a cold. Unfortunately I missed the sketch club.

3rd October 1942

If you have never thought me mad you will now, for what I'm going to tell you is very, very extraordinary: I'M IN LOVE WITH A GIRL IN MY FORM!!!!!!! No, I'm not joking. It's as true as my love for Roy was. This girl is called Audrey B., (my heart jumps at the sound of the name), and she's very much like a boy. I'll give you a brief history of Audrey: we've been in the same form ever since I came to the school but I never particularly

140

liked her. She lived at St. Joseph's for a short time, long before I did, and I was always told what a terrible girl she was - a real tomboy. She walks, talks, looks and sits precisely like a boy, and has very short hair. When I was lower down in the school I hated her because she was bossy and moody. I had then not yet discovered her charm. But gradually I got to like her better. I didn't think much about her but I admired her masculine behaviour and wished I could succeed so well in it. She's exceedingly pretty - the prettiest girl in our form. She has beautiful eyes and I adore beautiful eyes. (Mine are like a cow's). Well, last term our form performed a play about a Roman wedding and of course Audrey was the bridegroom. Betty F. was the bride. I like Betty very much too. Ever since that play, Audrey and Betty have pretended they are married and have a son! This strange marriage/friendship was to be the laughing stock of the form. They carried on like lovers; they were always together and Audrey usually had her arms round Betty or was kissing her or looking at her lovingly. Audrey always opens the door for Betty, lets her go first, in fact treats her exactly as a man does a woman. The girls in our form refer to them as 'he and she'. I think Audrey and Betty are devoted to each other. Betty once told me she wished Audrey really was a boy. (I've sometimes wondered if she *is* a boy, dressed as a girl!) It's rather thrilling to watch these love scenes between Audrey and Betty. As time went on I admired Audrey more and more. I was fascinated by her boyish manner and I watched every step she took in order to be able to copy it precisely. At the same time I laughed about her and teased her, along with the other girls. She took it well.

All this came to an end yesterday after school. There were a few of us left in the classroom after most had gone home, and Audrey and Betty were among them. Audrey was larking about and kissed all the girls to make them blush. I watched her and Betty having a love scene (they don't care who's there) and then Audrey, who has always been nice to me except that she tries to boss me now and then, came over to me and kissed me. Then I went home and knew that I had fallen in love with this girl. It was 10 minutes past 4 on the afternoon of Friday, 2nd October 1942.

At first I experienced a very strong and queer feeling for her which I couldn't quite understand. Then, this morning in town, I met her. I talked and walked with her. On the surface everything was the same, except that I noticed it whenever we touched. There's a lot of touching connected with love. In the afternoon when I was out I looked for her again, but in vain. Am I peculiar or mad, to love a girl in my form? But why? Can't one love anybody, if they are nice enough? Why must it always be sexual love? I read a story the other day about an old man of 75 falling in love with a *picture* of a woman, and he died for her! Why can't I then fall in love with a girl if she has the qualities I like? Perhaps I'm not mad, after all? Lieselotte doesn't think I am.

Now I come to think of it, there have been other women in my life. One was a young woman called Maria at a summer resort near Vienna. I have only the haziest memory of her. Then there was Frau Schrammel, my French mistress at school in Vienna. I was about 10 or 11. I adored her. When Hitler came she turned into a Nazi, and hated me, along with the other Jewish children. It nearly broke my heart. I'm certainly unfortunate with my loves! How will this one turn out, I wonder? I never expect my love to be rewarded or returned in any way, but I do want to be liked . . . I also *never* feel jealous of the friends of the person I love. So you see I am very modest - even if I'm mad.

I have decided never to marry but to have a career (e.g. that of an authoress), because this sex and bed business is loathsome - or people make it so.

8th October 1942

"Where are your stockings?" Audrey asked me on Monday morning as soon as I entered the cloakroom.

"At home," I said. "Why?"

"We are supposed to be wearing stockings. The notice was given out last Monday."

"Oh, I was away then."

"So was I, but I'm wearing them." She sounded critical of me, but then we looked at each other's legs - and laughed.

She sits in front of me in class. I noticed that she has been turning round a lot lately, and grinning and talking. I dare say she did that hundreds of times before I loved her, but one doesn't notice these things ordinarily.

A funny thing happened today: Betty F. came to my desk and

tried my pen. Audrey followed her and did likewise. Betty wrote the word 'you' in my rough book. Audrey grinned, took the pen and wrote 'I love' in front of 'you'. I said, "You fool," and crossed it out. Idiot, idiot! But I know she only meant it as a joke, and I couldn't bear it.

I've developed a silly habit: I want to show off in front of Audrey all the time. I want her to notice me. When I see her and Betty together I think to myself: "My God, if only she'd talk to me like that." Although I wrote last time that I don't expect my love to be returned, this sudden longing to be closer to her has come over me. In the days when we were just pally we discovered once that we both knew Wilfred P. and we used to have long conversations about him and call each other 'little Willie'. Those innocent days will never come back.

It's getting serious, my love for Audrey, my sudden mad love for another girl.

Next Monday my father is being converted. Lieselotte and I are going to the church with him.

10th October 1942

I think I've got a disease called inferiority complex. I'm a failure, a complete failure in everything. Already 15 and no aim in life reached whatever! Once I considered myself good at art and music - now I don't. Do you think there is any cure for this disease?

The other day I gave you causes for my happiness; now I'll give you some for my unhappiness:

The presence of the Disagreeable Person whom I hate and who disturbs my peace of mind.
The absence of my beloved mother from whom I have not heard for over a year.
The war.
My uncertain future. What will I do when I leave school?
My weaknesses and above named 'disease'.
My homelessness. (I want a *real* home).
Some school troubles.
My love for Audrey.
Whether to believe in God or not.

Are they very bad? I must stop now. I love you always, Wvmaro.

14th October 1942

My father has come across my little Utility Note Book which contains reports of Connie's and my detectiving expeditions. He was furious.

"Do you realise that you could go to prison if this is found? Do you want to ruin our lives? Have you forgotten that we are foreigners here, and there's a war on?" he shouted at me.

"It's only a harmless game Connie and I play," I said.

He slapped me.

"Connie is stupid, but you should know better. Throw away that notebook and don't ever do this again. Do you hear me?"

I did. I couldn't help it, he was shouting so. But I didn't throw the notebook away. Even if it *was* found, I can't believe that it would be taken seriously. It may sound like the work of a professional spy to my father, but I am sure no English person would think so.

19th October 1942

Although Connie does not go to my school (she goes to the Truro High) she has known Audrey for a long time. Yesterday we called at Audrey's house to ask her to come to the flicks with us. (My idea.) She lives in a nice house in Dracaena Avenue with her mother and older sister. Her father is in the RAF. She was wonderful, and quite different than she is at school where she spends so much time fooling and playing the boy to Betty (which I'm beginning to hate watching). While Connie talked to Mrs B. Audrey and I chatted, mostly about school, and she showed me her maths homework. We arranged a day, and I'm dying for it to come!

25th October 1942

I told Ruth about Audrey in my last letter and she said that it isn't love at all. But I say it is and it is! It feels exactly the same as loving a boy except of course I can't think of marrying her, but I don't want to marry, anyway.

I asked Pamela, my best school-friend, who's a good sport, to find out from Audrey if she's in love with Betty. Pam did, and came back with the following information: Audrey is *not* in love with Betty, she only carries on like that with her to amuse us and because she likes to be affectionate with her friends. If Pam had any more questions, Audrey said, then 'fire away'. As I'm sure that Audrey does not tell lies I believe what she says.

Next Saturday Audrey, Connie and I are going to the flicks and then to tea at Connie's. I can't wait!

31st October 1942

Is it right, do you think, Wvmaro, to be so happy? LISTEN! It started very badly, because the day appointed for our outing and tea party at Connie's turned out to be the day of Connie and her family's move back to Falmouth, for they'd been staying with her aunts in the country for some time, and so of course she couldn't have us. I didn't mind, did I, said Connie, we'd still all go to the flicks. No, of course I didn't mind, I lied. It was a terrific blow. Worse was to come. The next day Connie phoned me and said Audrey had invited her and her little brother Tony back to her house after the flicks. How I envied them! By this time the whole arrangement had turned sour and I didn't want to go any more.

Going home at dinner-time I saw Audrey pushing her bike up the hill. She called to me:

"Inky, I want you, come here a minute!" In a flash I knew what she would say. I don't know how I knew because up to that moment I hadn't a hope in the world.

"Do you think you can come to tea after the flicks?" Audrey asked me. Did she hear the joy in my voice as I replied, as casually as I could:

"Thanks, old stick. I'd love to." We then walked together up the hill, pushing our bikes, but I don't remember much about what we said because I was simply knocked silly by my happiness. On top of the hill we parted, I went home, had dinner, and an hour later I was sitting next to Audrey in the flicks. We saw *Jungle Book*, an Alexander Korda film with Sabu. (Not bad.) Three more hours, and I was right inside her house! Do you know what that meant to me? I sat next to her at teatime. Her mother had made a delicious chocolate cake out of stale biscuits - a wartime recipe, she explained. Mr B. used to work for Huntley & Palmers before the war, which perhaps explains the biscuit recipe. After tea we played Monopoly, laughing, fooling and cracking

g

jokes all the time. I was so happy! It was like a wonderful dream.

"Come again. I never have anything to do on Saturday afternoons," Audrey said when we left. I most certainly will!

Something else has made me happy. A few weeks ago our landlady, Mrs Tamblyn, said nobody was to touch the piano again because it had been scratched, and removed it. I was in a terrible state. If I couldn't practise then I couldn't go to music lessons any more. What could I do? It looked hopeless. I decided to have one more try. I asked Mrs Tamblyn again if I could use the piano if I promised to take great care. Yes, all right, she consented at last. That made me happy. It was a terrific worry removed.

It had been a good chance to find out if God existed or not. It looks as if there is one - a God of Love, Knowledge, Help and Refuge. Tonight I shall say a prayer and thank Him. I believe the scientific part is true too, but God is behind that as well. It is God who provides the mystery, and if it wasn't for this mystery we would have understood everything long ago.

7th November 1942

It is late in the evening but I must write something down, or burst.

A whole week has passed since that divine Saturday and throughout the week I returned to it in my thoughts. At school Audrey was her usual self - tomboyish, happy-go-lucky, full of fun. About the middle of the week Connie and I went for a walk in the evening and, as usual, we talked of Audrey and of Joan, the girl Connie is in love with at her school. We were walking in Dracaena Avenue (what a coincidence!) when suddenly I said to Connie:

"I dare you to go to Audrey's house and ask her to live with you when she grows up!" To my surprise Connie agreed. I didn't go with her, of course. While I waited for her I thought about the conversation we'd just had about two people of the same sex loving each other and living together, and wondered if this is possible. After 15 minutes Connie returned. I was very impatient to hear what had happened and bombarded her with questions. Connie related: Audrey's first reaction was that Connie was completely mad; when she heard it was a dare she burst out laughing. She was in a super mood and not a bit angry about it. She was still in a super mood the next morning at school but made

146

no mention of the incident. But later I saw her in a very different mood. She was dead quiet during dinner and hardly spoke. I don't think it meant anything, it's just her nature. She also talked of her 'wife' once or twice, meaning Betty F.

The fact that I've been inside her home, had a glimpse of her private life, has brought me closer to her and I hope in time will bring me closer to understanding her.

Last Monday was a half term holiday and Connie, Pam and I had lunch at the British Restaurant for a treat.

15th November 1942

Lieselotte and I went to a special Victory Service in Church today. All the church bells were ringing because the Germans are at last being thrown back in Russia. People are getting more optimistic now about an end to the war. Last Sunday there was a Peace Service on the seafront. Connie and I were there on our bikes. I spend most Sunday evenings at St. Joseph's, or go there for tea.

I know exactly why I love Audrey - she has that power over me, she fascinates and charms me. I'm like a frog hypnotised by a snake with her. And she can be like a snake. It is why many girls hate her. One of them is a girl in our form called Sally. Whenever Sally says something nasty about Audrey I defend her fiercely. But yesterday I came close to hating Audrey myself: I had invited her to tea, and she didn't even bother to tell me, until I asked her again some days later, that she couldn't come. I was deeply hurt and disappointed. Then I tried to make excuses for her - I always do for people I love. But, as you see, I am not blind to her faults. If I love her in spite of them it must be real love, mustn't it?

Pam is coming to tea instead. She was endlessly pleased to be asked. It's a very unjust world.

I wonder what I'll think of all this when I read it through in my old age? Do you think if a man loved me he would be jealous of a *woman* I loved? Perhaps he wouldn't understand.

In moments of happiness I forget everything, EVERYTHING: my mother, the war, my lost home, my future, my impossible father. As I did when Audrey asked me to tea. As I did on the 23rd of January 1941. And happiness it must have been, to make me forget all these troubles.

I had a row with Audrey at school. It was about something quite trivial but left me in a rage and shattered.

"I shall bang that girl's head one day," I raved to the class in general (when Audrey was out of the room, of course).

"Oh, I thought you *liked* Audrey, *'I'*?" said Sally sweetly.

"I can get mad with a person I like, can't I?" I said. I'm quite sure Sally is in love with Audrey herself and hides it by claiming the opposite. It seems to me everyone - the whole world - must be in love with her. As for me - do you suppose that I loved Audrey one inch less during my rage? No! (Can love be measured in inches? or weighed?) Well then, there's no more to be said.

The physical friendship, affection and extraordinary behaviour between Audrey B. and Betty F. are greatly on my mind. I discovered something else strange about them: they both believe in nudism, and would gladly go naked if it was allowed. Not me! I would hate it.

Could *you* lose your temper with someone you love, darling Wvmaro, if you were a human being?

23rd November 1942

Don't ask me whether it was a dream or not. Don't ask me *anything*. I'm in ecstasy. Audrey has been to tea! And I thought she would never come. It happened like this: On Friday afternoon I said to Audrey: "Can you come to tea tomorrow?" And she could! So, as arranged, the following afternoon she, Connie and I went to town. Walking beside her, it felt more like paradise than Market Street, Falmouth. Then we fetched Audrey's Monopoly and went to my place. We played for a bit and enjoyed ourselves. Then quite suddenly, we became serious, and started talking about sexual matters such as women changing into men and monthly periods. Audrey said she was glad she had at last found somebody with whom she could discuss such matters sensibly. After we had tea (Mrs Tamblyn had prepared a good one) we went upstairs to my room, meaning to come down again later to continue our game - but we never did. We passed the rest of the afternoon - hours - sitting on my bed, talking, with Connie mostly listening. And what did we talk about? Mostly about her and Betty and the girls in our form and their stupidity about boys.

Audrey doesn't like most of the girls in our form, she likes being alone or with Betty. No, she's not in love with her, she just likes her a lot. Was I clear about everything now? Why do they cuddle and huddle so much then, I ask. For fun, from affection, means nothing. *Now* was I clear about everything? Well, sort of. Would I tell Audrey exactly what the form thought of them? That they're soppy. What did *I* think of them? That they're soppy - and in love. Is Betty in love with her? Doesn't know. Would I ask her, and tell Audrey? (Great surprise!) No, I wouldn't, because it would be disloyal to Betty. OK, she'd ask her herself and then tell me at school - when we're alone. Shall we tell Betty about this conversation? asks Audrey. Don't mind. Did she tell Betty everything? Nearly. What did I think she and Betty did when they were alone together? Couldn't imagine. Would I like them to stop being soppy and sentimental together? I certainly would. She promises to try. I would hate all that kissing and fondling, I say. Whereupon Audrey gets up and, in spite of my resistance, kisses me . . . Oh, what that kiss meant to me! I said: "I expect anyone can fall in love with someone of the same sex as much as of the opposite sex." She looked at me for a long time. Then she said: "Oh, I wish all the world were like you, '*I*'. You have such sensible ideas." I laughed (with pleasure but also with embarrassment) and said: "I'm sure my father wouldn't agree with you! He thinks I'm stupid." For answer Audrey came and kissed me again.

Soon afterwards she left, and Connie and I accompanied her to her house.

"Poor Audrey," said Connie, when we were alone. "She doesn't seem to have or want any friends except Betty - and you."

"Did you notice how she wanted my opinion on everything?" I asked Connie.

"Yes, I did," replied Connie.

That I should have had such a confidential talk with Audrey was beyond my wildest dreams. It isn't half as nice writing it all down on paper as it was actually experiencing it, but it will be interesting to read in years to come. That night I couldn't rest. The scene in my bedroom with Audrey haunted me. I got out of bed and walked up and down. Finally I fell asleep at about half past midnight.

Now Audrey B. is truly my friend. Think of it! Think of it! How did I come to be so lucky? Do I deserve her? I thought her wonderful before, but I greatly underestimated her.

You are MINE now, Audrey, forever.

26th November 1942

Just a few words. I'm in a desperate hurry. Betty F. was absent from school until yesterday, so Audrey hasn't been able to ask her yet if she's in love with her. Audrey called on Monday after school to bring me back some film star pictures, and we had another conversation. She promised faithfully to ask Betty if she's in love with her (she agrees it's a difficult task), and then to tell me. We talked about love and I said *I'd* never admit to loving anyone, unless I wished to get married, which I don't. I said one can love passionately no matter whether your love is returned or not. She agreed. Then she urged me to ask her more questions. So I asked:

"Audrey, why are you so changeable?"

"Well, it's my nature," she replied, not objecting to this question at all. "I don't like people who are always the same. It's dull."

"You've quite the wrong idea about that. If you didn't change so often people would know where they are with you, and you'd be much more popular."

"I'll see what I can do for you, '*I*'. But remember, you and I have very different attitudes to friends - you want them and have them and care about what they think of you; I prefer being alone except with one good friend, and don't care much what others think of me." I had to leave it at that. What could I say?

Betty came back to school yesterday as I said, and I saw her take Audrey round the waist - and Audrey gently remove her hand and move away. "I haven't asked her yet!" Audrey whispered to me during the history lesson. I blushed terribly. Why? Because I'd hate Betty to notice that there's anything between Audrey - her best friend - and me. Later I saw them with arms around each other again. But today will be the crisis: I'm sure Audrey will ask her today - and what will Betty answer? I'm dying to know. Will her answer supply the missing piece in the jigsaw?

I still can't quite understand it all - the sudden new relationship between Audrey and me, the shared secret which Betty doesn't know about - I'm in a haze and a maze and a daze!

150

Yesterday, Saturday, I went collecting with Connie and then Christmas shopping with Lieselotte. I had 5/- pocket money and 7/- from the second hand shop in Killigrew Street for selling some clothes to them. Out of that I spent:

5d	On Pam's Christmas present
7½d	On Mrs Tamblyn's
11½d	On Connie's
3/9	On Lieselotte's
1/-	On Dad's
1/-	On Ruth's
7½d	On Christmas Cards

I put 2/6 into the Post Office.

I have also got my new pocket diary for 1943. That cost - nothing because, like last year, I took one from Woolworth's and didn't pay for it! It's very easy on a Saturday afternoon. My theory is that, as Woolworth's don't know I took it it won't make them unhappy, but it makes me very happy to have a diary without having had to pay for it. Is it wrong?

I plucked up my courage on Friday at school and asked a 'once more vague and eyes-for-Betty only' Audrey if she had asked the vital question yet. "Yes," was the answer. Well, and what did Betty say, I asked her. She took her time replying, and then only reluctantly, it seemed to me.

"She said she's not in love with me. It's just a deep friendship," Audrey said at last, and would say no more.

There are several Audreys for me:

1. Audrey as she probably really is or seems to be in the eyes of the world - a tomboy, unsentimental, happy-go-lucky.
2. A romantic Romeo, acting soppily with Betty and not her real self at all.
3. A good friend confiding in me.
4. An ordinary member of the form, an ordinary schoolgirl behind whose mask no teacher could guess the many faces.
5. Audrey in a bad mood, quarrelsome and denying our friendship.
6. Audrey in an exuberant mood, sweeping me off my feet.

Throughout all these stages I love her.

I played 'truth and dare' with my friend Pamela the other day and what do you think was the first truth she asked me? *Have I ever been in love with another female*! I said yes. That's all. Connie (who knows about me and Audrey) tried to find out for me if Pam suspected, but did not succeed.

Do you think Audrey has forgotten our conversation? She promised me to try and be less changeable but I haven't noticed it yet. But you can't expect people to change their nature within a week, can you?

I must finish now as it is about 8.45am on a Sunday morning and time to get up.

6th December 1942

Yesterday (Saturday) morning I went for a little bicycle ride at 10am, for that is the time Audrey finishes her music lesson with Miss Rogers. During the school week nothing much had happened between her and me, and it seemed as if she had quite forgotten our confidential talk. So I was determined to meet her yesterday morning - and I did!

"Hello, Inky. Where have you sprung from?" she asked me, as soon as we met.

"I've just been to see Connie off to her music lesson," I answered, which was true. We cycled home together. We talked of this and that. Then the subject of the school Christmas party came up, and the fuss the girls are making about what to wear to it; she and I are the only ones who don't care.

"Shall we wear our gym tunics?" said Audrey, laughing.

"Oh yes, let's," I replied, and laughed too.

"We mustn't let each other down, then," she said.

"Of course not. We'll both turn up in our gym tunics." I said.

So we shared a secret again, she and I. When we parted I realised I still did not know what had passed between her and Betty when Audrey asked her if she loved her. But one day I shall ask her again for I'm determined to know. Meanwhile I was happy. Some people say it's impossible to love one of your own sex. If this is true, I ask you, what is this peculiar sensation of mine for Audrey? Let people deny it. What do I care? I love her. And I love her in spite of the fact that I don't much like my own sex.

Yesterday afternoon Lieselotte and I went to Truro by train to

152

meet my father and his business partner Jane from London. We had tea and supper at the Royal Hotel, and we had a walk in Truro. Lieselotte and I returned to Falmouth on the 9.30pm train but my father stayed in Truro. Today, Sunday, my father and Jane came to us for lunch and tea. Jane gave me an order to design some Christmas cards. In the evening we saw them to the bus stop and they both returned to Truro. Next Thursday Lieselotte and I are going to have dinner with them again at the Royal Hotel, after the school concert at the Princess Pavilion, and as Jane returns to London on Saturday, my father is coming back to Falmouth.

15th December 1942

I had my last music lesson of the term today. Last week Miss Rogers said to me: "I'd like you very much to be in the recital next year." I asked if we *had* to be. Well, no, but she'd like all her pupils to take part. I don't want to, but what can I do?

We break up the day after tomorrow - hurrah!

I've taken some time off from designing Christmas cards and drawn a cartoon. Making up cartoons is my latest hobby.

17th December 1942 (Nearly 18th)

11.45pm. Can't sleep. Something important to tell you: Sally *was* in love with Audrey! I KNEW IT! She and I had a long conversation during which she confessed this, but said she doesn't love her any longer. Anyway, it wasn't really love, just a terrific crush. How queer that two people - possibly three - in one form should be in love with the same girl. I'm sorry Sally had that crush. I wanted to be the only one to love Audrey but at least *my* love for her is *real*.

I've heard that Roy Lovell is home . . .

Tomorrow, the first day of the Christmas holiday, I'm going to St. Joseph's and then Miss Davis is taking me to a play in the Catholic Church Hall in which she has a part.

24th December 1942

Pam and I cycled to Maenporth to pick holly. We found quite a lot

A cartoon: "And 'ave you 'eard, my dear, they feed them ATS girls some bad, poor things!"

with berries on. Yesterday Miss Davis brought our Christmas presents. Tonight we're having our Christmas dinner and presents here, my father, Lieselotte and I, and tomorrow, Christmas Day, Lieselotte and I are taking our presents to St. Joseph's and going to church, and in the afternoon I'm going to Pam's for Christmas tea - Christmas cake and mince pies and other goodies (not that I like them too much).

I'm beginning to think that Roy Lovell was only a vision. He's gone back and again I haven't seen him. I have one consolation: the last time I saw him was that glorious 23rd of January 1941. If I should never see him again I have this happy memory of him - and nothing afterwards. It's a long time since I talked to you about anyone but Audrey!

Tomorrow is Christmas Day. I'm worried. There's my poor darling mother somewhere in Poland, perhaps not alive any more, and here I am, thinking about Christmas and presents and a girl in my form who is like no other, and, and, and . . . In the evenings in bed everything goes round and round in my head and I can't sleep. What can I do, dear Wvmaro? Can't you tell me?

27th December 1942

Mrs Bath, Pam's mother, gave me an *orange* for Christmas!

Yesterday I was at Miss Davis' Boxing Night Party. It was very good and went on until 4am! David and Denzil and others were there. Denzil was nice - but it is surprising how separation interferes with friendship. We aren't the good pals we used to be. Fighting, teasing, laughing - we still do a bit, but it isn't the same. I can't stick David. He kept kissing Lieselotte again while we played 'Murder'. (We played it for 4 hours!) I was in his arms and also in Denzil's once or twice for quite a long time, but I think they must have taken me for the wrong person. I tried to get away but was in a hopeless scuffle. It was a jolly good game. Denzil murdered me once. Father Wiseman and Miss Hankin also played.

If I were a boy I'd ask Audrey to marry me at once.

30th December 1942

An unexpected piece of luck! Connie and I met Audrey in town!

She walked a little way with us (pushing our bikes), then asked us which way we were going - and went the opposite way! A strange creature. But later we met again and she asked us (yes, for once *she* asked) if we'd like to go to the flicks with her tomorrow. My heart stood still. We then went to her house to arrange things and stayed for about a quarter of an hour. So tomorrow we are going to the Odeon to see *Saboteur* with Robert Cummings.

And so the year 1942 is ending very nicely for me. What could be better than spending the last day of it in the company of Audrey?

I earned 6/- for the Christmas cards I designed. 2/6 went into the Post Office.

There's a list of jobs I have to do written down on the last page (Memoranda) of my 1942 pocket diary. They are:

> Wash my brush and comb.
> Write something in Margaret's autograph book.
> Cut my toenails.
> Write 3 letters.

I shouldn't like to end the year with these tasks undone. On the very last page are printed the words: 'Notes for 1943'. But how on earth do I know what will happen in 1943? Tell me that, Wvmaro.

31st December 1942

Much to my surprise, I felt like hugging and kissing Audrey all the time at the flicks today. I don't usually feel anything so soppy. I don't know what happened to me but it was as much as I could do to keep my arms to myself. She was delightful the whole time. I'm shivering as I write, remembering her closeness. I'm absolutely shaking, honestly.

5th January 1943

I go everywhere on my bicycle - to school, to cookery in Penryn, to music lessons, to the town, to the pictures - unless it's wet. Last Friday evening there was another party at St. Joseph's, and a play with Miss Davis in it. It was great fun, and I didn't get home till 1.30am, much to my father's displeasure. I have been to the pictures twice with my father and also for several walks, as of course he has no friends here and no one to go out with. But tomorrow he leaves again. We shall see him off at the station.

Last Saturday I met Audrey in the library and I recommended her a book, which she took out. Connie thinks Audrey likes me a lot.

7th January 1943

I'll come straight to the point. I had invited Audrey and Connie to tea for Monday the 11th. I was dying for the day, but never mind that. This morning at 10.45 I was playing the piano when the door bell rang. Thinking it was Connie, I went to the door - and saw, through the glass panel, not Connie but - AUDREY. The world stopped. Everything stood still - for a split second. I thought it was a dream, because I so often imagine Audrey coming to see me. As I opened the door my mind was totally blank. I said "Hello," and knew I was blushing. My voice shook and my knees were sinking. I just stood and gaped at her and she probably thought I had gone off my head. And then I knew in a flash why she was here. I said:

"I suppose you've come to say you can't make it on Monday," I said. She said: "Yes." And with that 'yes' it was all over for me. Everything. She proceeded to give me a long explanation of why she couldn't come - her father and sister were home on leave, was all I took in.

"Couldn't we arrange another day? I asked hopelessly.

"Sorry, not during these holidays any more," she said. "I'm really sorry, Inky." After she had gone I cried bitterly. It was such a bitter disappointment that I *had* to cry. All these feelings that I described to you are true and not exaggerated. I may seem sentimental - but then, love *is* sentimental. This feeling I had when I saw Audrey through the glass panel is impossible to describe. It keeps coming back to me, as though it was happening all over again.

This afternoon I was out with Pam, when we saw Audrey on the other side of the street.

"Why are you blushing?" Pam asked me.

"I'm not!" I cried.

It was terrible. I've lost utter control of myself. I blush when I see her, I cry when she disappoints me, I tremble when I think of her. This must stop, or I shall give myself away. And what *is* the real reason why she can't come to tea? Why can't she be out for one afternoon if her father and sister are on leave for the rest of the holidays? Doesn't she want to come? Isn't she allowed to come? Don't her parents want her to be friends with me for some reason? Perhaps because I don't live in a normal home with a father and mother?

No, no, no, no, no! I must not listen to these thoughts. Everything is all right. She'd love to come but she can't, she'll come another day, she's as sorry as I am, because she likes me too . . . This is what I must believe.

13th January 1943

It has been pouring for days. School starts again tomorrow and I won't have so much time. On Tuesday I saw *Gone With The Wind* for the second time with Pam. What a glorious, marvellous, film! Moira McLeod is in Falmouth and we've been out together twice.

On Monday, 11th January, the day Audrey should have come to tea, Pam, Connie and I were in the British Restaurant having tea. I was sitting near the window. I glanced out - and saw Audrey. She was walking down Market Street, alone. WHY then couldn't she come to have tea with me? The question went round and round in my head. I was talking to my friends absentmindedly; I said:

"These chips are good, aren't they?" but I was thinking: "Doesn't she *want* to come for some reason?" I said:

"Yes, I'm going home at five," but I was thinking: "Perhaps she doesn't like me?" I said:

"Shall I get some buns for us?" but I was thinking: "Going into town for a minute isn't the same as going out to tea. She probably went on an errand . . ." I said:

"You can have my bun. It's not very nice," but I was thinking: "Yes, that's it, that must be it. For God's sake don't misjudge her . . ." And so it went on.

But in the evening, when I was back in my bedroom in my so called home - the Tamblyns' boarding-house - I suddenly thought: "How silly of me to love a girl of my age (she's 10 months younger than me). I can't help it, but that doesn't make it any better." And I wanted to shake off this love burden, as a dog shakes off water when he comes out of the sea.

16th January 1943

The other day I had a mysterious letter containing an Errol Flynn picture, (my favourite film star) but no writing with it. I'm sure Robin T. sent it. If he did, I wonder if he's still in love with me? In a way I hope not because I know the damnable feeling . . . I wrote him a card today and asked him if he sent it.

I've got some news: Alan is here! I went to St. Joseph's today and there he was, and Denzil too. He was as nice as ever. He said: "We're coming to see you and Lizzy (Lieselotte) this afternoon. Shall we come round about teatime?" What a surprise!

"Yes, do," I replied, and of course had to invite them to tea. Just like Alan. He always invites himself to wherever he wants to go and does it with such charm that nobody minds. So this afternoon they came and we four had a jolly good time. Alan was in naval uniform and looked very handsome. We had tea, laughed, joked and then they played the piano. It was a very nice afternoon.

On the first day back at school Audrey was delightful. We were together a lot. Betty F. was absent. It didn't affect me. (Or did it? I'll leave it open.) Having been occupied in doing my utmost to fall out of love with Audrey for the last few days, it seemed success was very far away. Before going to sleep I would tell myself she's not worthy of my love, she's mean, false, changeable - then I have to stop. I never get any further. It hurts me to think badly of her. There must be another way.

There was general uproar in my form when I said I didn't want to marry. Most girls are so stupid. There were only three or four others who don't want to marry, and Audrey was one of them.

Miss Davis returned from Bath today. St. Joseph's always seems empty without her, however many people are there.

19th January 1943

One day when my father was here he asked me:
"Are you happy?" Before considering my reply I blurted out:
"No, not really."

"Why not?" he demanded. "Haven't you got everything a young girl could want? You go to a good school, you have a home with me and your sister, I'm making money now and we're not poor. So what's the matter?"

"What about what Hitler did to the Jews, and the war?" I said.

"Those are world problems, and no concern of yours," he snapped. The conversation was closed. Not a word was said about my mother. I would not use her holy name to him, and he - he has forgotten her, I think. I was left feeling that I was stupid and ungrateful not to be happy.

I'm going to do a bit of detective work because - listen: Betty lives with Audrey now (lucky thing) during the week, for some reason. One of the girls in our form said to me: "This is some queer business. Why can't Betty live with her parents in Helston?" Yes, why can't she, for that is where her home is but she's always staying somewhere else. Perhaps her parents are divorced. "They get on my pot, these two," another girl in my form said to me. "They're utterly soppy and absurd. Why, anyone would think Audrey was a boy. They're the talk of the school. Everyone is laughing at them!" Audrey knows that, but she doesn't care. Some time ago, during our intimate conversation, Audrey had said to me: "Anything more you want to know? Go on, ask me anything." I'd like to ask her a few things now! But the door has closed on me and I have instead to do some detective work. Nobody likes Audrey very much because of her silly behaviour with Betty. She promised me to stop but she didn't keep her promise - something I can forgive no one but her. I who am in love with the girl whose reputation and popularity are at stake ought to defend her but I don't, for fear of betraying myself. Oh, what a coward I am, and so weak, so weak! But I shall change that, I shall defend her in future, to prove my love to myself, and because I feel it's my duty.

Excuse me for writing in such a muddled way today but I can't seem to regulate my thoughts. I just have to put down what comes into my head.

Alan has gone back and Denzil was extremely nice the last time I saw him, when Jo the sailor was also at St. Joseph's and we played cards.

I'm never going to marry.

See what I mean about my muddled thoughts?

30th January 1943

I've dropped Needlework at school and I've started going in to Prayers in the morning. Audrey has been absent for the whole week and school life without her is unbearable. I'm on the way to finding out why Betty is staying at the B's but shan't say anything more about it until I do.

2nd February 1943

Audrey came back to school yesterday. It was lovely to see my darling again. During break she was looking through a book of mine in which she saw a nice fancy bookmark which Lieselotte had given me the day before - quite new. Audrey admired it greatly. I like it very much myself. I said: "Would you like to have it?" Then followed a long dispute for she wouldn't take it at first, but was finally persuaded, and couldn't thank me enough. I felt lovely afterwards - it's the first thing I've given her. She gave me a whole packet of chewing gum once.

Sally A. told me she liked Audrey very much.

"Has your crush returned?" I asked her.

"Oh no. Just as a friend." I told her to think hard about it and make sure she isn't mistaken again. I was angry. I had another surprise too. Audrey and Betty didn't walk to school together, and weren't on speaking terms today. If this was intended to puzzle everyone it certainly succeeded.

Towards the end of the day something unpleasant happened. It was before going out to games, and a few of us were left in the cloakroom. I said I'd change all the hats round for a joke. They all said: "Oh no, you mustn't, because it's mean," and tried to stop me. Then Audrey came in and when she heard what the argument was about she joined the chorus of "Oh no, you mustn't!"

"What, are you unsporty too, Audrey?" I said, and by now I was hurt as well as angry.

"It's indecent," said Audrey. "I never thought you'd do anything so indecent, Inky."

"Indecent?" I cried. "It's a joke!" To end the argument Joan, a mild, kind and gentle girl took me by the hand and said: "Look, Inky, don't do it, because some of the girls might be bus girls and if they can't find their hat they might miss their bus. See?"

"Yes," I said. "I see." But, looking at Audrey, I couldn't help adding, "but it's not indecent!" So with the others playing wise old aunts and looking on, I returned the hats to their rightful places. Reluctantly, of course.

7th February 1943

Last night Connie and I went for a walk, bought some chips and then went Gassarding. Guess who opened the door of the first house we went to - Mr Seaward, my one-time art teacher! I was very embarrassed because I'd been avoiding him since I left the Art School, and hoping I wouldn't meet him.

"Why don't you come to the class any more?" he asked me, after I had explained our 'errand'.

"My father thought I ought to concentrate on school work," I answered, which was partly true. I couldn't tell him that my father thought I wasn't learning anything at the Art School. After that experience I had no more taste for Gassarding, which Connie entirely appreciated.

24th February 1943

I know I've told you this many times before, but I do so long for my mother. I have so little hope of ever seeing her again. Whenever I'm in trouble I speak to her in bed at night and ask her for advice. Sometimes I can see her quite distinctly, and she is ready to answer and help me in her kind, loving, motherly way. She consoles me. This is a great help to me.

I must speak to her tonight.

Various people have been staying here for odd days, such as commercial travellers and business men. Last week an airforce man stayed for one night. We had breakfast together. On Sunday I was at church with Lieselotte and a Special Prayer for Russia was said, because of the suffering of the people there under German occupation.

1st March 1943

I still don't know who sent the Errol Flynn picture - no word from Robin.

On Saturday I went collecting in town in the morning; in the afternoon there was a birthday tea for Connie at St. Joseph's. Afterwards Connie, Pam and I went for a ride, explored an old ruin near the Castle and picked daffodils. The Castle itself is out of bounds as the Army has taken it over for the duration. Unfortunately, I ran into a cat on my bicycle, but neither of us was hurt. Today, Monday, was a half term holiday and five of us from my form cycled 20 miles to the Lizard and took our dinner and tea. We stopped in Helston and visited the aunt of one of the girls, and didn't get home till 7.30pm. It was a lovely day. But tomorrow it's school again, I have to start revising, I have an appointment at the dentist's at 4.30pm, and one with Mr Robins at his office. Enough nasty experiences to make me forget today's happy ones.

6th March 1943

The other night I had a vivid dream about my mother. I embraced her and she was wonderfully soft. The dream haunted me all day, and the soft warm feeling stayed with me. Otherwise I have almost forgotten motherly love.

I think I'm unjust to God sometimes. I blame Him for everything that goes wrong, and afterwards I'm always sorry. But who *is* to blame? The devil doesn't exist (although Miss Davis believes he does!) God is all powerful and the cause of everything. Therefore He is to blame. Some people say that everything God does is for the best if only we would see it. That excuses God, but is hard to understand. I don't understand the nature of God.

I expected Audrey to be at Miss Rogers' rehearsal for the concert this morning but she didn't come. That put the lid on a day on which everything had gone wrong. She was absent again one afternoon last week, to my despair. When she returned the following day I experienced a deep feeling of pleasure on seeing her. I asked her if she was better. She answered in the affirmative - very coolly. I was so happy to have her back I didn't mind. I would do anything in the world for her.

My father returned today. Lieselotte and I fetched him from the station. Afterwards I went for a short bicycle ride on my own.

12th March 1943

I've had to go to the Police station as I'm now 16 and have to register as an Alien.

We had an ATS lecture at school today - in a lorry - and I started up a motorbike! Ironically, my bicycle had a puncture, I discovered at the end of the day, and Beryl Crew lent me hers to go home on, which was really nice of her. Tomorrow Lieselotte and I are invited for tea at the Gibbs'. Mary Gibbs is Lieselotte's friend and Anne is mine.

Last Saturday we heard gunfire again after a long time. We haven't had an air-raid for ages.

There's going to be a dance at the Grammar School and some of the girls in my form are going, but I hate these things as you know - and so does Audrey, and we swore we wouldn't attend it. By the way, she very much enjoyed the book I recommended her in the Public Library which was by Hugh Walpole. I've recently read *Goodbye Mr Chips* and *The Prisoner of Zenda*, and now I'm reading *She Stoops to Conquer* and *The Vicar of Wakefield* by Oliver Goldsmith.

22nd March 1943

Audrey has been to the Grammar School dance! I couldn't believe it when I was told. My first thought was "I'll kill the boys who held her in their arms!" My next one: "Why did she lie to me?" It appears her mother was going because she knows some of the Grammar School masters and didn't want to leave Audrey at home alone. She told me this after a rehearsal at Miss Rogers. Then suddenly I told her something which I have told nobody else: Lieselotte wants to join up and my father intends to send me to a boarding-school in London. I can't bear the thought and naturally am very worried about it. So that is how I came to tell her of this plan. She looked at me for a minute. Then she said, "Oh Inky! Inky Polly, don't go! You'll do your best not to, won't you? Oh, I hope you won't go!" You can imagine how I felt. I said stupidly:

"Why? Would it matter to you if I went?"

"Of course it would! Good heavens, there wouldn't be any fun or anything at school if you went. We mustn't lose you."

I decided then and there that, if I did have to leave Falmouth, I would write and tell Audrey of my love for her. I know now that she likes me a little which is more than I ever expect from those

I love. If there is any justice in the world, if God really is a God of love, He won't permit me to be separated from yet another person who means so much to me. Audrey, Betty and I are the only three in our form who have kept up sending Sheila C. to Coventry. Girls are weak creatures! Actually I feel a bit bad about it because Sheila is the daughter of the President of the Rotary Club, and the Rotary Club is financing my education, and helped to bring me to England.

I saw Denzil yesterday. He is, I'm afraid, no longer a subject of importance. Times change, don't they?

My father goes away again tomorrow.

25th March 1943

I only had 65% for my Art exam - and I'm supposed to be the best in my form. Everyone - my father, Lieselotte, my friends and relations, even Miss Frost, my headmistress - strongly believe in my artistic talent. If I protest they put it down to modesty. But I know I have no real talent and now I have proved it. It was very humiliating because of my reputation, but it has proved me right. Which is not to say I'm not extremely upset about it - so much in fact that when I bumped into the netball post today and nearly broke my nose it hardly mattered at all and seemed a slight thing, despite the pain, when compared to the disgrace of my Art exam result.

30th March 1943

Miss Davis put on a play at St. Joseph's in aid of the Red Cross to which I went. That was on Friday. At the weekend Pam and I went primrosing in Primrose Lane. We found masses and I took a large bunch to Miss Davis. Betty Crothers, Lieselotte's friend, came to tea on Sunday, and yesterday Lieselotte went to London for an interview at a hospital as she has decided she wants to do nursing. She is determined to help the war effort. I had tea at St. Joseph's after she left, and played Tiddly Winks with the children there. My only contribution to the war effort is collecting on Saturday mornings. Sheila Arnold came with me last Saturday.

This morning something very funny happened at school. It was during a Botany lesson. We were dissecting an onion. As usual we worked in pairs and as usual Pam was my partner. When we had finished dissecting it and I thought there was nothing more to learn about an onion, Miss Coward, the Science teacher, started talking about something else. It was nearly lunch time and Pam and I were hungry. What did we do? We ate the onion, and felt much better. Imagine our feelings when suddenly Miss Coward's voice droned out: "Now, girls, look at your onions again!" Pam and I looked at each other, stifled our laughter and pretended to be studying our nonexistent onion on our table, hoping to remain undetected. No such luck, however.

"Pamela and '*I*', where is your onion?" Miss Coward demanded. I was about to say we'd lost it and climb down from my stool to look for it on the floor, when Pam, who refuses to tell a lie, said, loud and clear:

"We've eaten it, Miss Coward." The class roared with laughter but Miss Coward's face remained stony. She was visibly shocked and very angry. Fortunately the bell went just in time and without another word Miss Coward opened the lab door and called out, as usual: "Pass out, girls." Judging from her face as we went by, she probably wished Pam and I really did pass out.

31st March 1943

I do wish Lieselotte wasn't going to London to be a nurse. I've dreaded her going away for a long time and now it is coming true. She has made up her mind to help the country win the war. I'd be interested to know what God is driving at, separating me from the person who is closest to me since my mother. There I go again, blaming God! What shall I do, how shall I carry on without her? My father is now talking of sending me to live with a German baroness who lives just outside Falmouth. Better than boarding-school, anyway.

Perhaps I should stop worrying about everything - my poor mother in Poland, this terrible war, Lieselotte going away and possibly being killed in an air-raid in London, my awful father, my homelessness, my school troubles - and just sit back and wait for better times?

I think Betty F. likes me. Not only has Audrey said so once but she seems to be very friendly with me lately. Today I had a long in-depth conversation with her. She told me that she adored her father but didn't think much of her mother, preferred boyfriends to girlfriends (true female!) and that she tells Audrey nearly everything except about her mother, because she doesn't think Audrey would understand as she has such a nice mother herself. She also confided in me that she and Audrey quarrel often, and it upsets her. She appears to know nothing about my conversation with Audrey. It's strange, isn't it, that they both share secrets with me unbeknown to each other and yet they have this devout friendship. I seem to be stuck in the middle of it. Betty said she would hate me to leave, when I mentioned this possibility to her. I asked her if she was in love with anyone and she said no. "And you?" she asked me.

"No. I'm not in love with any boy," I answered truthfully and giggled under my breath.

Since my collision with the netball post my nose is a bit crooked. This morning Audrey stood by my desk and implored me to go to the doctor's. "Do go, Inky, please," she kept saying. "Do go." I longed to ask her why she cared.

Lieselotte came back from her interview in London today and I fetched her from the station. I'm so glad she's here again.

1st April 1943

I'm not fooling you even though it's April Fool's day. Audrey and Betty really are very nice to me and we seem to be a threesome now. They always want me to be with them. Coming back from Cookery in Penryn this morning the three of us went on the Western National while all the rest went on the local bus.

We break up next week.

8th April 1943

On Monday I twisted my ankle in a mock duel with Audrey. You should have seen how concerned she was! She helped me up and made me put my arm round her and supported me down some steps. The next day I stayed in bed as my ankle was very sore and I also had a cold. Today I went to see Dr Johnson and Lieselotte came with me. I went about my nose and he gave me some drops.

It's the first day of the Easter holidays tomorrow and some of us are going to watch a match at the Grammar School.

I had a heavenly day on Friday. It was like a dream. In this dream I found myself first of all fetching Audrey from her house and chatting with her nice mother a bit. She gave us some grub to take with us and then Audrey and I cycled into the countryside to pick primroses. The weather was fine, the primroses were plentiful and delicious smelling, and Audrey was lovely. When we had picked a huge bunch each Audrey suddenly said:

"I feel like lying down and dreaming."

"What do you want to dream about?" I asked her. "Boys?"

"Oh no. I never give one thought to boys."

"Neither do I." A moment's silence. Then Audrey said:

"You know, Inky, I think about girls much more than about boys. In fact I think a lot about girls." Another short silence, this time for me to take in what she had said and digest it. Then:

"That's funny, Audrey. So do I," I said. "Perhaps it is because we know more girls than boys."

"Perhaps." Another pause. Then loud and clear from Audrey:

"You know, I think I could fall for a girl much more easily than for a boy . . ."

"Well, that *is* strange," I answered. "You see, it's exactly the same with me. And yet we both prefer the masculine sex, don't we?"

She agreed and remained thoughtful for a minute or two. Then she suddenly asked me:

"Do you like anyone, Inky?"

"I?" I stammered. "Well, yes I do."

"Who is it, Inky?"

"Oh, I won't tell you that. It's funny but one never likes to admit one's feelings, does one? I don't know why not because they aren't one's fault. Love, hatred, anger, fear they just come. We don't tell them to."

"One can stop oneself from loving someone by telling oneself not to be so damned silly!" said Audrey fiercely.

"That's impossible," I said.

"It isn't. So who is it you like?"

"I'm not going to tell you." All this time we were sitting on the ground and I had my back to her and was nervously picking bits of grass. Now the conversation was over and we jumped up and it was like abruptly waking from a dream. I'm mad with myself for having admitted I like someone. Does she suspect the truth - or, worse still, does she suspect a boy? But what was I to do? Lies don't come to me readily.

I related all this to Connie and she said I'm either too modest or too stupid to see what Audrey was driving at. Of course, I don't believe her. Connie and I cycled to the Stack and read in the sun today.

I'm more than in love with Audrey: I worship her. I want to do things for her. I never felt that before for anyone.

Certainly not for Denzil, whom I never see now, but he seems to be going insane. I hear he isn't doing anything at all and he ought to be helping the war! I despise him for that. I'd like to send him a white feather.

Mrs Kent, the Tamblyns' daughter, and her fourteen-year-old son Melville, are here this week, and yesterday we all played the piano. Mrs Kent is a brilliant player but her son is an annoying boy.

Every time he sees me he says: "What shall we argue about?" He likes nothing better than an argument, and I hate it.

17th April 1943

Although it is after 10pm I must write a little now. I'm going to use a word which I know sounds soppy. The word is 'suffer'. I suffer mentally. Often during the night I throw myself around in bed and speak to myself and walk up and down in my room and look out of the window. The funny thing is that in the daytime I have no difficulty in pretending to be my usual self towards my friends and other people. I laugh, I joke, I chatter - but only on the surface. Inside I'm haunted and worried. Lieselotte, who means all the world to me, is going away. No one can possibly under-stand how deeply that affects me - in fact so deeply that I can't talk about it, or only in an off-hand, casual sort of way. The more deeply I feel, the less I show it. Certainly Pam suspected nothing when we cycled to the Stack today, in terrific heat, and took our lunch and read for ages in the hot sunshine. I was my normal, apparently cheerful self.

Lieselotte, who is very excited about going to live in London, says things like: "Darling, we must have a nice last week

h

together," or "Will you see me to the station?" and I can't answer. If I did I might cry. I pretend to my friends - and even to Lieselotte - that I don't care. I can't talk about it to anyone. This has never happened before. There has always been at least one person to whom I could speak about a worry. This time you are my only listener, dearest Wvmaro. I try not to think about it. But I do, and then cry. I determine to make the best of it. I console myself with the fact that *she* will be happy. But at other times I think I can't stand it. God is taking the closest person I have from me. Why does He do it? We shall see each other in the holidays, of course, but it won't be the same.

I can do nothing. I am powerless. I give in to fate, defeated, and may it do with me what it likes.

Once I was a silly little flirt - today I'm changed, utterly. Since I named this diary after Denzil (he doesn't deserve it) I must say a few words about him. I've long wanted to. Now let's go back to 'old times'. Denzil hardly ever goes to St. Joseph's any more because everyone there is mad with him for not doing anything in the war. He has always been a queer customer with a mysterious family and background. For nearly four years I tried to make him out, and failed. What a pity that nice, sporty Denzil from the good old days has turned into such a . . . what shall I say . . . detestable character. When will I learn, oh when will I learn, nothing is forever!

22nd April 1943

I've been busy organising a cycling trip for about 15 of us from my form, and Connie, and today the big event took place. It was a great success. We cycled to Penzance and had our picnic at St. Michael's Mount. Connie wondered whether it's possible to fall in love to order, and decided to put it to the test today. I picked Deanne for her - the cleverest girl in the form. She was on the trip too. When it came to buying drinks we each shared with another girl, and Connie shared with Deanne. (I didn't have any.) Afterwards she told me she thinks she might succeed in falling in love with Deanne if she keeps at it. I really enjoyed the day even though Audrey wasn't with us (she had scarlet fever when she was younger and is not strong enough for such a long ride) and even though it began to pour with rain in the afternoon and most

170

of us returned by train! Back at Tamblyns' boarding-house I was joined by a commercial traveller at tea, who was staying for the night. He told me: "When I was driving between Penzance and Falmouth this morning I met a swarm of cyclists and had to slow down. It must have been the local cycling club."

"Were the cyclists all girls, about sixteen years old?" I asked.

"Yes, about that."

"That was me and my school-friends!" I said, and we both laughed.

I went to bed early and read.

26th April 1943 - (Easter Monday)

Audrey told me that a little girl of 11 or 12 called Diana always follows her around, never leaves her, gives her flowers and generally embarrasses her. "She has a crush on me," she said. I didn't wonder at that and said nothing. I suddenly felt how ridiculous it is of me to love her. I may not show it like Diana, but I'm no better. I think I'll write down that promise I made to confess my love to Audrey after the war, as this will make it more honourable.

> I, *I.P.*, TAKE A SACRED OATH TO CONFESS TO AUDREY B. MY DEEP LOVE FOR HER (whether I still love her then or not) WHEN THE WAR IS OVER, PROVIDED WE WIN THE WAR.

Today I went on a boat trip to Percuil with Connie. Audrey should have come too but was away. I prayed hard last night that she would be back on time but my prayers never do get answered. We visited Percuil Church; there was a piano in it, and I played it for about 10 minutes as there was no one about. Before going on the boat trip I went to school at 8.30am to look for a tennis ball Pam and I lost on Saturday. Mr Martin, the caretaker, helped me look for it but without success. That spoilt the rest of the day a bit. When we got back from Percuil I went to tea at St. Joseph's. Denzil was there. He played the piano and it was like old times. His weaknesses and faults seem to disappear when he's playing the piano, and I forgot that he deserves a white feather. I still have a soft spot for him. And Roy? How long it is since I wrote about him. He was a passing ship.

On Sunday afternoon, when Connie and I were on the seafront

with our bikes, we met Mr and Mrs Eggins with their French naval cousin. I spoke some French with him. Mrs Eggins asked why Lieselotte and I haven't been to see them for so long, so we're remedying this tomorrow.

28th April 1943

To think that if my heart stopped beating - just such a simple thing - I would be free from all troubles and cares - nothing more to worry about. Yet I'd miss this world because I love life in spite of everything. Never to go to the flicks again, or for bicycle rides and on outings, never to see my friends again or play the piano or tennis, never to draw and read again - heaven, if there is such a place, could never make up for all this. Heaven for me are all the beautiful things that can be had on earth if only people wouldn't spoil them. But enough of that. This topic is too sentimental.

Well, Lieselotte has gone. She left for London this morning. Yesterday we talked till late into the night. In the morning I was quiet and calm. I accompanied her on the train to Truro and Connie came with us. For a minute, after her train left and she was out of sight, I truly wanted to die. But then I remembered all the happiness life has to offer, all the excitements that are just around the corner. I felt just like this coming to England and leaving my mother. Perhaps everything *will* come right in the end after all? For Lieselotte a new life is beginning, anyway.

Connie and I went to Truro Cathedral and then took the train back to Falmouth. We had a chips feast, called on Pam and sheltered from the rain at her house, and then we had tea at Mrs Tamblyn's boarding-house.

Tomorrow I'm moving into Lieselotte's room as it's bigger than mine.

30th April 1943

I went to bed hoping and praying I would see Audrey the next day and I did! But not the way I meant, for I only *saw* her, and her family, from my bedroom window. They were walking past and of course didn't see me. Audrey, as usual, had her hands in her trouser pockets. (My father never allows me to have my hands in my pockets when I'm out with him.) She looked wonderful. I'm still hoping and praying to see her soon and *speak* to her, too. Let there be no more misunderstandings. I think God either has a sense of humour or there is some mischievous spirit about.

I cut my hair for the first time today, and think I made quite a good job of it. Yesterday Pam and I went to a lecture in the Public Library given by an Austrian. Afterwards I talked to the Austrian and his wife and told him I enjoyed his lecture, which I didn't much, and he asked me where I came from. I didn't seem to have much in common with him, though Pam thought I would have.

8th May 1943

Today is the day of the famous Helston Floral Dance. Pam and I were going to cycle to Helston but it was raining hard and Mrs Bath, Pam's mother, wouldn't let Pam go. Yesterday we were going to assist with an air-raid practice at school but that was rained off too. I've had my first letter from Lieselotte and she likes her new life as a nurse very much. I miss her terribly.

I was out with Connie the other day, when who should come towards us but Audrey. I had a second for the thought to flash across my mind: "This is the moment I have longed for," and then she was here. When a dream becomes reality you're momentarily left speechless. We hadn't seen each other for about a week and something struck me about the way she looked at me when we first greeted each other. . . But it was probably imagination. We stood around talking and popping in and out of the telephone kiosk nearby and reading names from the directory aloud. Suddenly Audrey asked me:

"Are you leaving Falmouth, Inky?"

"Why?"

"Well, are you?"

"I don't think so."

"Are you sure?"

"I don't think I am."

"Are you *quite* sure?" Connie nudged me. Then Audrey told us she had been staying with Betty and when I asked her if she had a nice time she didn't seem at all enthusiastic in her answer. Connie suggested we walk on and Audrey readily accompanied us. She walked next to me and we touched several times. Outside Woolworths we met some girls from our form and stopped again.

173

One of them said something about a Grammar School boy and I jokingly said: "What a flirt you are!" Suddenly Audrey broke in: "I think you're daft about boys, Inky."

"That's only your opinion," I replied, inwardly shaking.

After the other girls had departed I asked Audrey to explain what she meant when she said I'm daft about boys. So she began:

"There are three types of girls. The first type are dreadful flirts, cheap and vulgar, and look exactly what they are. The second type are nice girls who go out with boys but behave nicely. Nothing wrong with that. The third type never goes out with boys, runs everyone down who does and thinks even speaking to a boy is flirting. And that type is you."

I thanked her for the description of my character but said she had got me all wrong.

"Well, you once accused me of going out with a boy and made a fuss about it," she said.

"That's a lie!" I cried. But then I said. "Or, if I did, it must have been because I thought the boy was not nice enough."

"That's a good one," she exclaimed sarcastically.

"Oh, let's forget it," I said. I certainly didn't want to get involved in an argument about a boy, the chief topic of the majority of girls' conversations. Soon after that we parted. That night in bed, as the name Audrey B. sounded in my ears, it had an icy ring to it.

15th May 1942

We've been back at school for over a week now. Pam had her birthday party on Sunday. I didn't get home till 10.30pm. Connie has moved into her new house with her mother and Tony. Monica, her elder sister, is in the Wrens. This morning Miss Rogers had a rehearsal for the recital in which I'm (reluctantly) taking part. Audrey was there. We are both singing in the choir. We practised 'Oh no John, no John, no John, no!' I'm also playing a duet with Miss Rogers. I'm dreading it. I refused to play solo.

The last time I played tennis at school with Pam I had a glorious surprise. Listen, my darling Wvmaro, and I will tell you about it. We had been playing for about three quarters of an hour when Pam hit the ball over the hedge. We had to go into the school to get a ladder. We tried two doors but they were locked.

We tried a third (3 times lucky) and who should be there but Audrey! I felt as if an electric current had been passed though me. She had come to help the dentist but he wasn't there and she had been about to lock up and go home. We found the ball and Audrey joined our game. Afterwards we chatted for ages - with poor Pam just looking on - and then cycled home together. I felt marvellous. On such occasions, when we're in harmony, I feel I could fight the whole world and win. David must have felt like that when he fought and killed Goliath. It is not always like that between Audrey and me as you know, but even in the middle of my anger last time, when we had the argument about boys, I realised that I want to go on loving her, that this love is enjoyable and exciting, and that I am lonely without her - even though she often doesn't want to go out with me - and loneliness kills. So I must keep PEACE at all times. In this spirit I parted from her today and in the same spirit I am going to leave you now.

20th May 1943

My father telephoned from London today to tell me he is coming to Falmouth on Saturday, and when to fetch him from the station. Another mishap was that I had a puncture. Mr Tamblyn helped me mend it in the cellar.

I told you about a little girl called Diana who has a crush on Audrey. Walking to school the other day I met her and her friend Lizzie and she continuously talked about Audrey to me. She said she was mad on her, that she'd die for her, that it was no fun being anywhere where Audrey wasn't. She tells everyone about her love for Audrey. I mentioned it to Audrey. I said:

"That little girl Diana certainly loves you. Strange, isn't it, for a little girl to love another girl like that?"

"I agree with you, and I wish I wasn't the girl," said Audrey.

Would she say that if she knew I too loved her? What is it about Audrey that sets so many hearts on fire? And she's not supposed to be very popular!

I've written a letter to Audrey telling her I love her and given it to Connie, who is to give it to her if I die before the war ends. There were some planes flying over very low today and I was scared stiff. One forgets how close one constantly is to death during a war.

Pam, Betty, Audrey and I play tennis together every break time. Audrey wasn't in a good mood today. That is, she wasn't in high spirits and she wasn't in a really bad mood, but something between the two. I don't understand why so many people are often in a bad mood. Here I am, with no home, no family around me, no settled life, no idea where my mother is, no future, and yet I'm always cheerful and never show it when I'm sad. I hate to speak of this and you will have noticed I don't often. I don't want to feel sorry for myself but when people give vent to their bad mood for all to bear the brunt of, and I keep my good humour under nearly all conditions, it makes me angry, because I know perfectly well that I have more reasons to be unhappy than most. The art of life is to control your feelings. Everyone always tells me what a good sport I am and always gay and cheerful, but why should I bother other people with my troubles?

Audrey always asks me to be her partner in tennis. Do you remember that Roy always wanted me to be his partner at ping pong? If that's anything to go on, it doesn't mean much.

22nd May 1943

Mrs Bath said to me: "It's a shame. It's not right, you living by yourself in that boarding-house place. You ought to have a nice home with your mother and father instead of living all alone over there." What could I say? I have given up hope. I have grown hard and bitter. I never feel sorry for myself and I don't want other people to either, but I do resent the injustice of it all. Why has this happened to me? Why me? I ask myself the question over and over again. No result. I've said that I'm always cheerful and so I am but at night I often cry, as I lie in bed, and think of all the things that could have happened to my mother. I implore God to save her.

We have a new Art mistress and she as good as told me that I'm not really good enough to take up art as a career. That confirmed what I already knew. She doesn't like my style. Anyway, I've lost confidence in myself and that's what matters.

Lieselotte loves her work and is very happy in London, which makes me happy too. I hope we shall always love each other and never grow apart.

'Wings for Victory' week started today. Connie, Pam, *Audrey*,

176

Pauline Mitchell and I went to the Parade on the Moor. In the afternoon I fetched my father from the station and - guess whom I met there? Well, can you? I heard footsteps, the waiting room door opened - and Audrey entered! God help me, I thought, how can I face her? She had come to meet her mother who was also coming from London. My life with my father during the brief periods when he is here, and my love for Audrey are totally irreconcilable, like two separate existences, led by two different people. We spent about five minutes talking, during which time I recovered a bit, and then the train arrived and we parted, she to welcome her beloved mother whom she adores, and I to 'welcome' my father. We went home by taxi.

Is Audrey really totally unaware that she is the centre of my life, does she have no inkling of her valuable presence? Is she a fool? Am I a fool? There are others who love her - Betty, Sally, Diana and goodness knows who else - but surely not as much as I do?

I could go on writing about Audrey till I have not another sheet of paper left, or my hand drops off. But I won't. Therefore, goodnight.

2nd June 1943

I'm so ashamed of having no proper home and no mother and of being foreign. As if that weren't enough, God, when He saw that I had nevertheless learnt to cope with that and made the best of it, sent me a handful more troubles. I mean things like a difficult father, Lieselotte's departure, not being good enough at art, not being good at anything, and so on and so on. The injustice of this world is insupportable. I envy everyone who has a home and a family.

I don't know whether I told you that Robin did send me that Errol Flynn picture.

A few days ago at school Audrey was in an exuberant mood. During a free period, with no mistress in the room, she hung around my desk and called me "Inky - Pinky - Nanks - Tiggy - Poo" till she almost made me blush. She stood on the platform, played the fool and made everyone laugh. She stood on a chair and told jokes. She went around pricking people with a pin. The sporty ones took it well, others called her daft. Then someone

177

pricked *her* with a pin. She was furious. Betty looked sympathetically at the girl who had done the pricking, but said nothing. She
never openly takes sides against Audrey. The same goes for me.

Some Airforce men have been staying here. My father doesn't
like it when other people come to stay as I suppose it reminds him
that this is not his own house.

Today, for the first time, I cycled up all of Dracaena Hill! Quite
an achievement. My father has been going to the Holdichs'
(Tommy Müller's guardians) for musical evenings. He plays the
violin.

Miss Rogers' dreaded recital takes place on Saturday. I'm sure
I'll disgrace myself.

Last but not least, one of my favourite film stars, Leslie
Howard, has been killed in an air-crash.

5th June 1943

The recital is over! What a day it was. In the morning Connie,
Audrey and I went to town on our bikes. In the afternoon Audrey
called for me and together we went to the Women's Institute to
take part in Miss Rogers' big event. We sat next to each other
awaiting our turns, and we both felt very nervous. In fact I was
shaking with nervousness. At the same time I longed to take
Audrey into my arms and comfort her. The hall was crowded with
spectators. They had come to hear and see *us*, all 50 students of
Miss Rogers' music classes. My father was in the audience, and
so were Miss Davis and Miss Kitty and of course all the parents
and friends and relations. I wore my green and blue check taffeta
dress with the big collar from Vienna which is still my best dress.
Audrey's turn came first. She played a Tchaikovsky waltz beautifully and got a lot of applause. My duet with Miss Rogers came
fairly near the end. I was shaking so that I don't know how I got
through it without a mistake. The very last item was the singing
of the choir. Then we had our photographs taken and then it was
all over. Audrey and I went home together. She was herself again,
in high spirits and laughing. I loved her. I thought: when she was
nervous I loved her and wanted to soothe her, when she is high
spirited I love her and admire her, when she is in a bad mood I
love her and want to cheer her up. However she behaves I love
her. Without her I feel dead. She keeps me alive.

Portrait of Leslie Howard.

When I got home my father said my performance was the best of all. Did he really mean that? I was amazed. It wasn't the best but I didn't contradict him. He is not usually very generous with compliments so I shall treasure this one.

Tonight I shall go to bed feeling very close to Audrey. As close as our two names are on the printed programme of the recital.

10th June 1943

Today I had strawberries for the first time this summer. You have to queue for them.

Well, my father has gone again. He returned to London last Monday. I seem to have done nothing but go for walks and to the pictures with him while he was here. Yesterday I had supper at Connie's house. It was Monica's birthday and Janet Tresidder and Miss Davis were there too.

Audrey has been extremely nice to me lately. She asked me to sit next to her in Prayers. She invited me to go to the flicks with her (I couldn't unfortunately). She brought a little clockwork animal to school and said I could have it. She writes me notes, usually in mirror writing, and leaves them on my desk. She wrote her name and mine on a piece of paper and played that game girls usually play with boys' names, crossing out the letters that occur in both names and then counting the remaining ones like this: friendship, love-ship, courtship, marriage. It revealed that she wants to court me and I to marry her. Audrey said: "Ha, ha, Inky wants to marry me!" I was quite stupid and could only think of saying: "This game can't be played with two girls." I can't make it all out. If I knew nothing about love among people of the same sex it would just seem to be a silly joke. But I know otherwise. Does Audrey suspect me? That she loves me too I refuse to believe. I would have to hear it from her own lips. Is it all imagination? I can't make myself believe that either. Let's look at the problem like a Geometry Theorem and see if I can 'prove' anything:

Definition: Love among people of the same sex.
Given: 2 girls, Audrey B., *I.P.*, aged 15.5, 16.3 attending the Falmouth County High School, Form IV A. Fairly good friends.

180

To prove that: 1. Audrey is in love with '*I*'.

                  2. Audrey is not in love with '*I*'.

Proof: **1.**   Audrey is very nice to '*I*'. She is inclined to show preference for her company on many occasions. She played the 'letter' game with her own and *I*'s names. She has ceased being soppy with Betty. She has admitted often thinking about girls. She is not interested in boys. Connie suspects Audrey's feelings for '*I*' are more than friendship.

          2.   Audrey is already said to have a lover - Betty F. Audrey is often anti-'*I*'. She frequently refuses her invitations. She often seems to be annoyed with her. She does not always tell her the truth.

Q. E. D: Don't know. I never could do Geometry.

16th June 1943

I love Audrey and I love her and I love her and I love her and LOVE her and LOVE her. (Latest news item.)

Mr Tamblyn has gone on holiday and I have been shopping for Mrs Tamblyn. Monday and Tuesday were half term holidays. Pam and I spent all of Monday together - on the beach, playing tennis and, in the evening, at the flicks. We saw *Star Spangled Rhythm* with Bob Hope and Bing Crosby at the Odeon. It was very silly. When we cycled home Pam had a puncture. Before I left their house Mrs Bath gave me an egg. She's a really kind person. On Tuesday we cycled to Perranwell and visited Pauline Mitchell, a girl in our form.

Last Sunday was my mother's 45th birthday.

When I was at St. Joseph's last time Miss Davis told me that Miss Rogers' concert had a good review in the *Falmouth Packet*. It said: 'Fifty of Miss Rogers' pupils played and sang beautifully to a distinguished audience.' This made Miss Kitty laugh.

"What distinguished audience?" she asked. "Your father, I suppose," she said to me.

Distinguished because he is a foreigner?

"Or perhaps Dr Johnson," I said, for I'd seen him there.

The war is going well and there has been a wonderful victory

181

in Africa. Allied troops have ejected the Germans from there. But when, when will it end? Sometimes I think never.

18th June 1943

This is what happened yesterday: Audrey had often asked me to go and see her kittens, and that's what I did yesterday after school. Walking between her and Betty I remembered how at one time I hardly dared speak to them when they were together. Now things are very different. I never expected they would move in this direction. The strange thing was that Audrey and Betty hardly spoke to each other except to quarrel. After a bit I said:

"What's the matter with you two? Are you *pretending* all this?"

"Pretending what?" asked Audrey.

"Well, you're always on at each other." I received no answer and Audrey changed the subject. When, at Audrey's house, she and I were playing with the kittens, Betty stood at some distance like a statue and never said a word. She looked pathetic and I was sorry for her. Once or twice Audrey flew at her for some trifling thing. It crossed my mind that I was witnessing something mysterious and unsavoury but as it made her all the nicer towards me I didn't care. Or not much. After we had finished playing with the kittens Audrey and I went into another room. Betty didn't follow. I don't know how it came about but we were sort of fooling around and then we acted out a love scene and rolled about in each other's arms, stroking and caressing. In fun only. But what lovely fun! Also, something nice happened during a lesson at school yesterday: some ink was spilled on the floor near my desk and as soon as the mistress entered the room Audrey cried: "It wasn't '*I*'s fault!" Then she turned round (she sits in front of me) and said: "Was it, Nanks?" (her new name for me).

I might be going camping on a farm in the summer, and Audrey too. We should be together day and night. To sleep with Audrey! I cannot imagine anything more wonderful.

24th June 1943

Audrey has been absent all week. She is the centre of my life at school and if this centre is missing everything else falls apart. The air-raid siren went during Cookery at Penryn today and we all went to the trench. End of Cookery lesson. Also today, this time without interruption from Hitler, we had our photographs taken at school to send to American penfriends. In the morning two clergymen attended Prayers and afterwards talked to us. One of them was the father of Beryl Crew, a girl in my form. By a coincidence I'd arranged to go to Beryl's house after school today to see her chickens.

Instead of Science lessons this week Miss Coward took us to Gyllingvase beach when the tide was out to collect seaweed. This seaweed is supposed to be a substitute for agar agar which we used to get from Japan before the war and is used for medicinal purposes. So we were helping the war effort and having lots of fun besides. As we gathered the stuff we sang *Maresidotes and dozidotes*. It was raining and the seaweed had a very unpleasant smell but I didn't mind. It was much better than sitting in the Science lab. If only Audrey had been there.

On Monday I was sick three times in the night. Perhaps it was the seaweed. Or maybe the tomato sandwiches I had had at Pam's for supper the previous evening. I probably ate too many. It was such a treat.

26th June 1943

Oh my God, I've seen her! I've seen her again after one whole week. This is how it was: I was waiting for Connie in town when I spotted Audrey in the distance, coming down the hill. At that moment she saw me too - we had seen each other - AND SHE CAME RUNNING TOWARDS ME. I needed every bit of self control. In a moment we would be face to face and I must quickly hide my feelings. She greeted me in high spirits. We were so pleased to see each other. She called me Nanks. I said: "Ah, Audrey, I haven't heard that for years."

"Years?" she repeated. "It was only a week."

"Well, it seemed like years," I said. It just slipped out. I couldn't help saying it. She said:

"Did you miss me all that much, Nanks?" By this time Connie had joined us, and I received a nudge from her and blushed and stammered something unintelligible. Soon afterwards Audrey left us.

Connie and I spent the afternoon on Maenporth beach, reading. Miss Davis and some St. Joseph's children joined us later. In the evening Connie, Pam and I went to the pictures and saw *Random Harvest* with Ronald Colman and Greer Garson which is on at the Grand for one week. It was lovely. A strange lady there gave us 9d as we hadn't enough money. Wasn't that kind? As if I wasn't feeling romantic enough, the film made me even more so. My thoughts flew to Audrey. I thought: she is mine, because I am holding on to her constantly with all my strength; I am hers because she can do with me what she likes.

29th June 1943

Tommy Tothill and his Norwegian friend are staying at St. Joseph's. It was nice seeing Tommy again.

Yesterday I dyed a frock for the first time in my life. So now instead of a white dress I have a navy blue one and I feel I have a new frock at hardly any expense. Today we were allowed to wear summer frocks to school for the first time, but I prefer wearing my uniform.

On Sunday Mrs Bath and Pam took me to Berkeley Chapel for a Special Anniversary Service. I wonder if they are hoping I'll become a Wesleyan? Afterwards I went for a short walk with Pam, Peggy, Joyce and Deanne.

2nd July 1943

I must write! I must write at once, and you must listen! Listen! I was just going to sit down and tell you that I went to the pictures with Audrey and Betty yesterday after school when Mrs Tamblyn told me a friend had come to see me. The friend was Audrey! She told me she had called earlier when I was out to ask if I could go for a bathe with her. We had a little talk and then I went to her house with her to see some film star pictures. We stayed for some time, looking at film star and other photographs, playing the piano and playing with the kittens. At 9pm we got on our bikes and cycled to the seafront. The sun was setting but it was still very hot. The sea was like glass.

"Shall we sit down?" I suggested, when we arrived at the beach where Connie and I often sit and gaze at the sea.

"Already? I don't want to make love to you *yet*, Nanks!" said Audrey, laughing. But we did sit down. At first we spoke little. I looked at her from time to time to make sure it really was her and not one of my other friends. Presently I said:

"Did you know that Oscar Wilde had a physical condition which caused him to fall in love with members of his own sex, and that he was imprisoned for it?" She seemed very surprised. She thought it wrong that he was imprisoned. Me too, I said. Then she wanted to know about my family and home in Vienna, and I told her a few things. She again asked if I was leaving Falmouth. And then we talked about YOU - yes, you, dearest Wvmaro.

"What do you put in your diary?" she asked me.

"Oh, this and that."

"Such as?"

"Mostly secret things."

"Would you let me read it?"

"No! Never!"

"Oh, Nanks." I changed the subject then. I had got too close already to betraying my innermost secrets.

I know now that Audrey likes me too. It is almost too wonderful to believe. I certainly couldn't be as charming to anyone as she was to me without loving them. I want Audrey to think of what happened between us tonight when she goes to bed. I want her to think of me, as I shall think of her.

I didn't get home till after 10pm, and went straight to bed. I shut my eyes and saw her face, her lovely laughing eyes that looked into mine, steady, loving, serious, and deep. Her look went straight into my heart and I didn't know how to receive it. I don't expect to sleep one wink tonight.

Tomorrow we're going out together again.

3rd July 1943

I've just come home. Do you know where I have been? To Maenporth beach with my Audrey, just the two of us. We cycled there and took our tea. We bathed. We talked. No doubt there were other people there but as far as I was concerned we were quite alone. We went back to her house and played with the kittens in the garden. We talked about Betty. She gets on Audrey's nerves. "But she's your best friend," I said.

"Well, you don't necessarily need to like your best friend best," she replied. And then she said: "Who do you like best,

Nanks? In our form, I mean."

"I don't know," I said. It is painful to have to lie to someone you love.

11th July 1943

Exams start tomorrow and I've been revising all week.

Yesterday Audrey and I went to the pictures alone together for the first time. It was a wet, horrible day but I don't notice such things when I'm with her. We saw *Rebecca* which I've seen before and could see again and again. It's one of the most marvellous films ever made.

Last Tuesday I and seven others from school went to Truro by bus to represent the 'Red Cross' and meet the Duchess of Gloucester at the Truro Drill Hall. It was very exciting. On Sunday there was a Cadet Parade on the seafront to which Connie and I went but which was very tame in comparison with the Truro event.

I have a PLAN - but not a word about it yet - not even to you, dearest Wvmaro.

Wonderful war news - today we captured Sicily!

17th July 1943

(Just after a glorious thunderstorm - 10.15pm.) Unfortunately I was out this afternoon when my darling called. We hadn't arranged anything. She desires my company. She no longer waits to be asked by me. She knows I have other friends, so rescuing me from loneliness is not her reason for calling on me. I have achieved something. I have reached my aim. I asked for her friendship, and she gave it to me - she, who is so difficult to make friends with. Why did she accept me? Is she offering me more than friendship? I ask myself that question a hundred times a day.

I believe in friendship more than in almost anything - more than in religion, marriage, nationalism. 'You can live without a brother but not without a friend,' Pam wrote in my autograph book.

I haven't told you that there have been some changes here: a cousin of my father's, Aunt Liesel Frank, is staying at Tamblyns' for I don't know how long. I fetched her and my father from the station last Wednesday. I think my father wants her to chaperon me. Today Jack and Jane, my father's business partner and her husband, arrived for one week and are staying in Truro. Tomorrow we are all having lunch at the Red Lion Hotel in Truro. Jack and Jane brought me some cherries! I haven't eaten those for years.

I may never actually have put it into words but you must know by now how much I love England. People say to me: "Never mind, dearie, soon everything will be over and you can go back to your own country again." But I don't want to go back to my own country! Can't they understand that? I want to be English. I want to do things for England. It has done a lot for *me*. after all. I love everything English - the language, the towns and country-side, the sea, the shops, and above all the people - their polite good manners, their reserve, their sense of humour, everything. I'm often taken for English and I love that. I can't get on with foreigners, except of course with Lieselotte, who's so English herself. The other day I was listening to my father and aunt talking - they were listing all the things they didn't like about England! I was quietly fuming. Do you think it's funny that I've made England my own country? In preference to my once beloved Austria?

A word about music: as you know, I'm learning to play the piano and I love it. But why is it impossible for me to play in front of people? My father asked me to play to Jack and Jane and I couldn't. If I did, I know my fingers would refuse to move across the keys. I'm not particularly shy by nature, so why about this? Needless to say, my father was very angry.

19th July 1943

Exams finished today. I couldn't do the Geography one so I handed in an empty sheet of paper, with just my name on it. Sally Alderton did the same with her Religious Knowledge paper. She didn't get into trouble but I did, the reason being that Miss Frost, who teaches Religious Knowledge, is lenient, but Mrs Bowen is not. However, I was cheered up by having my favourite hymn *Onward Christian Soldiers*, played at Prayers on Friday morning, by special request.

Today we went seaweeding again with the school. After school I went to see a Miss Gooden who is going to coach me in German

187

for the School Certificate. I envy all the girls who have left school and do not need to take the School Cert. They, with the exception of Audrey, Betty and Rosemary Johnson who are staying on, are all the girls who come from good and rich families and who have no need to study because they won't need to work - they'll lead exciting lives riding, travelling and going to balls. How I wish I were one of them!

25th July 1943

Janet Tresidder is going to be married to her sailor, George, on Saturday.

My father's schemes of sending me to boarding-school or to the German Baroness have come to nothing. He has been to see Miss Frost, with the result that, last Friday, she gave out a notice to the school that a home is needed for me. I'd like to live at St. Joseph's again but I think it's full up, and my father doesn't like the idea because there's no discipline there, he says. At the moment Aunt Liesel is 'looking after me', but I haven't noticed any difference. Her consuming interest is the News. As there is no wireless here she goes across the road to Kimberley Park and stands outside the park keeper's lodge twice a day where she can hear the News from his wireless through the window. She also goes to the pictures only to see the News and often doesn't stay to see the film. When I go with her she always pays for me. She is a great talker, especially about the past, and when we go for walks she tells me all about the wonderful life she led in Austria before Hitler came, and the holidays she spent in Ascona with rich friends. She certainly appears to have had a glittering life, and Falmouth must seem very drab to her. I don't think Mrs Tamblyn likes her much, and aunt Liesel doesn't like Mrs Tamblyn's food.

Yesterday, Saturday, Pam and I went house to house collecting for the blind in the morning. In the afternoon I went rowing with my father, Jack and Jane. We got a boat at Prince of Wales Pier and my father started rowing. The sea was fairly calm. When we were quite far out I took over - and I learnt to row! It's quite easy really. However, the sea was rougher by now and my father thought he had better row again. As we changed seats the boat rocked violently and I almost fell overboard. Jane screamed and grabbed me. What an adventure! I was glad to arrive back on land safe and sound. There was a man selling newspapers on the Pier and my father bought one. "After what we've just experienced," my father said, "The war news will seem very tame." We went to a café and had tea, and afterwards Jane bought me a bathing costume. I needed a new one badly. In the evening I went to the flicks with Aunt Liesel and saw *The Amazing Mrs Halliday* with Deanna Durbin, and she actually stayed to see the film, and paid for me, of course. Jack and Jane went back to London today and my father and Aunt Liesel and I accompanied them to Truro by train, and then stayed there for lunch.

We break up next Thursday.

1st August 1943

Today I wrote a *vital* letter to Ruth. I think it may be the most important letter I have ever written in my life, and it is connected with my PLAN - but no more of that now.

I've been rowing again with my father and am quite good at it now. No mishaps this time.

Mrs Tamblyn's grandson Melville arrived on Wednesday to spend some of his holidays here. Luckily I haven't seen much of him. On Saturday I went to church for Janet's wedding. I thought Denzil might be there but he wasn't.

For my holiday reading I borrowed *Anna Karenina* and *Romeo and Juliet* from the school library. Aunt Liesel was very impressed with my taste in literature but thought I ought to read something more light-hearted in between these two tragic love stories. The day before we broke up we had our Sports' day at school, postponed from last week when it was rained off. A pity it wasn't rained off again. I was in the slow bicycle race and came second.

Jane is coming again on Tuesday for one week, this time with her sister-in-law Doris. As my father expects me to spend much of my time with his visitors I can't go out with my friends so often. I am, however, meeting Deanne and Sally at school tomorrow morning to do a scrapbook about the war.

6th August 1943

Ruth's answer has arrived. But that's all I'm telling you so far.

189

She says she cried bitterly when she heard about Leslie Howard's death.

Miss Davis and Miss Kitty came to tea today. What a nice change from my father's London visitors.

When I went for a walk with Aunt Liesel yesterday evening, after she had listened to the News outside the park keeper's lodge, it started to rain. This reminded her of a similar occurrence in Ascona, when she was young and beautiful (she says). I listened for a bit and then my attention wandered, but I stayed in Switzerland, which seems such an idyllic place. Would my life have been a gay whirl from morning till night, I wondered, had I been able to stay at home in Vienna? Would my parents have sent me on holiday to rich friends in Ascona who had nothing to do but give me a good time and wait on me hand and foot? My imagination is incapable of completing this fairy tale, and I have to make do with Aunt Liesel's account of her glorious past in better times, when there was no war and no Hitler and the worst thing that ever happened to her was being caught in the rain when she was only wearing a thin summer dress and no hat.

11th August 1943

Today I have two most wonderful happenings to relate. First of all my father, Jane and Doris left on Monday - but that's not one of the happenings, though by no means unwelcome. Before I tell you where I went in the afternoon I must mention that Connie and I recently saw the film *My Son, My Son*, and couldn't stop talking about it. It is based on the book by Howard Spring. I knew that Howard Spring lives in Mylor. I said to Connie:

"Let's call on Howard Spring and tell him how much we enjoyed *My Son, My Son*. She looked horrified.

"Oh *'I'*! We can't!" she said.

"Why not? We can get his autograph at the same time."

"He won't give it to us. He'll be too cross, having complete strangers come to his house."

"He won't be. I'm sure he won't. Oh, do please come with me, Con." She did. We cycled to Mylor and took some grub. We couldn't find his house and had to ask some people to direct us. Connie was all for turning back.

But it was too late, for there was his house, standing in a

beautiful garden. We went through the gate and up the drive and rang the bell. Now even I almost regretted having come. The door was opened by an elderly lady with grey hair.

"Is Mr Howard Spring in, please?" I said. She asked our business and I said that we would love to meet Mr Spring as we were great admirers of his books. We were invited in and in no time a shortish slim man with a mop of grey hair appeared. He was Howard Spring. He smiled at us and he didn't seem to mind one bit that two unknown schoolgirls had come to see him.

"We loved *My Son, My Son*, I told him.

"Have you read the book?" he asked.

"No, not yet," I said. "But the film was lovely."

"You must read the book," he said. I felt ashamed that I hadn't.

We chatted a bit longer, even Connie adding a few comments, and then I asked for his autograph, which he wrote on the back of his visiting card. We thanked him very much, promised to read the book and left. Wasn't that a thrilling experience? An even more thrilling one was to follow on the next day, however.

I had heard that film stars had been coming to Falmouth for their holidays instead of going to the Riviera in the South of France, as they did before the war. And I had further heard that Anna Neagle and Herbert Wilcox were staying at the Falmouth Hotel on the seafront. I told Connie.

"Oh no!" she said. "You don't want to go and see *them*, do you?"

"Of course I do! You're coming with me, aren't you?"

This time she didn't raise so many objections. We arranged to go yesterday evening. We didn't tell anyone just in case we were unsuccessful in our mission. I had never set foot in the 'Falmouth' or any other of the large seafront hotels, some of which have been taken over by the forces, though we pass them regularly on our bicycles. It was an even more awe inspiring experience walking up the long drive and arriving at the entrance of the hotel than our visit to Howard Spring's house had been. We lingered a moment in the foyer.

"Oh *'I'*, I don't think we should," Connie whispered.

I secretly agreed with her, so I quickly went to the reception desk, before my courage failed me, and asked if Anna Neagle and Herbert Wilcox were staying at the hotel. The answer was yes. I asked if we could see them. "Just a minute," said the woman at the desk, and disappeared. Less than five minutes later, I was talking to the two famous film stars in the foyer of the poshest hotel in Falmouth. She looked exactly as she does in her films. He's an ugly little elderly man but was very nice. She was charming. She seemed to be quite flattered by our visit and both readily gave us their autographs.

Even Connie was quite excited about what we had done as we cycled home, but said she would never have gone without me. News spreads quickly, and Pam and Audrey got to hear about our meeting with the famous film stars. Can you guess where I went the next day? You can't? I'll tell you - to the Falmouth Hotel with Pam and Audrey! They wouldn't go without me either. Connie came again, too. Anna Neagle and Herbert Wilcox once more appeared promptly after being summoned.

"Hello, it's you again," she said when she saw me, in a very friendly way.

"I've brought some more friends to meet you," I said. This time we had an even longer chat. She told us about a new film she was going to be in called *Yellow Canary* and said we must be sure to go and see it. I got her autograph again and now she asked my name and wrote on a piece of paper: 'Best wishes, *'I'*, Anna Neagle, Herbert Wilcox.' I asked where she lived and she replied:

"I can always be reached at Denham Studios," and she added it on the piece of paper. 'Denham Studios, Denham, Middlesex.' Then she asked me where I came from, because of my name.

"Vienna," I answered.

"Oh, lovely Vienna," said Anna Neagle. "A beautiful city. I was there before the war."

As we went home, Connie, Pam, Audrey and I, we felt like film stars ourselves.

I told Aunt Liesel all about it when I got back and I think she was quite impressed, and didn't mention Ascona for the whole day. In the evening she and I went to see water-sports at Swanpool, and a dogshow. But I kept thinking of Anna Neagle and Herbert Wilcox.

15th August 1943

Today the clocks were put back one hour.

Sometimes I wake up in the middle of the night and I can see Audrey's face distinctly, as if she were in the same room with me, and then I wonder if I'm in my right senses. I never knew it was possible to love a person of one's own sex so much. She is the light of my life, she is my life-line, and I cling to her as though I were drowning. The more I know her the more I love her. I may not have my own country or a house with parents in it, but I have Audrey. My love is my home.

And she? How does she feel about me? She likes me well enough, that much I know. You should have seen us walking hand in hand along the street three days ago, you should have seen her look at me, put her arm around me, stroke me . . . you should have heard how tenderly she spoke to me - but is it love on her part? She must tell me so herself or I shall never believe it.

I love her to the end of eternity, and it is driving me mad.

And yet I must go through with my PLAN. But I must not speak or even think of it yet.

I've been losing my temper a lot lately. Audrey noticed it.

"What's the matter, Nanks?" she asked me. I said I didn't know. Truthfully.

20th August 1943

The weather is lovely and I've been swimming every day. On Tuesday the sea was very rough. It was marvellous. The waves were taller than me and swimming over them is the most thrilling experience I know. On Sunday at Maenporth beach Pam and I were cut off by the tide and had to make our way over the cliff tops. Pam went on holiday on Wednesday, and today Audrey is going away for a few days. She promised to telephone me! I can't bear the thought of not seeing her for some time.

Aunt Liesel and I made the acquaintance of a Viennese lady on Maenporth beach. She lives in a tiny bungalow just above the beach with her husband and two children and is called Mrs Thompson. She invited us for tea. Aunt Liesel said Mrs Thompson was probably a servant girl in Vienna.

I accompanied Aunt Liesel to the doctor's today. She has not felt well and puts it down to Mrs Tamblyn's food.

22nd August 1943

Audrey has telephoned! She's staying at Betty's and she doesn't

j

much like it. She's coming to see me as soon as she gets back on Saturday . . .

Moira McLeod came to visit me today. Her life, from what she says, is a continuous round of riding, sailing, watching cricket and dancing. Lucky girl. She has a boyfriend called Rafe.

I sent a story to Howard Spring and asked for his opinion on it. He returned it quite soon and enclosed a short letter. He wrote:

Dear Miss P.

I have read your story from which it is clear that you are still very young. Thank you for letting me see it, but, believe me, there is only one thing to do if you want something published, and that is to send it to a publisher . . .

27th August 1943

Aunt Liesel has gone. I went to the station with her this morning.

"You're pleased I'm going back to London, aren't you? Admit it, go on," she said to me, just before we said goodbye. How did she know?

"Of course not." I lied - kindly, for how could I speak the truth without offending her?

"Anyway, you can always turn to me if you need any help. Don't forget to write and tell me if you have any problems or need advice," she said.

"Thank you," I said. "I will."

She was gone. I fetched Connie and we cycled to town. In the afternoon we went to the beach and read. I had my bicycle pump stolen off my bike and was furious. We went to the police station to report the theft but we could have saved ourselves the trouble. No hope of finding the thief or the pump, I was told. So I shall have to buy a new one.

We went to Helford by bus yesterday, Connie and I, and wanted to treat ourselves to tea at the Ferry Boat Inn but there was none available. So we came back and bought chips.

If anyone ever says that I am a coward - an utter and complete coward - I shall shake hands with them and agree heartily. You see, Mrs Tamblyn doesn't know that I'm Jewish and the other day she was running down Jews, saying what money grabbers they are and that she doesn't like them.

"We don't understand them," she said to me. "Their ways are

different from ours, aren't they?" And I never had the courage to say: "I am Jewish too, Mrs Tamblyn." I, who profess to be so strong and brave, who call on famous authors and film stars without a qualm - and I could not admit I was Jewish. So, now I know - I'm weak, hatefully weak, and I shall despise myself for this for the rest of my life.

29th August 1943

She's back, and I've seen her! She called the day she returned and I was out; I called on her and *she* was out - and then by chance, we met. And tomorrow life will be worth living again because tomorrow she and I are playing ping pong together at St. Joseph's and there will be no one else there. I shall have my pet, my treasure, all to myself.

Some time ago I asked Connie to tell Audrey that I've had a bicycle accident and been killed, and note carefully how she reacts to the news. This Connie flatly refused to do. I shall have to find another way to discover Audrey's true feelings for me.

Tomorrow I'm going collecting for National Savings.

31st August 1943

I remember the first time I was ever *really* unhappy. It was when I arrived in England and was travelling from Exeter to Falmouth in Mr Robins' car. I remember looking out at the fields and trees and houses we passed but not really seeing them because my eyes were full of tears and my mind was on my mother left behind in Vienna. I think I knew then that I would be parted from her for a long, long time.

I can see my mother now standing at the railway station in Vienna and waving to us as the train began to move. We waved back, Lieselotte and I, and craned our necks to see our mother for as long as possible, until she became quite small and was finally out of sight. I have loathed railway stations ever since. And that was the last time I saw my mother.

I've been thinking about what life is really all about. Why are we here? Where did we come from? Which is right, science or religion? No answer can be found. And why am I personally here? What good have I done in this world? Again, no answer. In

Vienna life was normal and I had no thoughts about such things. Then, after Hitler, normality ended and so did happiness. I was suddenly introduced to the dark side of life. But in England, at Miss Davis', I glimpsed the other side again. I regained contentment - until a certain person came along and destroyed it all again. So that is why I made my PLAN. That is why I want to start a new life, to regain my freedom. As long as Lieselotte was here things went smoothly enough but without her I am entirely at the mercy of a certain person. But you must forget all about this PLAN for the time being, please. I will tell you when the time is ripe.

2nd September 1943

Yesterday I went for a walk with Connie in the evening and whom should we meet, coming along on his bike, but - Denzil! (Ah, you thought I was going to say Audrey, didn't you? Wrong!) We had a long talk, arriving at the usual subjects of love, marriage and religion. He came home with us. He has shut himself off from the world and never goes to St. Joseph's now. While talking to him I tried to remember our shared past, when we used to see each other almost every day. It made no difference, I never could make him out. People never really change, and he's still the same Denzil - by turns religious, narrow-minded, flirtatious, childish, false, funny - a peculiar character. I have never, of course, loved him but we've been good friends. I've never known a boy better than Denzil, and yet I never really knew him. Now there's just a little flickering flame of happy memories left of the days of our friendship.

Today I went to Mylor by ferry with Miss Davis, Moira, Keith and Sheila. Miss D. treated us to tea there and afterwards we went blackberrying.

Tomorrow is the 4th anniversary of the war.

Why do I have an urge to see Betty F. and talk to her? I'm very angry with myself about this.

8th September 1943

Allied troops have invaded Italy! Perhaps the war will soon be over now, and Germany defeated. No harm in hoping.

I've had my first letter from my American penfriend. She's a girl called Corinna who lives on a farm in Vermont. When the war is over she wants me to visit her.

On Saturday morning Moira treated me to coffee and cakes at the 'Old English' café in town. Later we cycled to the Stack and spent the afternoon there, reading. I read until quite late in bed sometimes - the other night until 1.45am!

Connie and I met Audrey's mother and another lady outside the post office a few days ago. Audrey's mother introduced the other lady as being Audrey's aunt. Then she said:

"And this is '*I*', one of Audrey's best friends."

"I've heard so much about you," said the aunt. I thought about that for the rest of the day.

All my father's plans for my future have come to nothing and I'm moving back to St. Joseph's on the 13th! I'm delighted as this is what I wanted.

Denzil came swimming with Connie and me yesterday. He didn't stay in the sea nearly as long as I did as the water was too cold for him. Afterwards we climbed rocks. It was a bit awkward getting dressed and undressed with him around. Connie managed much better than I did. Pam gets back from her holiday tomorrow and we're going to the flicks in the evening to see *The Life and Death of Colonel Blimp* with Anton Walbrook and Deborah Kerr. It's in colour! I adore Anton Walbrook.

10th September 1943

Audrey called. I wasn't in. I telephoned her. She invited me for tea on Sunday. I'm going to tell her of my plan! She must know me and all about me. I shall put all my cards on the table and then there'll be nothing for it except to hope she'll understand. I know she likes me though I mustn't say that too often - but will she understand?

Although I'm madly looking forward to Sunday, something always holds me back, and that is a fear that I'll do something wrong. I'm so unequal to Audrey. How dare I, a fat, ugly lump of a stupid refugee girl, fall in love with that beautiful, impressive child - that most wonderful creature on earth? This thought crushes me often, but then I say to myself: "But she likes me, she wants to be with me . . ."

197

Pam and I cycled to Maenporth today, had tea at the Thompsons in their little bungalow and then went blackberrying with them and their children. Mrs Thompson told us that she and her husband spent their honeymoon cycling through Holland on a tandem. Before the war, of course.

12th September 1943

Where shall I begin? Where shall I end? I'll try and tell you about the wonderful day I had today but as it was like a dream I am very hazy about everything.

She - my beloved Audrey - called for me at 2.30pm. We cycled towards the Stack, left our bicycles at the shop and climbed to the top of the cliffs. There were hardly any people about. A wild wind was blowing. As we climbed Audrey fooled around and put her arm around me. When we reached the top it was sunny and we lay down on the grass. It was very quiet except for the wind and, now and then, some gunfire in the distance. Audrey said she loved lying on the rocks in the wind, especially with somebody she liked. I said nothing. We lay next to each other quietly, only talking now and then almost in whispers, like a pair of sensible lovers. I worshipped her. All the time I was debating whether to tell her of my PLAN or not. "Now," I said to myself several times during silences. "Now!" I couldn't. I didn't want to break the spell. I was so happy lying there next to her, exactly as I had imagined it so often, the wind blowing about us, the sea below us, the rocks, the gorse, the sky . . . I loved every moment. It began to drizzle. Slowly and reluctantly we got up. Now or never! And before I had time to think, there were the words, pouring out of my mouth, and I heard myself say:

"I've got something to tell you, Audrey. I haven't told anybody and it's a dead secret because you see I'm planning to run away because I want to get away from my father, and - oh, I can't go on . . ." She stopped dead, looked at me with her wonderful grey eyes and forced me to continue. So, with that horrible, silly grin on my face which always appears when I'm nervous and which I could not get rid of until I was well into my story, I continued:

"One evening in August," I began, "I felt pretty desperate about things, about having no home and no future, about not being able to cope with schoolwork, and most of all about my father forever

198

looking over my shoulder and ruling my life. So I wrote to my friend in Portsmouth and asked her to find me a job there. Some time later Ruth - my friend - wrote to say that she had found me a very nice family where the mother needed help with her children. I would be treated like a daughter in the family and they would buy me clothes and pay me £1 a week. They would also pay my fare to Portsmouth. There's only one difficulty, and that is I have to get permission from the police to live in Portsmouth as it is a protected area, which means foreigners can't go there. That is how things stand now. So now you know everything." We were standing on the grass among the gorse bushes where a few minutes earlier we had been lying, and now the sky was grey and threatening. I looked into Audrey's grey eyes, waiting for what she would say, and tried to compare her reaction to what I had expected it to be, but found that I had really expected nothing.

"Oh Nanks," said Audrey after what seemed an age. "You can't run away. You mustn't."

"You don't know what my father is like," I said.

"But what about the School Cert., and all your friends here, and Miss Davis?"

"I know. I've thought of all that. But I want to make a new life for myself, Audrey, where my father can't get at me."

"I still don't think you should do this. But if it means so much to you, then I hope you'll get the permit."

"Oh, I knew you'd understand, Audrey, I'm very glad, but I'm sorry to involve you in my troubles."

"I wanted to run away too once, when I was small."

"What happened?"

"Oh, nothing. I didn't run away. And honestly, Nanks, I hope you won't, either."

It was time to go. We clambered down the steep hill, got on our bikes and rode to Audrey's house. She has a wonderful house and a charming family and I love everything connected with her.

"What a nice home you have," I said to Audrey, during tea.

"Look here, Nanks, you really must come as often as you like. Mother said to me only the other day: 'Why don't you invite 'T' oftener?' Make this your second home." Never have any of my other friends said this to me - NEVER. I could only murmur:

"Thanks, Audrey."

After tea we played Monopoly. It was pouring outside.

Suddenly there was a brilliant flash of lightning, followed by a terrific clap of thunder, and then the lights went out. I couldn't convince myself that everything that was happening and had happened earlier in the afternoon was really true. We sat in the dark for a bit and now I was sure everything was only a dream.

I stayed for supper. Much later, when I walked home wearing Audrey's mackintosh because it was still pouring - I left my bicycle at her house - I was thinking: "Now we are great, loving friends. There is something between us which does not exist between me and any of my other friends, but I don't know what it is. I still long to do things for her - and I haven't even got a home where I can repay her hospitality. I'm alone and lost and left to myself, and yet I am not, so long as I have her. If anyone ever reads this and still refuses to believe in love among members of the same sex, they must be mad. I don't know what she sees in me but it is obvious she has a great liking for me . . ."

Back in my bedroom, for the last night at Tamblyns' boarding-house, for tomorrow I'm moving to St. Joseph's, my thoughts continued to race around in my mind. They went like this: "I know she likes me, but I don't understand what she sees in me. I know we are friends, but we cannot be *real* friends so long as I'm in love with her. It's terrible to say it but my abnormal love for her is actually in the way of true friendship. In true friendship you feel at ease and comfortable with the other person, but when I'm with Audrey I feel anything but that - I feel wildly happy or anxious, often restless, often weak and powerless and a bit afraid. Love is not all wonderful. Every joy has to be paid for." So ran my thoughts.

As I lay in bed trying to fall asleep I wondered if she too was now lying in bed thinking of the hours we had spent together today? Or is she fast asleep? I hope not. Think of me, Audrey, think of me and love me, love me.

It is midnight. I've just eaten an apple. I'm not at all tired but I had better stop writing. At this time tomorrow I'll be at good old St. Joseph's again.

13th September 1943

Well, here I am again, not in the big double bedroom in the front which Lieselotte and I shared, but in one of the little back bedrooms. This morning Connie and I moved all my things in the pouring rain, making several journeys from Tamblyns' to St. Joseph's, luckily only a five minute walk. In the afternoon we went to town and then I went to the flicks with my love Audrey. We saw *Anthony Adverse* with Olivia de Havilland and Frederick March - a good film; unfortunately it was on in 'St. George's', nicknamed the Fleapit. Naturally I always feel itchy when sitting through a film there. In the evening Moira McLeod and her father were here, and so, to my surprise, was Denzil. Moira's father is called George and he is what I think is called brash. Miss Kitty likes flirting with him! They knew each other when they were young.

True to my promise to Howard Spring, I'm reading *My Son, My Son*. It was lent to me by Mrs Thompson. I'm not sure whether it is better to read the book before or after one has seen the film.

Janet and Father Wiseman are coming to supper tomorrow, and school starts on Thursday. I shall be going to the British Restaurant for dinner with the school this term.

14th September 1943

My plan has crashed, and with it all my hopes. It's all over. Fate was in my way. My permit to live in Portsmouth has been REFUSED. My bitter disappointment is indescribable but, as usual, on the outside I'm just the same - I just keep smiling, even though I'm born under an unlucky star.

Although I've tried, and often thought I succeeded, an inner voice tells me repeatedly:

> You will never be English!
> You will never be English!
> You will never be English!
> YOU HAVE FOREIGN BLOOD IN YOU!

You don't know what an inferiority complex is, do you, so I will tell you: it's dreadful. I may enjoy art, writing and music but I'm no good at any of them, in fact I'm no good at anything. I'm a failure, one of God's feeble creatures only here to make up numbers.

18th September 1943

Denzil came to say goodbye to us yesterday as he's going to

201

Wales today. This time he didn't kiss me. He has been terribly nice to me lately and we've been for long bicycle rides together several times. I think Roy is coming to Falmouth next week. I'd give a lot to see him again.

All is not over! Ruth has found me a family in London who need a girl to live in and help with their children, and today I had a letter from the mother, a Mrs Gaiman. It sounds wonderful and I'm keeping my fingers crossed that nothing goes wrong.

Today Connie and I went to a dog and horse show at Mylor. We saw Howard Spring there. I was more excited to see him than by the dogs and horses.

Yesterday we went seaweeding again on Gyllingvase beach with the school. We've nicknamed Miss Coward Miss Agar Agar. My piano lessons start again on Tuesday. Good.

I called at Tamblyns' as I hadn't said goodbye to Mr T. They gave me an egg. I also called at Audrey's as she wanted to show me her latest film star pictures. We had another talk about my 'PLAN'. She is very interested in it but is not in favour of it. She tells me to wait.

"Wait?" I said. "I've waited and waited and waited."

"Wait till you've finished school," she said.

"Not me. I don't want to finish school." Then I told her about the new family in London, and that there was now a real chance of my getting away. She told me to think of the consequences. What if I'm not happy, what if my father comes and drags me back? I'll risk it all, I answered.

"Oh, Nanks, you're very silly," she said. "I wish you wouldn't get such brainy ideas. You must have been reading schoolgirl stories."

"I've done no such thing!" I cried. But my anger passed quickly for I realised that she was trying very hard to understand and be sympathetic. One wants people one loves to behave like Gods, which is most unreasonable. It is enough that she listens to me sympathetically and gives me another point of view. She wanted me to promise a few things but I couldn't. She looked at me beseechingly.

"At least you won't go without telling me? You'll have another talk with me about it? You'll think it over well? You won't do anything rash?" she said. I promised those things. Then I had to go and her mother came to the door to say goodbye to me. As I went out I turned round and met Audrey's eyes - I shall never forget her look. It was comforting, understanding - loving! Then I left and I heard the front door being closed. I didn't look back again.

26th September 1943

Miss McCreight is here for lunch every Sunday. She's clever and funny and everyone likes her. On Wednesdays I have my German lesson after school with Miss Gooden. She lives in a little wooden bungalow in a huge garden just a few minutes from the High School. I think my German is better than hers! This is certainly not true of my piano playing in comparison with Miss Rogers'! My piano lessons are every Tuesday.

Miss Kitty came back from her holidays yesterday. Today Connie and I were on the seafront with our bikes, reading. We had an argument, and I went home without her. It really upset me. On the 22nd we had our first air-raid of the term at school and spent about an hour in the trench. It was the best part of the day. We also had a Red Cross meeting that day.

Miss Kitty's favourite cat, Peter, is dead. He was very old and sick and the vet took him away to be destroyed. When Father Wiseman was here for tea he noticed how sad Miss Kitty was, so she told him the bad news.

"Why don't you bury him in the garden?" he suggested. So I was quickly dispatched to the vet's to fetch Peter back, before the vet had time to incinerate him or whatever vets do with dead cats. Miss Kitty was quite excited at the thought of having Peter back, dead or alive, and begged me to hurry, giving me a large sack to bring the body back in. I didn't relish the thought of carrying a dead cat on my bicycle, but of course I went. Luckily Peter had not been disposed of yet, and Mr Smythe produced him from some back room. Although I was revolted by the whole business I bravely held out the sack and the vet dropped the cat in - and it dropped straight through and crashed onto the floor. I screamed. The sack had no bottom to it. Without saying a word, Mr Smythe picked up the cat, went away with it and returned with a neat parcel which presumably contained Peter. I took it from him, quickly put it on my carrier at the back of my bike and cycled back to St. Joseph's. It was the most unpleasant ride I ever had but

Miss Kitty's delight at having Peter back and being able to bury him in the garden made up for it. Naturally, I attended the funeral ceremony in the garden later.

30th September 1943

I had to see her. She had been away for a day and I was cycling back to school after the British Restaurant where we had had the usual boring dinner of roast beef and cabbage and apples with custard, and I had this sudden burning desire to see Audrey. I arrived at school, went into the cloakroom to leave my things - and saw her hat on the peg. She was here! I rushed to the form room - would she be there? Perhaps it was someone else's hat? Oh God, let her be there, I want to look at her. She was. She saw me and smiled.

"Hello, Nanks."

"Hello, Audrey."

I was alive again.

My whole school life depends on and centres round Audrey - and Betty, for Betty is so much a part of Audrey's world, and I like her, too. As for their relationship, that continues to be very cool.

As you know, I've loved quite a few people in my life. When I look back there is one person who stands out, and that person is Otto Seifert, the Viennese Jew who is about 46 years old now. He's in China and I shall never see him again. Perhaps because we endured that terrible time under Nazi rule together he will always be my most sacred memory. To think of him now is like cutting a wound open. My mother liked him too, and when I was eleven I wanted him to marry her - or me! The day he left us to emigrate to China was the day I really hated the Nazis for the first time.

3rd October 1943

Connie and I are reconciled, Janet is having a baby and there's an American camp in Falmouth; Beryl and I went to see it, as she knew exactly where it was.

On Thursday afternoon I was at Mr Robins' office after school; he had to sign a document in connection with my Aliens status.

This afternoon, Sunday, after a nice lunch with Miss McCreight entertaining us with her amusing chatter, Connie and I cycled to the Thompsons' bungalow in Maenporth where we were invited to a party. We had a lovely tea - delicious open sandwiches and Viennese cakes such as I have not eaten since I left Vienna.

I went to bed early with an aspirin as I have a bad cold, and wrote my book.

4th October 1943

Talk about cutting wounds open - I saw Roy today! We just said hello. He was with his wife. I would like to have all the people who have meant a lot to me lined up. I would then inspect them closely and try to discover what exactly it was that made me love them.

Everything is ready for my secret departure on the 8th, and the only person who knows about it is Audrey. She is coming to discuss it with me after school today. I have packed a case and am leaving instructions about the things I'm leaving here. I am catching an early train on Monday morning and Mrs Gaiman is meeting me at Paddington Station. On the way to the station I have to call at the Falmouth Police as aliens over 16 years old have to inform the police if they move to another town. That is the trickiest part. I'm excited, thrilled, but also very nervous. Everything has to be very carefully arranged. One mistake on my part and the whole plan may go wrong. My suitcase is hidden under my bed. The police must not be informed until the last moment, in case they get in touch with St. Joseph's. A hundred little things like that. I can't wait to live in London, air-raids or no air-raids, and be free and independent, and near Lieselotte, and yet I feel mean walking out on Miss Davis like this, and a bit apprehensive about my new life ahead, and about leaving everyone and everything I like in Falmouth. Will Audrey and Betty come together again when I'm gone, will the ice between them melt?

Later. She has been, and we talked about my plan. For a time we were in each other's arms. She helped me fill in a form for the police. Then we played the piano. There wasn't much more we could say or do. I accompanied her home in the dusk. Everything had become so important and precious, I wanted it to go on for ever. Instead of that everything was coming to an end. Now that she is my friend and confidante and we love one another it is coming to an end. If I have made her unhappy or worried her I wish I could die. But she said she was with me - always and forever.

I have just finished writing a very sad book called 'Ambitious Failure.'

6th October 1943

I can hardly believe that, in two days' time, I shall no longer be here. No more school, no more science lessons. I loathe science. The other day I messed up an experiment. I had no idea what I was supposed to be doing. Miss Coward - 'Agar Agar' is too good a name for her - said:

"Are all Austrians as stupid as you? No, they can't be, because your sister wasn't."

I certainly shan't miss *her*. And she won't miss me, either. I wonder if anyone will? My father is coming to Falmouth on the 8th and he's under the impression I'm meeting him at the station. In fact, all being well, I shall be on my way to London.

8th October 1943

It's not real at all - it never happened - it's only a dream, a very bad dream, and presently I shall wake up and find myself walking down the street with my mother, arm in arm, a happy child, who never left Vienna.

Last night, as you know, was to be my last in Falmouth. Everything was ready for my great adventure, my new life. In the evening Janet came and we all chatted and nobody had the least idea that I would no longer be here on the following day. For several days I'd been in anguish, and on this last evening I felt feverish with excitement and anxiety, but nobody suspected anything so I must have concealed it successfully. That night I could not sleep. I tossed and turned. At 8am sharp I was ready to leave. I locked the bathroom door and hid the key so that they would think I was in there and give me a chance to get away. I had written a note explaining everything to Miss Davis and put it in her room. Case in hand, I crept downstairs while I knew the others were in the kitchen, having breakfast. In a few minutes I would be at the police station to obtain my permit to travel, and within an hour I would be on the train to London. I reached the front door - and to my amazement found it locked. I turned the key - and the kitchen door opened and Miss Kitty appeared.

"What are you doing? Where are you going?" she cried. I cannot describe to you how I felt, nor can I recall in detail what happened next. There was a great hullabaloo, Miss Davis and one or two children came rushing out, I was forced back and held, all the doors were locked and Miss Kitty went to the police while I was bombarded with questions by Miss Davis who was very excited and upset. I didn't kick up a fuss. I just stood there, drained and motionless, and refused to speak, or was too stunned to speak. I realised then that there must be some God to arrange a situation like that, for do you know what my first sensation was when I was caught? Relief! A great weight fell from my shoulders. I had wanted to run away really badly and I was driven to it, but I hated the whole idea of it. After about 10 minutes, when things had simmered down a bit and I began to feel more myself, I said to Miss Davis, who was still pinning me against the wall outside the kitchen:

"I didn't want to run away from you, Miss Davis, honestly. You know I love St. Joseph's. It's because of my father." She was very understanding, and I told her everything, and we both cried. Miss Kitty returned with Father Wiseman, who she thought might get something out of me, or knock some sense into me, as she said. Apparently she had suspected I was up to something as she had noticed my strange behaviour for the last few days, and that is why she locked the front door. Thinking back to the last few days, or rather months, it seemed to me I must have been mad, out of my senses. As I slowly felt normality return to me, I was overcome with a desire to make peace with everything and everybody, above all with my father, to have a quiet, sensible talk with him, settle things, be friends.

The rest of the day I spent in bed. I ate nothing all day. Pam came to see me after school and I told her everything. In the evening Miss Davis went to meet my father from the station. He came into my room and sat down by my bed. He looked angry but at the same time puzzled. He asked me why I had done what I did. I said I didn't want to stay at school because I knew I would fail the School Certificate and I was anxious to embark on a career and be independent.

"Looking after somebody's child is not a career. It's being little more than a servant," he said. He said I must take the School Certificate as I would never be able to embark on a worthwhile career without it. I did not argue. Then, his nostrils still dilated in anger, he said it was very childish to try and run away and I was much too old for this kind of thing. He knew this would humiliate me.

Just before he left he noticed that I had bitten a few of my fingernails again and he slapped me across my face and my glasses fell off.

I am not ashamed of what I have done. I failed, and yet I feel just a little bit of courage has been shown. My darling Audrey was right, of course, it was bound to fail, and yet it has left me with a tiny sense of achievement.

But perhaps it was all only a dream.

10th October 1943

The three of us - Connie, Audrey and I - sat on the seafront yesterday afternoon while I described what happened on Friday. It seemed so incredible that I hardly expected them to believe me. I am glad it is all over. Later I went to Trevethan - Tamblyns' place - and helped my father pack, and sorted out Lieselotte's things which she left behind. I shall have to go several more times to do this. I stayed for tea at Tamblyns'. Today, Sunday, my father came to Church with me in the morning and treated me to the pictures in the afternoon. Once when I was at the pictures with him he sent me out for lounging in my seat; I just went and sat somewhere else and he never knew. Today he was in quite a good mood, however, and in the evening he came to St. Joseph's and we played Nine Men's Morris. Miss McCreight has been to lunch as usual today and I gave her my book 'Ambitious Failure' to read. She made me laugh with some of her witty criticisms, and I enjoyed discussing it with her.

12th October 1943

When Audrey entered the classroom yesterday we all stopped

what we were doing and looked at her: her hair was newly washed and shiny and she wore a shirt-blouse and she looked so beautiful that I couldn't take my eyes off her.

I went to the pictures with her and Betty last night. Their friendship is still icy. We saw an absolutely daft film with Leslie Howard called *It's Love I'm After*.

I've finished reading *My Son, My Son*. It was wonderful, though very sad. It's the best book I've read for a long time, almost as good as *Rebecca* by Daphne du Maurier. I can't stop thinking about these two books. The same can't be said for *Good Companions* by J. B. Priestley, which I thought very boring.

17th October 1943

Last night my father came to say goodbye to Miss Davis and Miss Kitty and today he left Falmouth for good and went to live in London. In the afternoon Miss McCreight helped me make corrections in my book and then I went for a walk with Connie.

On Friday Monica W. came to tea. I've still never been to tea at her farm but as she's a very dull girl I don't mind. Figgy had a big part in a school play which really surprised me as, like me, she hates acting. She's a good hockey player and plays in all the school matches, and as that is performing in a way, I suppose acting is not such an ordeal for her.

My father gave me £1. I spent it on the following items:

1/1d	Mouthwater
1/2d	Apples
3d	Radishes
9d	Shoe repair
1/3½d	Chocolate ration
5d	Shoe laces
3/9d	Laundry
2½d	Stamp
2/6d	Orange squash
5d	British Restaurant

Next week I'm going to sell some more things at the second hand shop in Killigrew Street.

I had to take my Certificate of Registration to the police station so that they could enter in it: 'Permitted to possess pedal cycle until further notice.'! That's because I'm an alien.

22nd October 1943

What has happened to Audrey? She has changed. She has not been at all nice to me for the whole week. Figgy and I talked about her all the way back to school from the British Restaurant yesterday. There's something so sad about Figgy; I am wondering whether Audrey is the cause of it?

Today we had to dissect a rabbit in the science lesson. It was disgusting. When I was at Pam's house afterwards, before going to the flicks with her, Mrs Bath gave me *an orange*! It took away the smell of the dead rabbit in my nostrils.

27th October 1943

Miss McCreight is ill. Connie and I cycled out to Penryn where she lives and visited her on Sunday afternoon. We made her some tea and gave her a hot water bottle, for which she was very grateful.

During an English lesson yesterday we were each asked to name our favourite book. When it came to Betty F's turn she said loud and clear: 'Ambitious Failure'.

"Oh? Who's that by, Betty?" asked Miss Clift.

"It's by *I.P.*" said Figgy. My cheeks felt scarlet and I didn't know where to look. All faces turned in my direction. Miss Clift gave me a big smile.

"Tell us about your book, *'I'*," she said to me.

"It's just a short novel," I replied.

"I hope you will let me read it some day," said Miss Clift.

Afterwards all the girls said they wanted to read it.

I have to stay in after school on Friday and do my science test again.

30th October 1943

Today I told Pam about my feelings for Audrey. We sat on a bench in Kimberley Park and ate chips and suddenly Pam asked me: "Why did you tell Audrey about your plan to run away?" She knew about that. So then I told her. She said: "I suspected something of the sort."

"And you never mentioned it," I said, in admiration.

"Of course not," said Pam. You may not be swept off your feet by Pam, but what would the world be like without girls like her? She's always ready to help anyone, never loses her temper and believes that honesty is the best policy. On Monday, which is a half term holiday, we are going to cycle to Truro to visit her grandparents, who live in a very humble house with no garden and only a back yard. Nevertheless, whenever we go to see them they give us a shilling each, and a very nice tea.

Yesterday I had a quarrel with Audrey. I had written something on the blackboard during break and said it was Chinese and a lot of girls believed me. Maybe they thought if you know German there's no reason why you shouldn't know Chinese as well. Someone asked me what it meant, when Audrey came up and - quick as a flash - wiped it off.

"Why did you do that?" I asked, in a rage.

"Because it was probably something rude and you shouldn't write rude things on the blackboard," she said.

"So you can read Chinese, and you're all of a sudden a very good little girl," I replied, almost trembling.

"Don't be daft," said Audrey.

"You're a spoil sport," I cried. She walked away. It's so dreadful to love someone and then they suddenly show themselves to be ordinary people with nasty streaks in them and at these moments you see them no longer as divine beings but as a black monster with horns. All through the day my mind returned to the happy hours we've had together, lying in the sun on the grass, walking together, holding hands, talking confidentially, two in one person. I want to hold on to those happy memories desperately, as though I were afraid someone might take them away. I *AM* afraid. But that's ridiculous. Audrey herself can't change what has already happened. But why am I saying all this? Everything is the same . . . Only some little things lately which are not, and now this quarrel - but no, no, it's nothing. We've quarrelled before, my imagination is too fertile, everything will be all right . . .

In spite of all my attempts to comfort myself, I went to sleep last night knowing that Audrey has the power to ruin my already ruined life.

I didn't tell Pam anything of this, or course.

Gerrard and I, we go hand in hand - he's the hero of my book

'Ambitious Failure' for whom everything in life goes wrong until at the end, Jane, the girl he loves, deserts him and he commits suicide.

1st November 1943

Whether I die or whether I go on living, I feel as if my life is over. The reason - Audrey treats me as if there had never been anything between us. I thought I had won her for good but I forgot that she could escape any time she wanted to. And I think I know the reason for her changed behaviour: she imagines herself to be in love with a Grammar School boy called John. She has found a world she can't share with me. She looks down on me suddenly because I care nothing for flirting with boys. I must find a boyfriend if I want her to love me again, to be her Nanks again, but I don't know if that will be any easier than trying to blot out the memory of the past.

Go, Audrey, go. Why do I go on seeing your face when I shut my eyes? Will you *never* leave me?

5th November 1943

I've had a long conversation with Figgy and my eyes have been opened. She worships Audrey but Audrey doesn't love her back. In fact she bullies her and gives her a hell of a time. Figgy has been terribly jealous of me. I confessed my own love for Audrey and grief at her changed behaviour towards me.

"That's Audrey all over," said Figgy. "She gets besotted with people, then drops them without a word. I meant to warn you but I didn't want to interfere. I too have happy memories of her but she doesn't care, she has no feelings. She's rotten right through. She doesn't deserve to be loved but I do still." Then she told me that Audrey had been dropping hints about my PLAN - my secret!

"Perhaps she wanted help and advice," I said, after the first shock.

"Audrey is not a person to confide in. Don't trust her. Believe me, I know. My God, I know!" she said.

"Do you think I can stop believing in her just like that?" I asked.

"Oh, I know," she said again. And we both sat there behind our desks in the deserted classroom, understanding each other's feelings perfectly because they are so alike. I can't tell you how sorry I felt for Figgy. Like me, she says she will always love Audrey.

"Why has she suddenly dropped me like this?" I asked in hopeless despair. "Is it because of John?"

"You're not the first one, nor will you be the last. It's her all over. I saw it coming. I knew you were the next victim. I knew and saw how she liked you and treated you accordingly and I knew what the next stage would be. Now it's over like it is with me. She'll never come back to you. Never."

"Stop it," I said. "Don't say that."

"I once asked Audrey if she liked you," Figgy went on. I didn't want to know and I wanted to stop my ears but, with a lump in my throat, I was compelled to ask.

"And what did she say?"

"She said yes and no. Sometimes a lot. And she has no idea that she means so much to you. She thought you didn't like her much."

I don't believe it. But it doesn't matter now. I just wish I could lose my memory.

14th November 1943

It has been pouring the whole weekend. Despite the rain Miss Davis and I went to see Marlborough House and grounds yesterday afternoon. This house is shaped like a ship and was built by a Cornish sea captain. It is quite extraordinary, inside and outside. As we walked about in it, I felt at any moment I was going to be seasick.

Sadly I can now see for myself that the person I love has no good in her - not deep inside, where it matters. She ill-treats her once beloved Betty, she takes advantage of the weak, she has a heart of stone. Figgy asked her why she dislikes her so, and do you know what Audrey replied? "Mind your own business!" Oh Audrey, you are made of rusty iron even though you are covered in beautiful shining gold. It's because of your gold exterior that everyone loves you, but God help them when they get to the rust. I don't think I shall ever believe in anyone again.

18th November 1943

Some time ago - and you'll know by now that I don't always tell

213

you things in the right order, and have forgiven me - Margaret Lawrance and I went to a Red Cross Lecture on First Aid. Before the lecture began a uniformed Red Cross lady asked us all our names. When she came to me and I told her mine she said: "What?"

"*I,*" I repeated.

"What?"

"*I.*"

By this time Margaret was in stitches, but recovered enough to say: "It is, really. She's called *'I'*."

"How do you spell it?" asked the lady. I spelled it for her.

"*'I'*? I don't believe it. You're having me on." And she walked away. Margaret was still laughing. I laughed too, but only with my mouth. I hate my name, which no one here can pronounce. I should like to be called Jane and then perhaps I might meet a Mr Rochester and marry him.

The lecturer told us about a woman who told her little boy not to put peas up his nose while she was out. This had never occurred to the little boy, and as soon as his mother had gone he did it, and needed first aid to have the peas removed.

Figgy has stopped living at Audrey's. She whispered it to me during the Christmas Carol Concert at school today.

I still go to the sketch club every Monday after school. It is a privilege, and only girls above a certain standard in art are allowed to belong.

23rd November 1943

My father is back on a visit. He's staying in Truro, and on Saturday I went there by bus and had lunch with him and Jane at the 'Royal'. Afterwards Jane took me round the shops. On Sunday I went there again, this time for tea.

Nearly every day during the dinner hour Figgy and I walk around the town. Sometimes we buy a bun, as the British Restaurant dinners are not very filling. Pam goes home for dinner, but once she didn't, had a taste of British Restaurant food and then joined us on our stroll to the shops before returning to school. We feel very grown up on these expeditions.

Last week nearly half the form was away with flu.

28th November 1943

I was at home all day today, Sunday, drawing mostly. Connie and Father Luke came to tea. Yesterday Figgy, Connie and I went to the flicks in the Odeon and saw *Wuthering Heights* with Merle Oberon and Laurence Olivier. Marvellous, super, lovely but sad, oh so sad! I loved every moment of it. I was rudely awakened when, immediately the film ended, a silly advertisement for Maypole tea appeared. Then a dog followed us home and wouldn't leave us. Everything conspired to wrench me away from Cathy and Heathcliff.

6th December 1943

Audrey has been absent for about 10 days, days which I spent chiefly with Betty F, learning more and more about Audrey's savage character. Days of grief and worry but also of relaxation because Audrey was not there to torture me. At the end of last week I found myself at Audrey's house once more (my 'second home'!) - It had taken me a lot of courage but I had to find out what was wrong with her. Mrs B. opened the door to me.

"Oh *'I'*," she said. "Audrey has been wanting to see you, about the kittens." (I'd found a home for them).

"How is she?" I asked.

"She's at the WVS. Why don't you go down and see her there?" said Mrs B. She's a WVS member. So that is what I did. I arrived at the office, went upstairs, knocked on the door, heard her voice say "Come in," opened the door - and this was the scene that met my eyes: Audrey was sitting at a desk, reading, her head resting on her hand. I said: "Halloh, Audrey," in a normal sort of voice, to hide my feelings, and walked towards the desk. She sat up, she followed me with her eyes, but she didn't answer my halloh, or speak, or stir, or smile. I felt a little uncomfortable seeing her turned to stone like this and receiving me in this way when we hadn't seen each other for nearly two weeks. Although it seemed like an age, it probably only lasted half a minute, and suddenly the stone statue came to life, got up, smiled, offered me a chair, and talked and talked. We had so much to say to each other.

After half and hour I left with a feeling of complete satisfaction. She was back at school on Monday, and everything was as of old between us, it was Nanks this and Nanks that, she was

215

suggesting things we might do together at the weekend, we went to dinner together, we kept away from the others, we held hands, and she was totally loving. I dare not believe in her again, but it's wonderful all the same. Figgy was absent.

Sometimes I wish all this had never happened. If I can't love her in peace I don't want to love her at all. Even while we were together I thought of poor Figgy and how mean Audrey has been to her. Would she one day be as mean to me? Why not?

I convince myself that she still loves me and that we shall walk through life together. All those conversations with Figgy - they were about some unknown person with a horrible character, not Audrey at all. Even if she leaves me again she will leave me only in body, for in spirit we are united forever.

8th December 1943

Alan has come to stay for a few days. I wish I were like him. He's always the same, always pleasant. He gives me an inferiority complex. I mean, a bigger one than I already have.

Last Sunday Miss McCreight was here for lunch as usual. In the afternoon, Miss Davis, the children, and her bad tempered Dandy Dinmont dog Timothy and I went for a walk on the beach. How uninviting and different the sea looks in the winter. We collected shells for the children to paint. Connie has a large collection of painted shells on her mantelpiece.

Yesterday Pam and I went to see a fortune teller! We were very nervous - and rather pleased to find she wasn't in. I don't suppose we shall have enough courage to go a second time. Our School Christmas party is on Friday, we break up the following Friday - and guess where I'm going! To London! I'm going to spend Christmas in London with my father and Lieselotte and staying with Jane and Jack. And this time I don't need to hide my suitcase under my bed.

11th December 1943

I opened my eyes and, still half dazed from sleep, saw a streak of light. I watched it intently. Then I heard the word 'Vorzimmer! Vorzimmer!' echoing in my brain. That was it - I was home - HOME in my old home in Vienna, a happy child, my mother's goodnight kiss still fresh on my forehead as I lay in my bed in the nursery watching the light shining in from the Vorzimmer (hall). I heard footsteps and voices outside - that was my mother talking to my grandmother and Rosa, the maid. All was happiness, all peace. I was back there, from where I had been wrenched. The scene was vivid - almost real. I continued to stare at the streak of light, fully awake now. Then I recollected. I looked around the room, and was unable to connect the past with this life.

The light had only been the moon reflected in the mirror.

14th December 1943

A few days ago Audrey and I went to Penryn by bus to deliver her kittens. They went to 'Tremough' and afterwards a nun showed us round the school. I expect she regretted that her only converts to be were cats and not humans.

In spite of what Figgy had said, Audrey *has* come back to me, and I was ready for her and received her with open arms, as I had promised I would. But I know it will never be quite the same again. She has left me once, without explanation, as she has left others, and therefore I must conclude that I am the same to her as the others. Tomorrow she might leave me again.

Why do I love her? She has destroyed all my illusions of her. She has proved to me that she's not my ideal, perfect girl. But still I love her and live for her, live for someone not worth living for perhaps.

Enough. Enough of that. On that day she loved me and made me happy. This then is the situation. I may still love but my love is no longer blind. And how can I be friendly with both Audrey and Figgy? It's an impossible state of affairs. Figgy is jealous of me again because Audrey has come back to me. Figgy may be the better person, but my heart belongs to Audrey and where she goes I must follow, even if it is down a crooked road.

She has promised to write to me while I'm in London.

19th December 1943

I'm in London! I arrived yesterday, Friday, which was the last day of term, but I left a day earlier. Miss Davis saw me off at the station and Miss McCreight travelled with me as far as Exeter.

k

When it came to lunchtime and I became hungry I wanted to eat the sandwiches Miss Davis had given me but no one else in the compartment was eating. In the end I took them to the lavatory and ate them there. To my surprise I found a lovely bright red tomato in the parcel with a little note from Miss Kitty to say it was from her, and she hoped I would enjoy it. Wasn't that nice of her? I was anxious all the way in case I dozed off, or was on the lavatory when the train stopped in London, and I would miss it. But I didn't. The train arrived at Paddington Station 35 minutes late and I was met by my father and Lieselotte. We went straight to Jane and Jack's flat, where my father lives too, in Maida Vale, and stayed up very late, talking. It's a beautiful flat, warm and modern and with electric light, which takes some getting used to again. The next day I went shopping with Lieselotte and made my first acquaintance with an escalator and was at first frightened to get on, much to the amusement of the other shoppers. We had lunch at a restaurant called 'Old Vienna' with Jack and my father, and afterwards did more Christmas shopping with Lieselotte. Later she took me to Paddington Green Children's Hospital where she works, and introduced me to some of her nurse friends. In the evening there was a party for 30 people at Jane's flat, with dancing, for which I had designed the invitation cards. I was up till 3am.

Today I slept till 10.15am, we had lunch at 3pm, and Lieselotte was here for all meals, as she is on holiday. In the afternoon we went to Hyde Park and Kensington Gardens and saw the statues of Peter Pan and Queen Victoria. More sightseeing tomorrow.

20th December 1943

Today Lieselotte took me to Piccadilly Circus, we had lunch at Lyons and then visited Westminster Abbey and Cathedral - we climbed to the top and had a wonderful view of London - Trafalgar Square, the Houses of Parliament and Big Ben. Next time I play Monopoly I shall be able to picture all these famous places. In the afternoon we had tea at Buzzards with my cousin Herta.

22nd December 1943

Yesterday my father, Lieselotte and I went to Oxford by train for the day. Of course, my father had to spoil the journey by scolding me for having dirty hands, and telling me that his sister Grete never took her gloves off on a train! My father has two cousins in Oxford, Bruno Furst and Else Haas, and before visiting them we went sightseeing - Christchurch Library and several colleges. We had lunch at a restaurant with Uncle Bruno and his wife Erna, then we went to their flat and were joined by Else later. They gave us Christmas presents. We returned to London in the evening and this time the train was two hours late.

Today I went to Mme Tussaud's with Lieselotte, had lunch at Lyons, and in the afternoon my father took me to his doctor's for an examination as he thinks I have an overactive thyroid. Then we went to see Buckingham Palace.

23rd December 1943

Lieselotte, Herta and I went to St. James' Palace today to see if we could find out anything about our mother through the Red Cross. But we couldn't. We had lunch at the Quality Inn and tea, after another visit to Lieselotte's hospital, at 'Old Vienna' with her and my father. He said the waitress who served us would certainly not be allowed to work in a café in Vienna as he saw her put her hand in her dress to adjust her strap, for which he said she would immediately be sacked. Lucky waitress, not to be working in Vienna. In the evening Jack, Jane, my father and Lieselotte and I went to the theatre to see *Pink String and Sealing Wax* which was very funny, and afterwards we all had supper at the Hungarian Czardas in Dean Street - my father's favourite restaurant. I had a real goulash but Lieselotte only ate ham as she doesn't like rich foreign food.

Tomorrow, Christmas Eve, we are going to meet Mrs Laszlo, the wife of my father's business partner, and in the evening we shall give each other our presents, as my father prefers the Austrian custom of celebrating on the 24th rather than the 25th of December.

26th December 1943

On Christmas Day, after a late breakfast, my father took

Lieselotte and me by train to Southall to meet yet another cousin of his, Felix. In Vienna he was my favourite uncle and I used to go skating with him. We had tea together, and went for a walk. Today, Boxing Day, the three of us went to St. Paul's for a service in the morning and afterwards Lieselotte took me to see London Bridge and the Fire Monument. Jane's younger sister Betty was here for the day. She's a fashion model, tall, slim, blonde and beautiful. Herta came for tea, and in the evening she and Lieselotte went to a dance.

Tomorrow I'm going back to Falmouth.

My father said that he hoped soon to be able to pay the Robins' back every penny they spent on us - about £300.

27th December 1943

I'm 'home' again. My father and Lieselotte saw me off at Paddington Station. It was a wonderful holiday. London seems quite near, now that I've been there. I loathed parting with Lieselotte and shan't see her again until the summer. But it is nice to be here again. If I pass the School Cert. I'll probably live in London. Passing the School Cert. is now my greatest aim, and thereafter to have a career, perhaps in art. And if my stories ever get published perhaps I'll be famous one day! But I expect I'll fail in everything, however hard I try.

Miss Kitty and Sheila met me at the station in Falmouth.

30th December 1943

The day after I got back I went to see Connie, Tamblyns and Pam. In the afternoon I went to a Grammar School Concert with Connie and Pam, and Miss Hankin was at St. Joseph's for lunch and tea. She hasn't been sleeping here for a long time as we haven't had any more air-raids.

On our walk yesterday Connie and I watched some army manoeuvres. In the evening there was Miss Davis' Christmas Play at the Catholic Church. One of the Prendergast boys gave me a cigarette during the interval.

Today Sheila and I went collecting for the Red Cross, and in the evening there was a party here. We played 'Murders' until 3.45am!

31st December 1943

A thousand new Yanks have arrived! They are billeted in a large house just across the road from St. Joseph's.

Sheila Arnold has passed her entrance exam to the High School, and is delighted, of course.

Miss Davis and I sat up till midnight this evening (it's nearly 1am now) listening to the wireless and seeing the New Year in - Goodbye, 1943.

5th January 1944

Halloh, New Year. Do please bring me some happiness, an end to the war, victory and a reunion with my mother. I've started writing a new book and I wrote all day on Sunday except for a visit to Connie's who's ill in bed.

Miss Davis has gone to London with three of the children, and I saw them off at the station with Tony, Connie's younger brother. Miss Kitty and I have been to the flicks, and visiting Miss Hankin, and on a moonlight walk. We're having quite a nice time together, making the best of things alone in the large empty house. I've been helping her a bit in the Church, too. Today she took me to Miss Hennessy's (a friend of hers) fancy dress party, and I went dressed as a Chinaman, with a pigtail attached to an orange cardboard coolie hat. On the way home Miss Kitty told me the following joke: two soldiers on a battlefield were walking together. One of them placed a stone in his way and then intentionally fell over it.

"What are you doing that for?" asked the other in surprise.

"To make sure that I'll be included on that monument they'll erect one day, in honour of those who fell in the war," replied the soldier.

"I made up that joke!" I said. Miss Kitty didn't believe me at first.

"Tony told it to me," she said. So that was it. Jokes travel fast, even bad ones.

Miss McCreight said that *Wuthering Heights* is not a love story at all but a story about love for the Yorkshire Moors. This shocked me. People don't understand that, she said, and think it is just about the love between Cathy and Heathcliff. She implied that this would be much too unsubtle for such a great book, but what

221

is unsubtle about love between two people? Why are love stories always made out to be trash? It seems everything is more important - work, landscapes, wars, - and love is not a serious subject at all. But without love there would soon be no life. I said to Miss McCreight: "How do you know?"

"It emerges on every page if you read the book with insight," she replied. Not wishing to appear silly I said nothing more. I may have misunderstood the book but it doesn't alter how I feel about it.

6th January 1944

Oh my God, I've misjudged Audrey again! You see, she'd said she'd write to me in London and I waited and waited but no letter came. Then, yesterday, I met Mrs B. and she told me Audrey had written to me the very day I left and been very worried because she had no reply from me. And I had been prepared to hate her (without succeeding, of course) because she had, as I thought, broken her promise. It seems the letter was lost.

After three whole long weeks I've at last seen Audrey again and she was lovely. I still mean something to her, she still loves me and she is still my heart's darling, my great friend.

Robin was here today and we had a long talk.

I heard that Laurence Olivier and Vivien Leigh are on holiday at the Ferry Boat Inn in Helford, so this afternoon Connie, Audrey and I cycled there (and took our tea) but we didn't see them. Instead we met Miss Coward! What a consolation!

8th January 1944

I have seen them! And spoken to them! Listen: When Pam heard that Laurence Olivier and Vivien Leigh were at Helford she said:

"Let's cycle there and see if we're luckier this time than you were on Thursday." We went in the morning and arrived at the Ferry Boat Inn at about 11am. I asked the receptionist if it was possible to see Mr Olivier and Miss Leigh - and as I spoke they came into the foyer, looking exactly as they do in their films. We gazed at them, and were transfixed.

"These two young ladies would like to see you," the receptionist said. Both Olivier and Leigh turned to us.

"And where have you come from?" Olivier asked, with a wonderful smile. As Pam didn't speak I had to, though I didn't think I could, my heart was beating so fast.

"We cycled here from Falmouth and we'd like your autographs, please," I said. My voice sounded very strange to me.

"You cycled all the way from Falmouth? Don't call me to rescue you if you collapse on your way back, will you?" he said.

We laughed, and handed them our autograph books, which they signed. We thanked them very much but were too overcome to say anything else. They said goodbye and walked out of the hotel. We followed in a minute or two and watched them go onto the beach and get into a rowing boat. They saw us and waved.

"Want to join us?" Laurence Olivier called to us. We knew he was only joking so we just waved back and shook our heads. How I would love to have gone rowing with Laurence Olivier and Vivien Leigh, but my legs wouldn't have made it as far as the boat, as I felt quite weak in the knees with excitement. For the rest of the day I could think of nothing else, and I had to describe every detail of what had taken place between me and two of the most famous film stars in the world to everyone I met.

To make a perfect day even more perfect, Audrey came to tea in the afternoon, and as Miss Kitty was out we were alone together the whole time. Tomorrow I will tell you what we talked about.

9th January 1944

There's always something left in life when you think there isn't, there are always people who wake you up out of your despondency, to create new memories never to be forgotten. Yesterday was such a day.

Audrey told me about her affair with Betty - and I'm more bewildered than I was before. She was as scathing about Betty as Betty has been about her, and she refuses to believe Betty still loves her. Audrey hates her, and won't forgive her for telling lies about her family, for being rude to them and even cheating them over money. Audrey said she was aware how close Betty and I were recently and that's why she wouldn't have anything to do with me during that time. She considered it wasn't possible for me to be friends with both of them (my own opinion too), and she

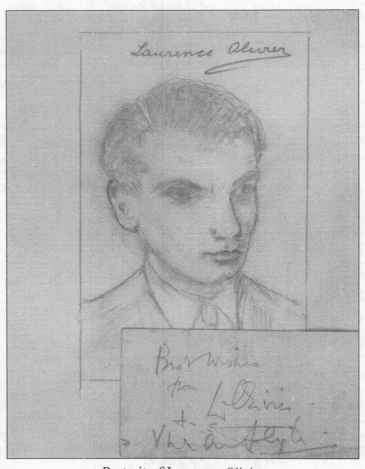

Portrait of Laurence Olivier.

may have to continue to ignore me at school so as not to clash with Betty. Their bust-up may be nothing to do with me but I'm hopelessly muddled up in it.

Oh, what can I do, what a terrible situation! I see no way out of it. I told Audrey that I felt differently about her than about all my other friends and she said she felt very flattered. She said she had wanted to tell me all this a long time ago, and I'm very glad she has done so now. I dared to ask her about John, and she said what John?

"The one you love," I said.

"I don't love anyone," she answered.

11th January 1944

We got free tickets to the 'Yankee Show' at the Drill Hall. Connie, Tony, Audrey and I went to see it and then had tea and supper at Audrey's, played Monopoly and listened to Laurence Olivier on the wireless - even more thrilling now that I've made his acquaintance.

Miss Davis is back. I fetched her and the children from the station yesterday. She had experienced nothing as exciting in London as my meeting with Laurence Olivier and Vivien Leigh.

Today I bought a book about Oscar Wilde by J. Reinier. At last I've found what I've been looking for, and I'm beginning to understand.

18th January 1944

School started on the 13th and one consolation is that I've been coming home for dinner. The sketch club, music lessons and German lessons have all begun again, after the nice long Christmas break. On Sunday Connie and I went for a ride; afterwards Connie came to tea, as did her sister Monica and Father Parkin. Miss Davis has so many ration books that there is never any shortage of anything at St. Joseph's, except of course the things one can't get, like bananas and chocolate biscuits.

Yesterday, at school, I found a letter on my desk addressed to 'Miss I.P, FCHS, Form IVb, from E.M. Lawrance, PRIVATE.' So I opened it when no one was around. The note inside said: 'Dear *'I'*, This is in strictest confidence (Hum hum). I've lent Muriel my

225

rough notebook to copy some history notes . . . Will you please ask her for the book and look back a few pages to an address starting 'Noel Buddle'. Will you *please* rub it out and forget it because we're not supposed to say where he is. I don't suppose Muriel would say anything but you know, 'Careless talk' etc. I know *you* wouldn't say anything. Thanking you in anticipation! Much love, Margaret. P.S. Don't tell Muriel why you want the book.' And I'm supposed to be an enemy alien! I felt very honoured. Noel Buddle is a relative of Margaret's in the Navy.

20th January 1944

It's all as expected - hell! I'm between Betty and Audrey all the time; if I'm with one I can't be with the other; if I please one I offend the other. Audrey won't go to the B.R. for dinner because Betty is there, Betty won't play hockey after school because Audrey is playing. I can never be with both at the same time. Each talks against the other to me, and I must remain neutral. But I will never give up one for the other. Betty is very decent. She said: "Go over to Audrey and forget about me, *'I'*. It will make things easier for you." I said I wouldn't. She said she very much appreciated my friendship. Poor Betty! According to Audrey, Betty is a wretched liar who doesn't speak one word of truth.

I don't believe it
IT IS NOT TRUE

It's only Audrey's bitter hatred towards Betty that makes her so unreasonable. But what can I do?

During prayers today both Audrey and Betty wanted me to sit next to them, so I had no choice but to go and sit somewhere different altogether. Next thing, Audrey followed me and sat down beside me.

Audrey says that Betty owes her 6/- and Betty denies it. So today I wanted to give Betty 6/- to give to Audrey. "Take it, give it to her, and settle the matter," I said to Betty. She flatly refused to take it. Another attempt at peace policy collapsed! I can't do a thing to help - I'm powerless. Having been dragged into this I don't know how to extricate myself.

29th January 1944 (Audrey's birthday)

Gladys E. was here to tea today. She's such a quaint girl, she always makes Connie and me laugh, and Miss Kitty teases her, but Gladys takes it well.

The 23rd January, which was last Sunday, is still a special day for me, and I mark it with a ring round the date in my pocket diary. This year it was an uneventful day. Miss McCreight was here for lunch as usual, and afterwards we had a long talk. I like talking with her because she's so interesting and amusing. She has a deep, loud voice, and always wears brownish sort of dresses that are too long for her.

Next week we're getting 1lb of oranges each! And tomorrow, Sunday, I'm going for a long walk with Margaret Cade and Rosemary Johnson (from my class) and Rosemary's dog.

4th February 1944

> 'If you can force your heart and nerve and sinew
> To serve your turn long after they are gone,
> And so hold on when there is nothing in you
> Except the Will which says to them: "Hold On!" '

As I've told you before, I'm no good at anything. I wish I could follow Kipling's advice, and I do hold on and fight back, and lose and start again at the beginning, but it gets me nowhere. I'm too young to think of such things, and yet I've often wondered how many aspirins it would take to die? 20? 50? 100? I don't want to run away from life with all its terrors and injustices, I want to have the courage to fight back, or better still to develop a thick skin and feel nothing, go through life like a block of wood, bumping against things but registering no pain.

It's school which mainly gives me my inferiority complex. Everything we do is competitive, and I hate competition. The very word makes me want to give up. I try to believe in people, but the more I get to know about them the more disappointments I suffer. There are so few people worth loving. Never mind about them loving me - I just want to love them, have them accept my love, believe in them. I'd like to believe in someone! There must be *someone*.

I am not even sure of God. Is He there? Does He exist at all? If so, why doesn't He make me believe in Him? If there's anything I truly believe in it's friendship. I'm very grateful for that.

There are four things which make me happy under any circumstances and they are: snow, music, sunshine and riding in cars, trains or buses. I shall now end this miserable entry with some questions:

> If one has an ideal, can one live up to it?
> Do some people get everywhere and others nowhere?
> Is religion a curse or a godsend?
> If there is a God, what kind is He?
> 'Fame is the spur' - is it? Or is that an illusion?
> Is there a heaven for everyone on this earth?

5th February 1944

I'm going to shock you now but I won't give you a long introduction. I'll come straight to the point:

I am NO LONGER A SLAVE TO AUDREY!!!

Do you realise what this means? I'm free - free from my madness. That is, I'm not quite free because I'm still very sensitive about what she thinks of me. It has been coming on for a long time, and when she ran down Betty so unreasonably and meanly, and dragged me into it, that put the lid on it. All my burning love has gone, leaving me burnt out and ready to close a chapter in my life.

Today, after going to the pictures with Angela Birch, she treated me to tea at the 'Old English'. We saw *Let's Face It* with Bob Hope at the Odeon. It was quite funny, but not really my type of film. The Odeon is more expensive than the Grand and the Fleapit, and when I took some more old clothes and things to sell at the secondhand shop in Killigrew Street the lady owner asked me: "Going to the pictures, are you?"

"Yes," I said.

"Which one?"

"The Odeon."

"Oh well, then I better give you an extra 6d." I thought that was really nice of her, and thanked her.

Monica W. was here to tea today. She still has those silly ringlets. I think she likes Robin T. Perhaps even more than likes.

I've started taking iodine for my thyroid gland. On Monday we all saw the school doctor. It was also Prize Giving Day, for which the Grammar School joined us. The next day we had our first hockey game of the term. Mary Prior fainted on the hockey-field. I saw her fall over but didn't know what had happened to her until later. I'd never seen anyone faint before. When she slowly keeled over I thought at first she was fooling.

Pam's mother had to come to school when Pam was examined by the school doctor. It took place in Miss Frost's office. Pam had to do exercises with nothing on - in front of the doctor, the headmistress and her mother - and she slipped and fell down. Terrible! Why is the naked human body so ridiculous? Poor Pam was very embarrassed, she told me later.

19th February 1944

Lieselotte is probably coming to Falmouth for a week's holiday. I can't wait!

When I lived at Tamblyns' I got to know a girl called Jean Lyon who was spending a holiday in Falmouth. She met a soldier on the beach and they got engaged. Today she and her uncle came to see me. She is getting married soon, in Crewe where she lives, and she has invited me to the wedding.

Who would have believed, years ago, that cheerful, happy-go-lucky me, now enjoys nights better than days? Most mornings I wake up very unwilling to face the day - the same monotony of every day: school, canteen dinner, school, home, practising, tea, homework - and to bed at last! And always studying and studying, worrying and worrying about the future, about everything. And horrible cold weather. But the nights are different, for then I live in my world of make believe, and here I feel quite at home. Here it is never lonely or cold or competitive, here there's no war and no cruelty, here I'm loved and happy and successful.

I wonder what and how people think of me and if they ever dream of me and what they say of me and if anyone hates me and if I really mean anything to anyone and what they will say of me after I am dead? Oh, I can just hear Miss Clift exclaim:

2nd March 1944

I've been terribly worried about Putzl - I've started calling Lieselotte by her old nickname again, which our mother called her in Vienna - because of the air-raids in London. I was so happy to get her letter. She's coming on the 22nd. (And she now calls me Uns or Unsl, my old nickname.)

How lovely it would be to get away from the horror of war, the horror of enemies, the horror of pelting rain and dark, dull days which people spend fighting or driving each other to distraction . . . How lovely it would be if everything turned suddenly around, and underneath the tumult and the mad fighting world a world of beauty and peace came to light, with sporting English gentlemen in knickerbockers happily playing golf or smoking by the fire, where one wakes up each morning to a laughing, sunshine place, where one can achieve what one wants to achieve . . .

My mind is made up about art. I'm NOT going to an art school when I leave school. I did very badly in the art exam - came third from the bottom with a C! What a humiliation. I shall never forget that feeling I had when I saw my name right down near the bottom of the list. I grew hot - frantic. The words "You mustn't let anyone see you like this, so humiliated," buzzed around in my head. There followed a long wet afternoon during which I managed to control my emotions. I was a little cheered up at the end of it to find that I had a Credit for English Language, and came fourth from the top out of 20. But I've finished with art. It's all my father's fault, anyway. He refused to listen to my protests and insists I should go to Art School. Well, I've been proved right. But it is a bitter victory.

4th March 1944

My father is back, on a visit. He's staying in Truro and Jane and Betty are with him. I fetched them from the bus today and afterwards we had tea and supper at a café in town and then went to the flicks. In the evening we visited Tamblyns and had cocoa and biscuits with them.

Connie had her birthday party last Sunday. Miss Kitty, Keith

The Ward
2.30 a.m
1st March 1944

My darling poor worried Urs,

Many thanks for your sweet letter & the 4 "La France". I also received your post card & telegramm, & am terribly sorry you were so worried. The raids really sound worse from a distance than they actually are. There was a lot of noise & a few incen? diaries round the Green, & on the Pad. Hotel, but otherwise nothing near. The Hospital that was hit, was a Maternity Home just outside London. Of course I don't think you soppy, darling; it does me good to know you think such a lot of me. But please don't worry too much, we can only hope for the best, & I promise to send you a post card whenever there has been a bad raid. As for your advice to take shelter, I'm afraid that is impossible, as I am on night-duty & have to stay on the ward with the children. However I am very glad to be on duty; it pre? vents me from thinking too much. You

Letter from Putzl.

231

and Sheila and I were there. The next day was a half term holiday. Miss Davis, the kids and Pam and I went to Lanner by bus and had a walk there. Later we had tea at the Eggins', listened to music on their gramophone and were taken home by Mr Eggins in his old-fashioned little car. Back at school on Tuesday, we were divided into houses. I'm in St. Michaels - the yellow one. I wanted to be in the red one, naturally. On Thursday we had our first house meeting. I couldn't go to the sketch club on Wednesday as I had my German lesson after school. In the morning we had a lecture by a Missionary. So much for school news.

I forgot to mention that, on the journey home in Mr Eggins' car, he said to me, I can't remember in what connection:

"You're not the only person in this car who's not English, you know."

"Who else isn't?" I asked, very surprised.

"Me," he replied. "I'm a Cornishman." That's close enough for me, I thought, but didn't say anything.

7th March 1944

Today I started learning harmony during my piano lesson with Miss Rogers. On my way home with Connie, who usually meets me after my music lessons, I wanted to discuss it with her as she has been playing the piano longer than I, but she wasn't much help.

Last Sunday I was in Truro for the day. I had lunch with my father, Jane and Betty at their hotel, and later we all went to a service at the Cathedral. They are returning to London on the 9th, my birthday.

My new resolution is to face life and everything in it with courage - face what I have to face, face it the best way I can and not avoid it. If I'm determined enough, perhaps I'll get what I want in the end. A few days ago I got two things I wanted - and my father provided them! The devil must have deserted him for a bit: I said I needed a pair of pyjamas and we went to town and he bought it for me. I said I wanted the art book *Serious Business* (12/6d!) and he took me to a bookshop and bought it for me. What am I to make of that? Perhaps he wants me to love him. Too late. I can never do that. He is now so well established in his business that he has had some little cards printed. He proudly presented me with one. I think he earns about £4000 a year!

Mrs Baden Powell is coming to the Princess Pavilion on Thursday.

11th March 1944

I had my birthday tea today, Saturday. Pam, Connie and Tony came, but I was studying all the time till teatime as exams start on Monday. After tea we played cards and then went to the flicks. Some Yankee soldiers sat near us and gave us chewing gum.

My father, Jane and Betty left on Thursday. I bought myself a little book called: *How to Draw Portraits*, by Charles Wood.

25th March 1944

Hurrah! Lieselotte is here, and Janet has had *twins*! I fetched Lieselotte from the station on Wednesday and she's staying 10 days. On Thursday she came to school with me to see some of her old mistresses. She wears lipstick now and I was a bit apprehensive about what Miss Davis and Miss Kitty would think of that. I don't think they liked it. Our exams finished yesterday. I celebrated their end with a flourish by upsetting a glass of water all over Miss Rogers during my music lesson - accidentally, of course. Today Lieselotte and I took our tea to the Stack and read there, and in the evening she went to a dance with her friend Betty Crothers. Tomorrow she's going to Betty's house for tea. Mr Churchill is going to speak on the wireless tomorrow. On Monday Connie's sister Monica is coming for tea; she and Lieselotte used to be quite friendly.

Miss Davis has been in a play again. Her sister Dollie Gray was in it too, or rather in the other play; it was a double bill. One of the other actors, George Collinge, works in Timothy Whites and is tall, blond and very good looking. Connie and I often go into the shop just to have a look at him.

1st April 1944

Today is a very sad day because Putzl returned to London. I went as far as Truro with her by train. After she left I looked around the

CORNWALL CONSTABULARY

Chief Constable's Office,

Bodmin.

14th March 1944.

Sir/Madam,

In view of the fact that you are a resident in an Aliens Protected Area, you have not been totally exempted from the provisions of the Aliens (Movement Restriction) Order, 1940, in accordance with the recent B.B.C. announcement, but it has been decided to exempt you conditionally from Articles 1 and 2 of the Aliens (Movement Restriction) Order, 1940, i.e. the requirement to obtain permission to be absent from your place of residence at night and the prohibition upon the possession of motor vehicles and bicycles.

You should, however, carefully study the conditions under which the exemption has been granted, as shown on the adhesive slip in your Registration Certificate, and in all cases of temporary absence from your registered address, except for fire watching duties, report to the Police in accordance with your obligation.

You are still required to obtain the permission of the appropriate Chief Constable before entering an Aliens Protected Area outside of Cornwall, and if permission is granted to you, to strictly comply with conditions set out on the permission. Separate permission will be necessary before using a motor vehicle or a bicycle in any other Protected Area you may be granted permission to visit.

Any Regulations which may from time to time be in force respecting entry into Defence Areas or Regulated Areas will apply to you as they apply to British Subjects.

Yours faithfully,

Major,

Chief Constable of Cornwall.

Miss I.S.P.
St.Joseph's ,
Kimberley Place,
Falmouth.

Letter from Cornwall Constabulary, exempting me 'conditionally from Articles 1 and 2 of the Aliens (Movement Restriction) Order, 1940, ie. the requirement to obtain permission to be absent from my place of residence at night and the prohibition upon the possession of motor vehicles and bicycles.'

town - and missed my train back to Falmouth. It was pelting. I had to go back by bus. Pam, Connie, Father Wiseman and Sally T., Robin's sister, were all at St. Joseph's today. They helped to take my mind off Putzl's departure. In the evening I called at Miss Gooden's for a book I'd left there, and was introduced to her handsome nephew who's a naval officer and was visiting her.

Tomorrow I'm going to a concert with Miss Davis (Audrey will be there too) and Denzil is coming home, and will be coming for supper. We break up for Easter on Tuesday - thank goodness. On Wednesday the 5th I'm going to the Labour Exchange to see what jobs are available for girls. If it doesn't rain Pam and I are going primrosing in the afternoon, and in the evening a Polish Catholic Airforce cadet boy is coming to stay at St. Joseph's, and Miss Davis and I are fetching him from the station. I wonder what he'll be like?

6th April 1944

Miss Kitty went on holiday today. Connie, some of the kids and I saw her off at Penmere Halt. After Connie and I had been to town on our bikes, she, Miss Davis, Tony, the Polish boy Michael, the children and I visited some friends of the Davis' called Horseford who live in a beautiful large house at Budock, surrounded by wonderful parkland. They have one daughter called Coraleen who's about 19. First we all went primrosing in the woods belonging to their grounds, then we had tea at the house, after tea Coraleen played the piano for us and afterwards we played ping pong in the Games room.

In the evening Denzil came to St. Joseph's. He treats me very politely now, as one might treat a young lady. Quite right too. I'm 17 now, no longer just a giggly school girl. No more fighting and romping.

Have I ever talked to you of smells? I'm very sensitive to smell. At this time of year I remember the smell of spring in Vienna, and it is so strong that I'm spirited back to the Arenberg Park, wheeling my dolls' pram among the lilac bushes on a warm spring day, wearing clean white socks and shoes. Spring never smells like that here. While we were living at Trevethan, the Tamblyns' boarding-house, my Uncle Felix once sent Lieselotte and me a wonderful box of chocolates from London. When we

235

Dramatic Entertainment

DRILL HALL, BUDOCK,

WEDNESDAY, MARCH 22ND. 1944

Doors Open at 7 p.m.   Commence at 7.30 p.m.

Programme 3d.

" THE REUNION "

(By Dollie Gray).

CAST

Matty (an old nurse)	EDNA HALSE
Lady Diana Charterhouse	KIT HANKIN
The Hon. Henry Charterhouse	GEORGE COLLINGE
Lucille De Valois	DOLLIE GRAY

Scene.—Mistress Lucille's Boudoir, London. Late evening, many years ago.

" LINDEN LEA "

(Produced by Mr. and Mrs. Gray.)   *(By Dollie Gray).*

CAST.

Antony Linden	H. REEVE
Janet ⎫	AGNES DAVIS
Cherry ⎬ his children	JEAN HADDON
Geoffry ⎭	FRED HOPKINS
Frances, his sister	EDNA HOPKINS
Bates	FRED HALSE
Peter Warwick	GEORGE COLLINGE
Katrina Poldini	KIT HANKIN
Trudy Layne	ELIZABETH WEAVER
Charmain Muller	DOLLIE GRAY

Scene.—The Hall at " Linden Lea." Spring, 1940.

Act I—9 a.m   Act II—7.80 p.m.   Act III—1 a.m.
One day later.

236

opened it I couldn't stop smelling the delicious chocolates.

"I could smell them and smell them," I told Lieselotte.

"All right, you smell them, I'll eat them," she replied. But of course we shared them, making sure we each had exactly the same number.

I've been going to the dressmaker's quite often of late as I'm having some summer dresses altered.

8th April 1944

We all went to Joan Cutler's wedding at the Catholic Church today. She's a friend of the Davis'. In the afternoon Connie, Michael and I went to town and afterwards I helped with decorating the (Catholic) Church for Easter. In the evening Pam and I went for a walk.

Yesterday, Good Friday, lived up to its name - it was a very good day: in the morning I was at Pam's with Connie. In the afternoon Denzil, Michael, Connie and I walked to her Aunt Horner's house at Penanze Point to pick some flowers in her garden - and returned home in a Yankee lorry! It was lovely. Not only did the Yanks give us a lift but also chewing gum and sweets. In the evening we all played cards. Tomorrow is Easter Sunday and a crowd of visitors are coming. I'll probably go to the Catholic Church with them all.

12th April 1944

Thank goodness, Michael has gone. We saw him off at Truro station today. Why do I say thank goodness? Because he fell in love with Connie and I was terribly jealous! Not that I specially liked him - he was only 16, spoke hardly any English and was short and ugly and very shy and quiet - but I was made to feel that I was worthless. I read somewhere once that we live in a world of rivalry and failure and by God, that's true. I'm not begrudging anyone anything, I only want some share of it. I didn't care two hoots about this Polish boy but I do care about being popular and do not wish to be put in the shade by other girls. Of course I know that different girls appeal to different boys, but every girl I know has some boy who likes her - I haven't. I'm not a flirt but I want fun, and boys are fun. It's obvious that I must be a very detestable person if Connie, who's unfeminine and doesn't care about clothes at all, is preferred to me. Miss Kitty says boys like Connie because she's a tomboy and a good sport. I think she (Kitty) felt sorry for me and tried to cheer me up. I'm quite old enough now to come out of my shell and get to know more boys. I've neglected it for so long. I'm determined to redress it when I've finished with school after the School Cert. - but I'm sure I'm not the type of girl boys like.

Just as the train moved off carrying Michael away - forever, I hope - he called out to Connie: "I write you letter!"

"You better send a dictionary with it!" she shouted back.

She doesn't care about him at all and seems hardly aware that he was so taken with her.

On Bank Holiday Monday, which was two days ago - I'm telling you things in the wrong order again - Connie and I cycled to Maenporth, where we picked primroses and visited the Thomsons. They're fun to be with, and very hospitable. The rest of the day I spent studying. On Tuesday we went to Helford by bus with Miss Davis and from there to Manachan by ferry, where we had lunch at a little art shop, went primrosing and had tea at a café. Miss Davis treated us. It would have been a lovely day, if Michael hadn't been there mooning over Connie all the time, and totally ignoring me!

I've been for a walk with Audrey. It was drizzling and windy and we watched Jeeps being unloaded from the U.S. ships over pontoon bridges onto the beach. We were to meet two of Audrey's 'boyfriends' but that didn't materialise. Afterwards I went to her house for tea and we listened to the gramophone. Quite like old times!

The boys we were supposed to meet were Jenkins and Tattersall.

14th April 1944

Today has been a rotten day. It poured non-stop and I was studying non-stop, apart from a short trip to the post office and a walk with Connie after tea. Do you know, today I felt I wouldn't mind being raped! Just to be able to boast of some sort of relationship with the opposite sex. If I said this to anybody but you I'd never again be allowed on their doorstep. But you know me so well and you know that I'm not really like that. I've been reading a book which was filthy in parts and it made me feel I want to be like that too. But I'm not. I feel much better now that I've written it down and opened my heart out to you. I no longer want to be raped.

Do you think I'll ever achieve anything? Ha, ha, funny. I wonder that I've hopes of anything still. No, I'm afraid I was not born with the seeds of greatness in me. These seeds are scattered all too scantily. I am near the bottom of the wheel and the wheel doesn't turn any more. God has other things on His mind. After all, there's a war on.

I have some pills in my room which I have to take twice a day - and they are poison - if you take too many, that is. It must be the incessant studying which brings on these black moods. Which reminds me, I must get back to my studies now.

20th April 1944

A road ban started today. I wonder how it will affect us?

Moira has been to St. Joseph's for a visit.

We've been going on different outings every day, taking lunch or tea and playing ball games, which is good fun. We've been to Flushing by ferry and to Devoran, Portreath, Mylor, Penzance and Maenporth by bus, children and all. Mrs Palmer, one of Miss Davis and Kitty's many sisters, came to breakfast today after early Mass. Mr Palmer always smokes Du Maurier cigarettes and he once offered me one.

This morning I was trying to mend a puncture in one of my tyres when two of the American soldiers billeted in the house at the bottom of our garden saw me - and came to help. They were called Rex and Sam. Sam is a huge fat fellow and very jolly. They mended it for me, for which I was very grateful.

Tomorrow I'm going to play tennis with Pam. We've decided that too much studying is not good for one, although she's much cleverer and doesn't have to work so hard. But I usually beat her at tennis.

27th April 1944

Back to school today, worse luck. At St. Joseph's we started having our meals in the garden again, last Saturday being the first time of the season. When the weather is fine I do my studying in the garden, too. Next week is 'Salute the Soldier' week and to mark the event there is to be a Grand Social at the Grammar School to which all at St. Joseph's - or most - are going. Keith Arnold (who still lives here) is a Grammar School boy.

Ruth has invited me to Portsmouth in the summer for a holiday! I'd love to go. We haven't seen each other since we were little girls in Vienna. I wonder what she looks like now?

On Friday 5th May my father is coming for a visit and staying in Truro as usual. Miss Kitty is coming back from her holiday on Tuesday.

One of the Yankees from the house at the bottom of our garden has given me some oranges! As if that wasn't treat enough, Mrs Bath gave me some chocolate the last time I was at Pam's house. So you see I've been lucky of late as regards food.

7th May 1944

Now that Miss Davis' school term has started too, I unfortunately have to have my dinner at the B.R. again. But on Saturday I dined in style at the Royal Hotel in Truro with my father, and today I had tea there and afterwards we went rowing on the Malpas river.

Tomorrow evening, after I've been to the dressmaker's, Miss Davis and I are going to visit the Lovells', Denzil's family. They never invite us to a meal; maybe they haven't got enough ration books. It's Pam's birthday on Tuesday and I'm invited to tea at her house, and shall have to excuse myself from my music lesson for once. I expect we'll do our piano practice and homework together.

10th May 1944

Today, after a long time, the topic of Audrey came up again between Betty F. and me. She said she loved her better than anyone in the world outside her family - still!

"Sometimes," she said pathetically, "I think if only she would smile at me - just once - I would kiss her feet."

I was terribly moved by that. For a moment I was ashamed of getting so much kindness and love from Audrey because I no longer long for it, or deserve it. Why does Betty continue to love

Audrey so much when she knows Audrey is not worthy of it? Reason has managed to conquer *my* love. I suppose there must be something magical about Audrey, there's no other explanation. When I looked at her after my conversation with Betty, I felt, for an instant, that I still - or again loved her. But it passed. We're very fond of each other, that's all. Poor Betty. I think the reason I really stopped loving Audrey is because I always felt inferior and slightly uncomfortable in her presence, and I couldn't take it any more. But as both Audrey and Betty have boyfriends now I don't see why I should feel sorry for either of them.

Roy has a son! Roy's name will shine brightly for me for a long, long time to come and I will treasure his memory forever. Perhaps as a tragedy, perhaps as a wound, but anyway as something very precious.

Don't ask me to translate all this into everyday, sensible language. I can't. So, goodnight.

13th May 1944

There is a sudden change in the weather today; after days of sunshine and glorious blue skies, it's raining hard. I went to the hairdresser's this morning. Usually I wash my own hair. When I was living with the Robins' they once took me to a hairdresser's and left me there. I was sitting alone in a cubicle for what seemed ages, and was terrified as I didn't really know what the place was and couldn't speak any English. I also fetched my repaired watch today. Every time I go to that watchmaker's he says to me: "The war will be over by Christmas."

"How do you know?" I asked him this morning.

"Wait and see. If I'm wrong I'll give you your money back for the watch repair." I'll keep him to that.

My father returned to London yesterday, his business in Truro being finished. He doesn't only come down to see me. On Wednesday evening he came to supper at St. Joseph's, although he hates the food there. When I walked to the station with him we talked about Miss Davis and Miss Kitty, whom he rather despises and calls poor spinsters.

"Miss Davis was engaged to be married when she was young," I told him, "but her fiancé was killed in the last war. She remained loyal to him and never wanted to marry anyone else."

241

"More likely she never found anyone else," he said, cruelly. He's always on about there being nobody for me to marry in Falmouth.

"Denzil certainly won't marry you," he once said.

"Denzil doesn't want to marry anyone," I had replied.

Yesterday I went to an art exhibition with my form, to see some French Impressionist paintings. It was marvellous. After school I played lovely tennis with Pam, Beryl and Margaret Cade and afterwards we went to Beryl's house to see her chickens.

When Miss Clift returned our English essays on Thursday she said only one person had an A. It was me. She read the essay out to the class. I was proud but embarrassed.

18th May 1944

Today has been a terrible day. I could do no work, I lost two games of tennis and I've been made jealous of Connie again because she has a Yankee admirer. Even my art mistress, Mrs Andrews', comment: "What a lovely drawing, 'I'," didn't help.

On Sunday I went to a boxing match on the Recreation ground with Connie to see Jo Lewis, the champion boxer - but we missed him. We came too late. Tomorrow I'm going collecting for the 'Mission to Seamen' with Pam. The area we are doing contains Yankee billets and the Yanks are always very generous, but we don't like going there at all.

I've decided that, since one cannot manipulate one's fate, one must always leave oneself an escape exit. If morphia seems the only way out but is unobtainable, look elsewhere. I'm not being morbid, just practical.

19th May 1944

Well, today I've made an utter idiot of myself again. As you know, I and Betty F. and some other girls usually have our dinner at the School Canteen in the town. Betty and I mostly don't wait for the others so we were in the front of the queue. We got our dinner and sat down at a table. We started eating and talked. Everything as normal. Suddenly Betty said:

"Shall I tell you something, Inky?" Thinking back now, I remember that a thought flashed through my mind, quick as lightning, a sort of premonition - I knew what she was going to say, and yet I didn't. I said, "Yes. Tell me."

"I like you," Betty said. She pronounced the words clearly, quietly and distinctly, and full of feeling. I could hear the emotion in them. I was so utterly taken aback despite my (correct) premonition, so confused, so dumbfounded, that I just sat and stared down at my dinner. No words would come. Then I laughed - I laughed and said the lowest, the stupidest, the meanest, the most inappropriate, the feeblest thing anyone could possibly have thought of:

"I don't believe it," I said. I caught sight of her face and she stared at me. Her eyes were full of pain. The laugh on my face disappeared. I realised what I had said, and I could have killed myself. I wanted to apologise, to explain, but it was too late - another girl had joined us and sat down at our table. I remained confused for the remainder of the meal - just as I had been when Audrey had once called on me unexpectedly. My mind stopped functioning. We ate our food more or less in silence and mechanically, and left as soon as we had finished. When we were out in the street I asked Betty to repeat what she had said. She repeated it, in the same tone as before.

"I'm sorry, Betty, I thought you might have been joking," I said.

"Of course not. I was perfectly serious," she protested.

"It's not that I thought you a liar, but I thought you might not have forgiven me for taking Audrey away."

"It never entered my head," said Betty. Actually it had never entered mine either - that was a white lie. I knew all along that Betty liked me - she had hinted at it often, and she always makes a fuss of me. But when she burst out with it so suddenly, I couldn't take it. Besides, compliments always confuse me.

"I like you too, Figgy," I said. "Very much." She smiled. Poor Figgy. I hope I am a satisfactory substitute for Audrey.

As you know, the Yanks are billeted near us and we've made friends with a few. One of them, a short, fattish, plain fellow called Charlie, stopped me the other day and asked me where my girlfriend was. Another time he asked me her name. He meant Connie. I haven't told her. Robin T., who has grown into quite a nice young man, called yesterday. I don't think he likes me any more.

I am going to look for God. I think perhaps He is there after all, and I need Him desperately. I'll gladly let myself be persuaded by anyone who talks convincingly on the subject, or even not so convincingly.

"If ignorance is bliss, 'tis folly to be wise." I'm going to be converted, too!

27th May 1944

I've won the whole school tennis tournament! Aren't you proud of me?

On Thursday we had a CEMA concert at school, with *real* musicians. It was wonderful. During the dinner hour I went to town to see about new glasses and met Robin T. He lent me a shilling.

I went to the pictures *alone* today, for the first time in my life. Sheila Arnold had her birthday party to which several kids came, and I was glad to miss some of it. Miss McCreight is sleeping here tonight because there have been air-raids in Penryn, where she lives, and she's frightened of being alone in the night.

I told Miss Davis I'm going to be converted. She said she was very pleased I was going to be a Christian but sorry I'm not going to be a Catholic.

In the evening I talked to some of the Yankees at the bottom of our garden. Miss Kitty gets on well with the lavatory orderly. There used to be railings outside the house the Americans have requisitioned but, like all the other railings, they've gone to be melted down for armaments. Similarly, also to help the war effort, people have been asked to hand in their old saucepans; these are needed to make into aeroplanes. It must be ghastly to be a fighter pilot - I'm glad I'm not a boy, as I was meant to be. Maybe, when things are at their worst, if a pilot of a spitfire says to himself: "I'm sitting in an ex-saucepan," it will make him feel better.

3am, Tuesday, 30th May 1944

What excitement! I haven't slept a wink tonight. First of all it was terribly, unbelievably hot all day and I couldn't get to sleep in the evening. I lay awake from 11-12.30, when all at once the siren went. There was terrific barrage and we all sheltered under the stairs - no time to go to the trench. At first I wasn't frightened at all, but when I heard the whistle of a bomb I thought: "Oh God, let us be killed outright, but not injured please!" They say if you hear the whistle the bomb won't fall on you, but that was no comfort then. The last night raid I could remember was when I was living at Tamblyns', and they invited me to sit it out in their bedroom, so the three of us sat on their bed for two or more hours, and the sight of Mr and Mrs Tamblyn in their night attire was so funny it took my mind off the bombs. However, tonight's raid was much worse. The bloody Germans got our oil tanks and the sky is simply ablaze with fire. I'm much too hot and restless to go to sleep and am not a bit tired, but I suppose I better stop writing now and try and get some sleep. School tomorrow. I had a lovely Whitsun weekend - more about that some other time.

I wish I could help put that fire out, but girls and women have to sit at home, waiting for the news the menfolk bring.

Goodnight. I mean, good morning.

2nd June 1944

Keith Arnold had his birthday party today; he's 14. Yesterday we had a bomb lecture at school, and house badges were given out. I got my horrid yellow one. I played tennis after school, and went to my music lesson. On Tuesday we were allowed to wear summer frocks to school as it is still very hot. Miss Davis and I went out after supper to look at the damage after the terrible air-raid of the night before.

On Whit Sunday, which was Sheila's birthday, I went to Church with her, and Miss Davis and Connie fetched us. In the afternoon Connie and I went for a bicycle ride and visited Tamblyns, Gladys E. and Audrey. In the evening two of the Yanks came to supper, which we had in the garden. The next day, Bank Holiday Monday, Pam and I played tennis and afterwards we went for a ride on our bikes.

Next week I'm going for an interview with the Rector of the Parish Church, Canon Roxby, as he will be instructing me on the New Testament before my baptism.

What are memories? They are unforgettable things, like Vienna, my life and home there, and summer holidays and school-friends and birthday parties and little incidents which stand out clearly forever. I am going back to Vienna after the war - but only for a visit. Just to tell her I have not forgotten her and never will. Only those who share your memories can understand them. And before they were memories I didn't appreciate them. Now the past has vanished except in my memory, the tide has swept it away. One day the tide will sweep me away too. I shall be completely washed away. Just a memory.

As I've said before, I'm not much good at anything. Every time I fail at something I think of my mother who bore me, of how upset she would be in her sweet way to see her beloved child doing so miserably. But I also see the mocking, annoyed face of my father, watching me, disappointed in me and my 'talents' which he so overrates. I hear his voice saying *"Na, das ist eine Schande! When *I* was a boy . . ." Then I know that failure must always be concealed.

Why do I only see myself as a failure and a good-for-nothing? Have I not succeeded at some things, with schoolwork sometimes for instance, have I not won a tennis tournament, have I not had a drawing sent in to a government sponsored competition? Can I not write good essays? Am I not popular with all my friends at school and make them laugh? Have I not had fun, occasionally, with boys? Yes, all this is true, and more. But it doesn't help. Even a failure sometimes does better than others and my 'better' indeed is very poor.

Enough of that. It is 9pm, I've just finished studying and not done two homeworks because I can't take any more in. Soon it will be night and bedtime and I shall be able to plunge myself into my imaginary world and for a time be at peace in my place of refuge from which I so soon have to wake. This other lovelier life, however, must by no means interfere with my daily routine.

> 'If you can dream and not make dreams your master,
> If you can think and not make thoughts your aim . . .'

I always try to keep this, the beginning of the second verse of Kipling's divine poem *If*, in mind.

---

* "You should be ashamed of yourself!"

One more thing, and then I must finish for tonight: The other day somebody was talking to me about their wonderful home and family and about an air-raid when a bomb just missed their house. For a fraction of a second, a dreadful sentence flashed across my mind, one I would never dare to repeat to any human being, and one which I know I didn't mean - couldn't have meant. It was: "I wish the bomb *had* dropped on your house and family!" Silence. Why did this enter my mind at all? I'll tell you why: every time somebody speaks to me of their home and family I feel enraged - and then ashamed - as I have none. I tell God that I hate Him and that He has yet to learn what justice means instead of expecting it of us. Afterwards, of course, I'm deeply sorry for my wicked thoughts, and feel that I probably deserve everything that has happened to me anyway.

5th June 1944

I might as well tell you now what I didn't want to tell you earlier but after all, I started you originally because I *had* to write everything down, though I didn't know that at the time, and gradually you became my confidante, and now I couldn't do without you, for to whom else could I tell everything? Well, let's get to the point: as I mentioned before, on Saturday, 27th May, Miss Kitty and I were in the garden; she was gardening, I was cleaning my bike. It was a glorious, sunny evening. After a bit the fat Yank 'Sneezy', the lavatory orderly, came out for a chat. Presently he was joined by another young soldier who told me all about the USA and Hollywood in particular. Then they went away and 10 minutes later Sneezy returned with another soldier and I heard Sneezy say, pointing to me: "There she is, that's her." The young soldier said "How do you do?" to me, and I greeted him back. That was all. But I felt strangely happy afterwards. Something new had happened.

The next evening, as I came up the garden path, I talked to Sneezy and out came the nice young soldier. He asked me my name and told me his - Jim Hoxey. Then we had a long conversation and I discovered that this exceedingly nice young man was not only different from most Yanks but also highly intelligent and, I'd imagine, well bred. That evening he and Sneezy came to supper.

I suppose you're waiting for me to tell you that I've fallen in love with Jim. Well, you're wrong. I've been thinking of him ever since, I liked him very much, and I'd love to see him again - but that doesn't add up to love, does it? Anyway, he hasn't shown himself since. He probably has no interest in me whatever, and I don't blame him, or maybe he is kept busy with the Invasion preparations.

And why didn't I tell you all this before? Will you believe me if I tell you it was because I'm a bit ashamed of being interested in a Yankee soldier?

6th June 1944

The INVASION HAS STARTED! And I am its first casualty! Not in Normandy, but here in Falmouth! This is what happened: I played tennis after school, had my music lesson, and was cycling home near the Recreation Ground when a huge American lorry struck me from behind and knocked me off my bicycle. It stopped at once, and several Yankees jumped out, helped me up, put me and my injured bicycle into the lorry and drove us to their own American Clinic. Here my grazed knee was attended to and I was then driven home. Later they returned my bicycle, also repaired. What an adventure! The Yanks may not be very popular here, but they certainly behaved well over this accident. I could have been killed.

The King spoke on the wireless today. The war is really coming to a head now. Surely it can't be much longer to the end?

I haven't seen Jim Hoxey again. How silly of me to think he might be interested in *me*! I could write pages on the theme of 'I'm no good'. Minor things are enough to discourage me nowadays. But one day I'll catch up with that other elusive good life, and I'll look back on the old one and wonder why I ever allowed it to torture me so. In the meantime, I *do not* wish to make a martyr of myself and I really must try not to moan so much.

What will people think when they read this diary after my death . . ?

7th June 1944

I was walking home this evening, when I met a young, laughing boyish Yankee Doughboy. We stopped and chatted - for quite a long time. About everything. Then . . . he asked me to go to the 'movies' with him . . . I thanked him and agreed.

The Yank was Jim!

10th June 1944

The 'Flying Bombs' have started over London!

On Thursday some ATS girls gave a lecture to us at school. In the evening I heard Liszt's *2nd Hungarian Rhapsody* played on the wireless. I love that piece of music. It inspired me so much that I composed a waltz today - my first musical composition . . .

Yesterday I saw Jim again. He had his coat on. Last time he said he was only waiting for his coat to come till he could go to the 'movies' with me.

But there's a difficulty. When I told Miss Davis an American soldier had asked me to go to the pictures with him she put her foot down and flatly refused to let me go. I argued, but she remained obstinate. I lost my temper and we had a terrific row. She said I should invite him to tea or supper or a game of ping pong first, so as to get to know him, but I was too angry by then to agree to this, even though that idea quite appealed to me.

"What will people say if they see you at the pictures with an American soldier we don't know?" Miss Davis cried. Of course there would be endless gossip, I know that. I would probably be called a prostitute. My name would be mud. This then is the situation. So, when I saw Jim again yesterday my first thought was: "Oh my God, he's got his coat!" I had no idea what I would say if he suggested the flicks again - but he didn't; and I said nothing about his coming to tea or supper at St. Joseph's. Stalemate. Nothing ever runs smoothly with me. But somehow, because of having met Jimmy, I'm almost convinced again that there is a God. All these little difficulties will soon pass - in fact they make it all the more exciting and romantic. (That these difficulties may get bigger and insurmountable I forbid myself to consider.)

People are always saying they wished the Americans would leave. But I don't.

13th June 1944

Sunday was a special Prayer Day for the Invasion, and Sheila and I went to Church. Miss McCreight came for lunch as usual, and the Horsefords (from Budock) and some friends of the Davis' called Bradley, were here for tea. Mr Bradley is the manager of Barclays Bank.

Today is my mother's birthday. Where is she, and how is she spending it? My poor mother. She was not born under a lucky star, any more than I was.

I haven't seen Jimmy since Friday. Charlie loves Connie but Jimmy can't love me or he would have come. I look for him every day, every evening. But he is nowhere. Yank after Yank passes by our gate but none of them is him. I watch endless convoys of lorries and jeeps go by, all ready to go to France taking men to face death in the Invasion, and I hope against hope that Jimmy is not among them. I stare at every soldier until the convoy has passed. I accompany them in my thoughts for they are going to fight my bitterest enemies, and I wonder if Jimmy is perhaps already lying dead on a battlefield in France. With every convoy leaving my hope of ever seeing him again is reduced. But I bet if he *was* in one of those lorries going to France he would be laughing all the way! *He* wouldn't sit there sour-faced and afraid like those others I saw passing by - no, he would laugh, as he always did.

17th June 1944

Today, just as I was going out on my bike, Charlie came over to me and said he'd made a mistake, he did know Jimmy (he'd previously said he didn't) and then he suddenly said: "Here he is coming right now . . ." I turned round - and faced Jimmy. Charlie went away, and we were left alone. "What about the movies?" he asked me. I told him that, as my glasses were being mended (true) I couldn't go just yet but could he come for a game of ping pong this evening? He could. He came promptly at 7pm. We played a few games and then we had a long talk in the garden shed. He told me that he's an orphan, and never had a proper home, being always boarded out with various relations. He comes from Rhode Island, America's smallest state. We also discussed religion and music. We learnt a lot about each other. He stayed for supper, and then he asked Miss Davis if he could take me out. SHE REFUSED! Very politely, of course, but she refused. Can you imagine it! Jimmy said nothing, but I, almost crying, flared up. I could have saved myself the trouble - Miss Davis, for once, was unrelenting. Jimmy and I talked for a long time in the garden.

At 11pm I saw him out. He pressed my hand and said:

"When shall I see you again? When *can* I see you again?" I thought for a moment . . . then . . .

"Tomorrow at 7pm at the Park corner," I said.

As this will be a secret meeting I expect Miss Davis will turn me out if she discovers, but I don't care. Jimmy and I want each other and will see that we get each other.

Will I ever have an inch of happiness without a yard of misery with it? I doubt it.

His real name is Jerome Hoxey.

20th June 1944

I didn't go to meet Jimmy at the Park corner.

Today is the 5th anniversary of my arrival in England. What a lot has happened since that day!

Although I haven't thought much about Aunt Liesel since she left Falmouth, I suddenly remembered that, when we parted on the station, she said I should write to her if ever I needed anything. Being desperate about Miss Davis' narrow-minded and unreasonable refusal to allow me to go out with Jimmy, I wrote to her asking for her advice. If she's on my side Miss Davis will have to give in.

Next Thursday I am going to the rector's for my New Testament instruction.

Charlie gave me an orange yesterday. When he once asked Connie what she would like him to give her, expecting her to say nylons or cigarettes or tinned food, she asked him for a telescope! She's interested in astronomy, and we've sometimes been stargazing together. A week later he presented her with a telescope! Connie is much luckier with boys than I am. Maybe I don't give out the right signals.

25th June 1944

I sulked for a week after my row with Miss Davis. I told my father the whole story in a letter and asked if I could bring Jimmy to Truro when my father comes down next week. *He agreed!* The thing was, how to get the message to Jim . . . I sent Keith and Tony up to the American billet several times, and at last Tony managed to get my note to him in which I asked him to come to St. Joseph's on Saturday evening at 8pm. He never came. I called it 'The Broken Tryst', after the poem by Arthur Symons. When one is sad, a sad poem can make one feel better, which is strange, isn't it?

Then I did something of which I am so ashamed that I nearly didn't tell you - even you! *I went to the billets myself!* I asked the first Yank I saw for Jim. Only God will ever know how dreadful I felt. I shudder to think of it. I must have been off my head. Presently Jim appeared and he was different! He wore not the laughing boyish face I liked so much but a dead serious mask, and he was quite abrupt. I told him about the arrangement I was hoping to make and apologised for coming here.

"I feel very cheap," I said.

"Well, that's up to you," he replied. He must have felt very awkward and been annoyed, to talk to me like that. Charlie writes Connie love letters but she doesn't care for him - maybe I should take a leaf out of her book. Jim said he would let me know through Charlie if he can come, but I don't want him to any more. I don't think I can ever face him again.

It's all Miss Davis' fault. I'll never forgive her for it. She has spoilt everything. I know he won't come. I'm quite ready for Charlie's message: "Jimmy says he can't come." No note, no greetings. All right then. Goodbye, for all I care.

27th June 1944

Today I had my French and German Oral Examinations for the School Cert. They were OK. Even the French was quite easy.

I visited my father at the Royal Hotel in Truro, and told him Jim was away. I had tea at the hotel, and we went for a walk.

I spend most of my spare time studying. Father Wiseman - who thinks I'm a heretic because I'm going to become a Protestant and not a Catholic - and Gladys E. were here for tea, but I didn't spend much time with them on account of my schoolwork. Tomorrow we are going to be given our School Cert. timetables.

The first exams start on 10th July.

A dashing Indian came to school on Thursday and gave a lecture on India. Today we had an art exhibition at school and some of my pictures were in it.

I had a house point taken off for fighting!

Aunt Liesel has written to say Miss Davis is making a mountain out of a molehill and she sees nothing wrong in my going out with an American soldier. Unfortunately her letter has come too late.

I've been consulting Miss Hankin, who's a social worker, about opportunities in social work for me when I leave school but it would take a long time to get qualified. I'd rather be an authoress, anyway.

Miss Davis is taking me to the pictures for a treat. I think she is sorry for what has happened between us.

9th July 1944

'Man proposes - God disposes.'

Before I explain, let me assure you of one thing: I'm never going to be a slave to any man who doesn't need me as urgently as I need him. Well, Charlie had apparently been talking a lot about me to Jimmy, and today Connie repeated to me the following conversation between them:

Charlie: "Have you seen your girl lately?" (He always calls me Jim's girl.)
Jimmy: "No, not lately."
Charlie: "Why don't you go to see her?"
Jimmy: "Because I'm not going to that house again." (I *knew* that was the root of the trouble.)
Charlie: "Well - do you want to see her?"
Jimmy: "Yes, I do."
Charlie: "OK, I'll talk to Connie and 'I'. and see what I can do about it."

The result - Connie's mother invited us both - Jim and me - to their house. When I entered their drawing room Jim was already there, waiting for me. He looked at me and smiled and in that smile all my troubles melted away. I told him that everything was OK now. Because of the others there we couldn't really say much else. Presently Monica, Connie's sister, joined us. She's 21 and very pretty. We all played cards. At 9.30pm I said I had to go. Jimmy got up and came outside with me.

I'm not a complete fool in these matters and, although I hate to say it, all the thrill has gone out of what little relationship we had, both for him and for me. His eagerness to take me out seems to have vanished too. All this I have Miss Davis to thank for but I'll forget that, like the good Christian I'm going to be. I'll obey St. Paul's Epistle and 'repay evil with good'. Anyway, we didn't make a date because he didn't know when he was going to be off duty. He claimed he didn't send me a message because he hadn't seen Charlie. But that's all over now.

My first real relationship with a man has not gone well, has it? It would have been surprising if it had: why should a handsome young soldier take on a plain, bespectacled, homeless refugee for his 'girl'?

14th July 1944

The School Cert. started on Monday and goes on till Friday the 21st with exams nearly every day. I didn't have any today, however, so in the morning I helped Miss Davis with the children during lessons, I spent the afternoon with Audrey at her house, and in the evening I went collecting with Sheila. My father went back to London on Wednesday. He has invited me to spend a holiday in Tenby with him, Jack and Jane and Jack's sister and husband, the McKennas. I shall be joining them there on the 22nd July, the day after the School Cert. finishes. I'm looking forward to it.

20th July 1944

Today an attempt has been made to murder Hitler, with dynamite, but it failed! Oh, why did it fail? Just think - if it had succeeded the war might be over today! There would be no more fighting, no more air-raids, no more rationing or blackout, we could get news of my mother, and then, and then . . . But what's the use of dreaming, Hitler is alive and the war goes on.

Sometimes, during my piano lessons, Miss Rogers plays a piece of music to me and then she asks me: "Did you like that?" She obviously does, and I always dutifully reply: "Yes," although usually it's some boring little-known piece by someone like Kuhlau or Diabelli or Field and I don't much care for it. The next question is: "Would you like to learn to play it?" Having said I liked it I now have to produce another lie, and again I say: "Yes." Last time this happened, as I sat listening to her, I thought the concerto or whatever she was playing was particularly uninteresting and I decided to be honest for once and admit I did *not* like it. She finished, turned to me with a smile and a hopeful look and asked me:

"Did you like that?"

"Yes," I replied, "it was very nice."

Who sent me a guardian angel at just the right moment?

"I'm glad," said Miss Rogers, "because I composed it."

There was an air-raid during the history examination and the whole school trooped to the trench bordering the hockey field. We were on our honour not to discuss the examination while in the trench, but we couldn't have done anyway because a mistress stood guard. The air-raid lasted nearly two hours and played havoc with the timetable, but as far as I was concerned it was a welcome interruption. Tomorrow is the last exam and on Saturday I'm going to Tenby.

25th July 1944

Welsh Holiday

I arrived here after a very long and complicated journey on a crowded train and was met by my father, Jack and Jane. We went straight to the hotel and had tea. Tenby is a small beautiful coastal town in South Wales. I have a delightful view from my bedroom window. It's wonderful not to have any more studying to do - I'm so relieved that the School Cert. is over, though I'm sure I've failed it.

On Sunday we went to see a Greek Temple in the morning and in the afternoon we played cricket on the beach. There was a very cold wind. I had never played cricket before and was hopeless and felt a fool. Later we went for a walk and fed the seagulls, which was much more relaxing.

Today my father was away in Haverfordwest on business. Jane took me shopping for a new bathing costume. I have only one horrid old one in which I'm very ashamed to be seen, so that I pray for bad weather even though I love swimming so much. Today the weather obliged, and I went sightseeing with Jack - to a church and a museum.

Yesterday was the most exciting day so far: we went sailing and fishing and I caught a mackerel! We caught ten in all. I've never fished in my life and certainly didn't expect to catch anything.

Jim McKenna spends all his time on the golf course, and tomorrow I'm going to watch him play golf.

29th July 1944

Tomorrow has been and gone - and it was wonderful even though there was a howling wind and it poured with rain and I got drenched. I went to the golf links with Jim McKenna, Jack's brother-in-law who's a doctor, and also there was a professional golf player, a soldier in the tank corps, called Sutherland. He's very tall with thick black hair, brown skin, large white teeth and dark eyes. He's about 25. He explained the mysteries of golf to me and he didn't treat me like a child, as I expected him to do. He was kind to me and that is why I liked him. I enjoyed his company, probably because I am secretly a bit sick of being with much older people all the time and was delighted to find someone more of my own age. After the round of golf, Jim McKenna, Sutherland and I went out to tea. I wasn't going at first but Sutherland smiled at me and said: "Oh, come on." So I went, and had a good time. Now, if I'd been a pretty, bright young lady, well-dressed as a girl of 17 should be, no doubt he'd have asked me for my address. As it was - what could I expect? Fat, plain, childish and dull that I am, the poor fellow could but be kind to me. I wish he had liked me though.

I've been sailing with my father and Jack again and this time it was very windy, we caught nothing, Jack was seasick and I felt it!

I get to bed very late every night - never before midnight - as we always have a walk after dinner and feed the gulls and then stay up talking in the lounge for ages - my father and I, Jack and Jane and Jim and Doris McKenna. The other night we were talking about whether people dream in colour or not, and this led to my telling them that I not only dream in colour, I also saw the days of the week and months in colour. This was met almost with disbelief. I was asked to name the days and months with their colours. I suppose Jim still didn't quite believe me because the next evening he asked me to go through them again, which I did - Monday blue, Tuesday white, Wednesday red, and so on. He had actually noted them down the previous evening, and as of course they were the same on the subsequent day he at last had to believe me.

One morning this week - it must have been Sunday - my father and I and Jack and Jane were sitting in the hotel garden and the church bells were ringing out a hymn tune. I sang the words to it as we often sing that hymn at school. Afterwards, when we were alone, my father said to me:

"I was so proud of you when you sang that hymn. Jack and Jane will understand now that we are no longer Jews." While I'm pleased that he has something to be proud of in me, this seems a very unworthy thing. He wasn't proud of me the previous evening, however, when he noticed that my pale blue dress was spotted all down the front when I came down to dinner. His nostrils dilated and he glared at me.

"How can you come to dinner looking like this!" he whispered to me.

"It's only water." I said. "I've just been washing my hands."

He said no more then, but later he gave me a lesson on how one should always wash one's hands before putting on one's clothes, or else cover the clothes.

I feel very dowdy and insignificant in the company of these friends of my father's, and the fact that he's continually out to impress them makes me wonder whether he doesn't feel a bit inferior to them himself. When I was watching them all on the beach the other day, the two sets of husbands and wives so loving and fond of each other, and my father there alone (except for his ungainly daughter), I felt sorry for him. I know how it feels to be out of things. But then I hardened again, and remembered that he never seemed to want his wife - my beloved mother - when he had her, and that all they ever did was quarrel. No doubt he still doesn't want her; he hardly ever mentions her, and if he does it

The Day of Judgement

... And when the end of the World came & all the inhabitants of the Earth were gathered together upon the meadow of Peace & Safety, there suddenly appeared a light & behind it was the Lord. And the crowd sprang up & sang beautiful words & fell upon their Knees & worshipped. And God came ~~closer~~ closer to His children & touched them with His hand & gave them His blessing. And the wicked were good & the evil repented.

And I rose from my knees to see God in His full glory & my feet trembled beneath me because there was fear in me of the Almighty. And I walked towards God & stood opposite the full & His full Glory & God said to me "my child", and I answered: "Mother!"

P.T.O.

Extract: The Day of Judgement.

isn't anything nice. But it doesn't matter to me any more.

Today we are leaving here. We are catching the 4.30pm train to Carmarthen and staying the night at the Ivy Bush Hotel. On Monday I'm returning to Falmouth.

I almost forgot to tell you that, last Tuesday during a walk, I saw, and recognised at once, guess whom? Richard Greene! He's as handsome as he is in his films. Unfortunately I had no paper on me, or I should have asked for his autograph.

I don't suppose I shall ever see this place again. It was quite a nice holiday. I don't suppose either that I shall ever see Mr Sutherland again. Perhaps I just told you about him to be able to say, romantically, as one might say in a novel: "I met a nice man on a summer holiday in South Wales . . ." But the truth is there was nothing in it at all.

1st August 1944

I came home yesterday, after a journey lasting all day. Miss Davis and Sheila fetched me from the station. In the evening Connie came over. Today I went to town with Pam in the morning and then we went to school and played tennis and cards there. In the afternoon we went to see *The Mikado* at the Women's Institute, performed by members of our school, and later Sheila came with me to fetch my case from the station - and who should turn up there, to help us carry it home, but Jimmy! He had called for me at St. Joseph's as soon as he heard I was back (from Charlie). Perhaps he likes me a little after all then?

Afterwards we went to the pictures together! My first date! I was in such a state that I wore the first things I could lay my hands on - a shapeless grey skirt I'd made myself during Needlework at school, and my school blazer. I was much too embarrassed and shy to dress up, anyway. Soon after the film started Jimmy put his arm around me. I told him not to, so he stopped. It didn't mean anything, it's what all the Yanks do when they take a girl to the flicks, but I didn't like it.

After we said goodnight he said he would call for me again soon.

3rd August 1944

Lieselotte and her hospital are going to be evacuated to

259

Birmingham because of the doodlebugs. Thank goodness.

Today was the last day of term, and my last day at school. I said goodbye to all the mistresses and I got my last ever report. Some of us 5th formers helped Miss Rowe with the Kindergarten. Tomorrow we, the 5th form, are going seaweeding with Miss Clift, and taking our lunch to eat on the beach. Afterwards I expect we shall have a swim, weather permitting.

When I went for a walk with Pam and her neighbours' dog last night we met John Tresidder, Janet's brother. He looks exactly like her. Pam thought him so posh that she didn't open her mouth

5th August 1944

I'm in bed, feeling ill with hay-fever or flu or sunstroke or something. Last night I dreamt I was with my mother. I threw my arms around her, as I used to, childlike, years ago when life still had mercy on me. I cried out: "Don't leave me, mother, don't leave me ever again!" I looked at her and she was standing there laughing at me, heartlessly laughing. Then she walked towards the door, away from me. I felt that she didn't care for me but I loved her so frantically that I ran after her and wouldn't let her go.

Perhaps, one day, mother, I will be able to pay back the unselfish love you gave me when I was a child; perhaps, one day, I will be able to make your life a paradise as you made mine so long ago, when I was a child.

Keith came home from camping today, and Connie is leaving for *her* camping holiday. I've never had any desire to go camping.

9th August 1944

I've entirely given up the idea of going to Art College. Some time ago I considered applying to Hornsey in London but I know I'm not good enough. I've been to see Mr Hooper who keeps a grocery shop and whose daughter Wendy used to be a pupil at St. Joseph's, about a job there until something else turns up, but I don't really want to work in a shop. Miss Davis is going to take me to see Mr Bradley at Barclays Bank to discuss the possibility of my working there, but as I'm no good at maths I don't think that will do either.

Denzil is home, Father Oddie and three of 'his boys' have

come to stay, I've had my first lesson with the Rector at his house on what being a Christian involves, and I've been to Flushing by ferry twice this week with Miss Davis and some of the kids, visiting the Kellys and taking a picnic lunch which we ate on the beach, once in a drizzle and once in a cold wind. It was fine on Sunday though, and some of the time I sat in the garden, writing a story.

The following story I didn't make up, but is said to be true: a British soldier and a Yankee one were having a drink at a pub in town, when the Tommy dropped sixpence. He got on his hands and knees and looked for it under the table. When he hadn't found it after some minutes of groping around in the dark, the Yank struck a match, lit a £1 note and said to the Tommy: "Here, you need some light down there to help you find that 6d."

10th August 1944

It was very strange. The day after I was ill in bed I awoke with a lovely feeling of peace and relaxation. It seemed as though I was a child in Vienna again, with no cares or worries. Something was comforting me but I don't know what. It won't last of course, so I better make the most of it while it does. I can feel it beginning to slip away already.

Denzil still hasn't been to visit us. I was looking forward to seeing him again even while I was at Tenby, and am very disappointed. When I was at the flicks with Jimmy I saw someone who reminded me of Denzil, and it was like thinking of home from a strange country. Denzil was 'home', Jimmy 'the strange country'.

Pam and I went to see a War Exhibition at the Drill Hall today.

I lent my bicycle to Father Wiseman as his had a puncture.

11th August 1944

This morning Charlie said to me: "I heard from Jimmy today." He always talks about Jimmy to me.

"*Heard* from him?" I said in surprise. "Isn't he in Falmouth?"

"No. He's left," replied Charlie. There were other Yanks about and I didn't want to ask any questions in case it got back to Jimmy that I'm interested in his whereabouts. If he doesn't take the trouble to say goodbye then I shall take the same attitude. A good thing I didn't like him better than I did. I'm only sad that *I* wasn't more to *him*. Oh, to hell with him, let him be gone and I hope he never comes back. I mean it.

Audrey was here this afternoon. The Yanks have a rubbish heap just beyond our garden where they dump all kinds of things they no longer need, and we spent some time there helping ourselves to what we wanted. Later Keith joined us and he found things of interest there too, which Audrey and I had rejected. There were combs with hardly any teeth missing, mirrors, knives with aluminium handles, a few pots and pans, tools, even some socks.

Tomorrow I'm going collecting for Miss Hankin's Society for Poor Girls.

15th August 1944

All the Yanks from the house at the bottom of our garden left today. Poor fellows, they looked awfully sad. Charlie called to say goodbye and we had a long chat. He said he'd write. He asked me if I'd like Jimmy's address. I said no. What should I do with his address? Besides, I have my pride. I'll never forget him though - he was my first beau. I can still clearly see his laughing, boyish face, and I remember how he consoled me and talked seriously to me in the garden after Miss Davis had refused permission to let us go out together, but it doesn't mean much any more. Poor Jimmy, he was lonely, he wanted a girl, and he found nothing in me to cheer him up. So he left. Simple.

We go to the beach every day - Miss Davis, Miss Kitty, kids, Connie, Pam, Audrey, I and anyone else who wants to come along. We swim, play ducks and drakes and eat our picnic. The best beach of all is Sunny Cove, which isn't a proper beach at all but a tiny patch of sand amid rocks, and I learnt to dive from there. Audrey is an excellent diver, and has been teaching me. I love Sunny Cove.

Next week I'm starting at Miss Hoare's Secretarial College at Truro twice a week, to learn shorthand and typing. Putzl went there too after she left school. My father thinks all girls should know shorthand and typing.

20th August 1944

This morning, Sunday, I went to Church with Sheila as usual and stayed at home in the afternoon, playing chess with a boy called Michael (another Michael) who's a boarder here, and a very good chess player. A new lot of Yankee soldiers has arrived at the house below. When Connie and I went out on our bikes in the evening some of them accosted us, chatting us up in their usual friendly way. I gave one of them a ride on my bicycle as he was very keen to try an English one.

Denzil still has not been to see us. Unless there's a very good reason for his mysterious absence the name of Denzil Lovell shall be banished from my thoughts.

If I wrote down what I felt about a certain subject I should, in ten years' time, call myself a stupid schoolgirl. In order to prevent this I shall say nothing about it and for once not waste paper on my silly thoughts. I feel better already for having suppressed them.

23rd August 1944

PARIS IS LIBERATED! It *can't* be much longer till the end of the war now.

Yesterday I spent the whole day in Truro at Miss Hoare's Secretarial College. There are about 20 girls in the class, all complete beginners like me. How I shall ever learn to touch type and write shorthand I don't know, because the one seems impossible and the other is unintelligible.

Oh God, I'm fed up, and I must turn to you - I don't mean to God, I mean to *you*, my darling diary. The future looks so barren and my life is not taking on any shape and all the time the rain is beating down. I feel like a maddened lion in a cage. I must get away, experience new things, meet new people. I like St. Joseph's, but I must get to know a wider world. I'm 17½ now and haven't earned one penny yet. What's more, I've probably failed the Cert. If there is a God I don't like Him any more.

26th August 1944

Life goes on normally and I'm by no means in the above mood all the time - it just comes over me now and again, when it rains incessantly and when I consider my bleak future. But back to the present. Last Thursday I was at Secretarial College and Miss Kitty was in Truro too, seeing her doctor. We met for lunch at Treleaven and I had a delicious mixed grill to which she treated me. The next day I got up at 5am to see Miss Davis off at Penmere Halt as she's going on holiday. Then I went back to bed. The rest of the day I spent with Audrey - we're the best of friends now - diving off the rocks at Sunny Cove, *smoking*, eating buns at the beach shop, going to the flicks and smoking again, having tea at her house and ending the day with more swimming, this time being joined by her friend, Kenneth Tattersal.

Now for something that's not personal for a change, at least not directly. Outside the Post Office this morning I saw a good-looking, well-dressed young man. I could see he was a visitor. Presently a pretty Wren came along. They went to meet each other. They smiled and seemed delighted to be together. I heard them talk quietly, in classy English. Then they walked off, hand in hand. Wasn't that a nice scene? I wonder if they were in love. I thought to myself:

Oh, if only I was that girl! If only I could have a good profession and a smart uniform for all to see where I belong (foreigners are not allowed in the Wrens), and a charming loving boyfriend to hold my hand and take me away to - - oh, anywhere! A job and a boyfriend, what could be more natural wishes? And yet nothing could be further away from me and more unattainable. Standing there outside the Post Office, I hated everything about my life, above all I hated my ignorant, good-for-nothing self.

I and my dreams! Dreams, dreams all the time. What am I doing here, dreaming and writing tommy rot about other people's beautiful lives instead of facing facts and fighting back? If I don't, how will I ever get out of that horrible life I've been born to?

30th August 1944

I've just come back from a Red Cross sale in Mylor which took place in Howard Spring's garden. He and his wife organised it. I went with the Kellys - Rosemary Kelly was in my class. He shook hands with me, as he did with everyone, but didn't remember me, of course. As I watched him walk about and talk to his friends, I thought: "Here is a genius, who was almost a beggar in his young days, who has grown rich and famous because he can use words to a wonderful effect and tell stories that make people forget their own lives. And yet, he gives no sign of feeling superior to us and succeeds marvellously in disguising his genius." But surely he talked about and did things which to him must be what baby talk and play is to the rest of us? The strange thing was, nobody else seemed to know or care who he was. He might have been a fish-monger. I wished I could have done something to make him notice me, but I was probably the least important person there. I'm a refugee, a foreigner, and though I have a tongue like everyone else I dared not use it, and though I have a heart like everyone else I had to silence it.

Howard Spring lives in a typical author's spot - one that befits the writer of that marvellous book *My Son, My Son*, which still haunts me. His house stands hidden behind the little Church, and there's a path right down to the rocky shore and the sea from his garden.

I forgot to go to the Rector's for my instruction on Christianity yesterday. I'd been to Truro all day at Secretarial College and that put it out of my mind, I suppose. However, I did a good deed and made a cake for Miss Davis.

There have been urgent appeals for people to give blood. You have to be 18, but I thought it was time I did something for the country, so on Monday I went along to the clinic on top of Killigrew Street. I was welcomed with open arms and ushered in. There were rows of people lying on sort of makeshift beds, looking white and lifeless to me. I got cold feet.

"What age do you have to be to give blood?" I asked the nurse.
"18," she said.
"Oh, I'm only 17," I said. "I better not then," and I turned to go.
"It doesn't matter, you can stay," said the nurse.
"I better ask my father first," I said, and hurriedly left. I felt very ashamed of myself afterwards. Did you know I was such a coward?

2nd September 1944

Father Oddie and his boys left today.

When Audrey and I were out on a walk on Thursday we made friends with a Yankee soldier called George, and he came to Audrey's house with us, had tea and afterwards we played

m

Monopoly. The next day George came again. This time we played cards and smoked George's American cigarettes and had supper. Afterwards Audrey and George saw me home.

I had a letter from the Refugee Committee today saying there might be a chance to find out my mother's whereabouts. I nearly wept with joy. I've imagined a reunion with my mother so often. Sometimes I think I shall go mad if I don't see her again soon. The letter almost made me forget the dreaded result of the School Cert. which is due quite soon, and the uncertainty of my future.

The Arnold children went on holiday today, and I've been to the dentist's to have my teeth checked.

3rd September 1944

Today is the 5th anniversary of the war. It was a Sunday too. We're all so tired of it, but we know we mustn't grumble. It will be over soon now - the news is so good.

There was a special celebration in Church this morning. The Lord Mayor was there.

Autumn has come. An awful gale has been blowing for two days but the leaves have not yet changed to their lovely colours. They are still wearing their green summer clothes. It is Sunday afternoon. There is no one in the house apart from Miss Davis and Miss Kitty. The children are all away on holiday. My life is my own, and - dare I breathe it - there's a chance of my going to live in Oxford at the end of September! I shall attend Secretarial College there and when I've finished the College will find me an interesting job. I still have nowhere to stay in Oxford, however. My father doesn't want me to live in London because of the bombs, and he thought Oxford would be a good idea as Uncle Bruno and Aunt Erna live there. Oh, how I long for a change! I hope nothing interferes with our plans, and that I shall have more success in my new life than I've had in my old.

As you know, Audrey and I are greater friends than ever and we go out together nearly every day. I can hardly understand any longer why I was in love with her. It's much better now, because I no longer see the extreme sides of her nature. Love makes you very vulnerable. Is it something to be avoided then? We often have serious conversations, and she told me once that the only boy she ever really liked was a Belgian refugee called René de

REFUGEE CHILDREN'S MOVEMENT, Ltd.

REGIONAL COMMITTEE No. 7

CHAIRMAN: LADY WARE
SECRETARY: W. BRYCE GIBSON
TEL: GLOUCESTER 2478.

Community House,
Gloucester

August, 1944.

Dear

     For the purpose of enabling German, Austrian and Stateless refugees to try and trace their relatives and friends in liberated EUROPE, a CENTRAL SEARCH BUREAU has been set up in conjuction with the BRITISH RED CROSS.

     We will help you with registering the names of people you wish to trace, giving preference to any of your close relations. If you want to register any members of your family or of your friends, we will provide you with the necessary Registration Cards and will gladly help you to fill them in should you require any assistance.

     Although we hope with you that this new Organisation will open up a new channel of communication between you and your people, we feel we ought to add a word about the difficulties of this task, especially in those cases where all trace has been lost for a long period; nevertheless, we hope with you that in the end we shall succeed in helping you to get news from those whom you left behind.

              Yours sincerely,

              W. BRYCE GIBSON

              Regional Secretary

Letter from Refugee Children's Movement.

Quaker, who used to go to the Grammar School. He was 20.

Today I heard the news that René was killed in enemy action in France. Poor Audrey. I shan't tell her.

I've taken to smoking lately - mostly secretly, but occasionally in public. Well, I must grow up, mustn't I?

7th September 1944

Mrs Hodgett, whom I had not seen for a long time, asked me to tea yesterday to meet an Austrian called Dr Stecker. He's an elderly man and had a very strong accent. We went for a walk together. I didn't want anyone to see me with him. How could I have anything in common with someone so un-English?

Today, during my lunch break at the Secretarial College in Truro, I went to a café for lunch with Miss Davis, Connie and Tony, which was much nicer than eating sandwiches over my typewriter.

8th September 1944

I've had a most wonderful and exciting day - thanks to my good friend Audrey. Listen: as you know (although why should you?) petrol is almost unobtainable and hardly anyone drives a car. However, the B. family have a friend called Mr Holloway who does have one, which he uses on business and can therefore obtain petrol for. He often travels quite long distances in connection with his work, and today he had to go to Fowey. Do you know who lives in Fowey? The authoress of *Rebecca* - Daphne du Maurier! Audrey said to me a few days ago:

"How would you like to come to Fowey in Mr Holloway's car, Nanks?"

"I'd love to," I cried. The car ride alone would be exciting enough, but Fowey! "Daphne du Maurier lives near Fowey," I said.

"I know, and I suppose you'd like to see her?" I didn't deny it and Audrey was quite keen, too. So, today we set off early in Mr Holloway's car. Connie came too. She and I sat in the back, which is where we like to sit best because we don't have to make conversation. We just sat back and gazed out of the window, our dreams and thoughts the only companions we needed. It was quite a long journey. We went by car ferry across Polruan, saw Sir A.T. Quiller-Couch's house, had lunch and then walked around the town while Mr Holloway was busy. We went to a bookshop and I bought a book called *Austria on £10*, by S.A. Clark. Last of all we went to see Daphne du Maurier. Mr Holloway knew where the house was. As we approached, I got more and more excited. My eyes were glued to the road. Any minute now I expected to see the iron gate leading to the drive that twists and turns until it reaches the house called Manderley. Perhaps Laurence Olivier and Joan Fontaine would be there to welcome us . . . And here we were at last. The real name of the house is Menabilly, and the drive, up which Audrey, Connie and I were now walking while our 'chauffeur' waited outside, was not nearly as long as I thought it would be. We reached the front door. Before ringing the bell, we looked at the large lovely garden surrounding the house. Some small children were playing on the lawn. Then we rang, and waited. I was appointed spokesman. A woman who I was quite sure was not Daphne du Maurier eventually opened the door.

"We'd very much like to see Miss Daphne du Maurier," I said.

"Have you an appointment?"

"No, we haven't. We'd just like to meet her and get her autograph."

"Just a moment." She went back into the house. We waited, without speaking, tense and thrilled. The woman returned.

"I'm sorry. Miss Du Maurier is busy, but if you give me your notebooks she will sign them." What could we do? We handed over our notebooks, and presently they were returned to us, duly signed. She had written in mine: 'Yours sincerely, Daphne du Maurier.' That's all. We thanked the woman and turned to go. She seemed to feel a bit sorry for us and accompanied us through the garden.

"Is Miss Du Maurier writing another novel?" I asked.

"Oh yes. She never stops," the woman replied. "These are her children," she told us, pointing to the little group we'd seen before. "They're all called after characters in Margaret Kennedy's *The Constant Nymph*. Do you know it?" We said we did.

"That's Tessa there," said the woman, pointing to the blonde girl nearest to us. I thought it a lovely idea to name your children after fictional characters. When we were part way down the drive the woman said goodbye to us, we thanked her for obtaining the autographs and rejoined Mr Holloway in his car.

"Well, did you see her?" he asked us, but I suppose he could tell by our faces - or at least by mine - that we didn't. I was very disappointed but it was a nice day all the same.

Miss Hankin, who's an actress in her spare time, has asked me to go to her house tomorrow and help her with her German accent as she's taking the part of a German in her next play.

14th September 1944

I've passed the School Certificate! What a relief. Among the few people who failed were Joyce G. whom nobody expected to pass - and Betty F. Poor, poor Figgy. Later today I'm going to the Rector's for a baptism rehearsal; the real thing is next Friday, 22nd September, at the Parish Church. On 28th September I'm leaving Falmouth! I can hardly believe it. All this week I've been trying to sort things out and do some packing. In between I've been going out with Pam and Connie, once to Feock, and been treated to chips and teas at cafés by various people, in view of my imminent departure. Last night Connie and I went to the Princess Pavilion to see *Rookery Nook*.

The Battle of the Flying Bombs seems to be over, for the time being anyway. Lieselotte will be moving back to London again now, with her hospital. These bombs never fell on any other towns, only London.

On the morning that I heard I'd passed the Cert. I went to town with Robin T. How much more I'd appreciate his love now than I did three years ago. That, of course, is long finished. I'd love to say to him: "Do you remember, Robin, when you were a little boy in short trousers, how you used to write me love letters, give me presents and call me 'darling' in your soppy schoolboy fashion?" Perhaps he's ashamed of that now. After all, he's a tall young man of 17!

I've never heard any more of Jimmy. I don't care. I was just a girl who helped him pass the time. It's a pity I was mistaken in him as I've been in so many people, but I still think he was a nice, intelligent fellow. I've often regretted that I wasn't dressed better the time I went to the pictures with him. You remember I'd just returned from the station with my case, and I went as I was - in my childish grey skirt, my shabby school blazer, a grubby blouse, and no stockings or socks.

That was how I appeared on my first date! But never mind the past now - I must face the future, and forget the past.

21st September 1944

Only two days ago I assumed it was all over between Robin and me, and today it seemed it isn't - quite. Although I've never particularly cared for Robin, when someone stops caring for you it is always painful, and I've secretly always hoped to win him back. That is because I'm such a vain creature. This I own. Anyway, yesterday, as every Thursday, he was at St. Joseph's for lunch after attending Art School. I was cleaning my bike in the shed when he saw me and came over to me and we chatted about this and that. We were quite at ease with each other and all the stiffness had gone, which had been the result of not seeing each other for so long. Later, when I was in my bedroom, there was a gentle knock on the door. It was Robin. He came in for another chat. He asked me to go to the Art School with him, and to the pictures afterwards, but I couldn't. He asked me to write to him after I leave Falmouth. He asked if he could borrow one of my books. He told me he had been taking Monica W. - that old fashioned girl with the ringlets - to the pictures, but he wasn't showing off, just confiding in me. Monica teaches at St. Joseph's school now. I must say I liked him better than I ever used to. I'd like to know if he still cares for me or if all his childish fancies have passed away? He will be here on the day of my departure. I wonder why it pleases me to think of our new relationship? You must think me a fool. No, not you - you understand. Anyway, I'll never be serious about love or men again, or not for ages and ages.

Last Sunday a new priest was here to tea - a German. Clocks were put back one hour so we have longer daylight now.

In the evening I went for a walk with Pam and Beryl. On Monday my father, Jane and Doris arrived. They are staying at the 'Royal' in Truro, as usual. I had dinner with them, going there by train and returning by bus. Yesterday I went again, and had some grapes! I had forgotten what grapes taste like. Jane and Doris took me to the shops to try and get me some shoes, but we couldn't.

I've been to school to see Miss Frost and the girls from my

form, who are now in the 6th form, and joined some of them in a French lesson. Pam is doing French as she wants to study it at University. (I got a distinction in French, Pam a credit.) I went with Pam to get her new bike after school and then I visited Miss Gooden. In the evening I heard Yehudi Menuhin on the wireless. He plays the violin like an angel.

Tomorrow is my last day at Miss Hoare's Secretarial College. And I'm being baptised.

23rd September 1944

So now I'm a Christian. Mrs Roxby (the Canon's wife), Miss Frost, Miss Davis and my father were at the Parish Church for my baptism. Miss Frost said to my father afterwards:

"You must be proud of *'I'*. - hasn't she done well to pass her School Certificate?" That, and my becoming a Christian, certainly make him temporarily pleased with me. The Certificate will launch me on a good career, and being a Christian means I shall never be persecuted again. And what *I* am most pleased about is that I now have a lovely, new, English name in addition to my horrible, foreign, unpronounceable one - JANE. It's my favourite girl's name. Now all I need is Mr Rochester to go with it.

On Thursday, 28th September, I am leaving Falmouth. I shall stay in London for a few days, at my father's, to buy some new clothes, and then, as soon as some digs are found for me in Oxford, move there and attend Secretarial College for about a year. What I'd really like to do is work in a library.

Now you know my plans. I shan't believe in them though until I'm actually on the train!

27th September 1944

What a week it has been! One round of seeing people and saying goodbye. On Sunday evening I went with Pam to a Harvest Festival at her Chapel (having been to the Parish Church in the morning). In his sermon the vicar said something about we didn't all need to go to Oxford to be educated and Pam nudged me and I felt very embarrassed.

"But I'm not going to the University there!" I whispered to her.

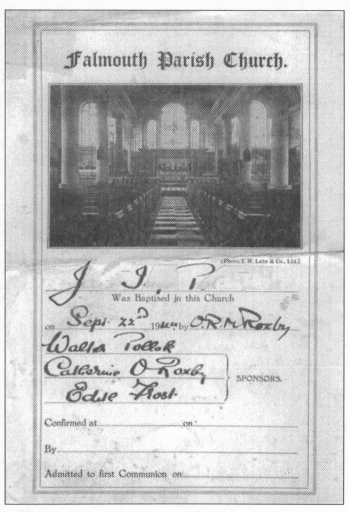

Baptism certificate.

Guess who visited us at St. Joseph's on Monday - Barbara Wilson and her husband! Yes, she's married now. Otherwise she hasn't changed. I didn't see much of her as my whole day was taken up with visiting people to say goodbye (and packing) - Eggins', Hodgetts, Thompsons, Roxbys, Miss Gooden, and goodness knows who else.

Yesterday the School Certificate results were published in the papers. I felt very proud when I saw my name, but my heart aches for Figgy. I'd so much like to see her again and talk to her but she has vanished. She was much more intelligent than many of the people who passed, myself included. I had tea at the Lawrances' for the last time. On the way there I met a Yankee soldier called Dick and made a date with him - just for fun. I had supper at Pam's and was very sad to say goodbye to her and her parents. Mrs Bath had baked a special cake for me.

Today the van came to take my large cabin trunk to the station. Connie and I accompanied it. Now I really knew that I was going. When this same trunk left Vienna for England I felt exactly as I did today - I wanted to go and I didn't want to go. But the trunk has gone and there's no turning back. I called at Tamblyns to say goodbye, and last of all at school, where I took my leave of Miss Frost and the girls. Audrey and I nearly wept when we said goodbye.

This is the last entry I shall make in Falmouth. It was your birthplace, and you have a right to feel a bit sentimental about leaving it. As for me - I don't know where I shall be sitting when next I write this diary.